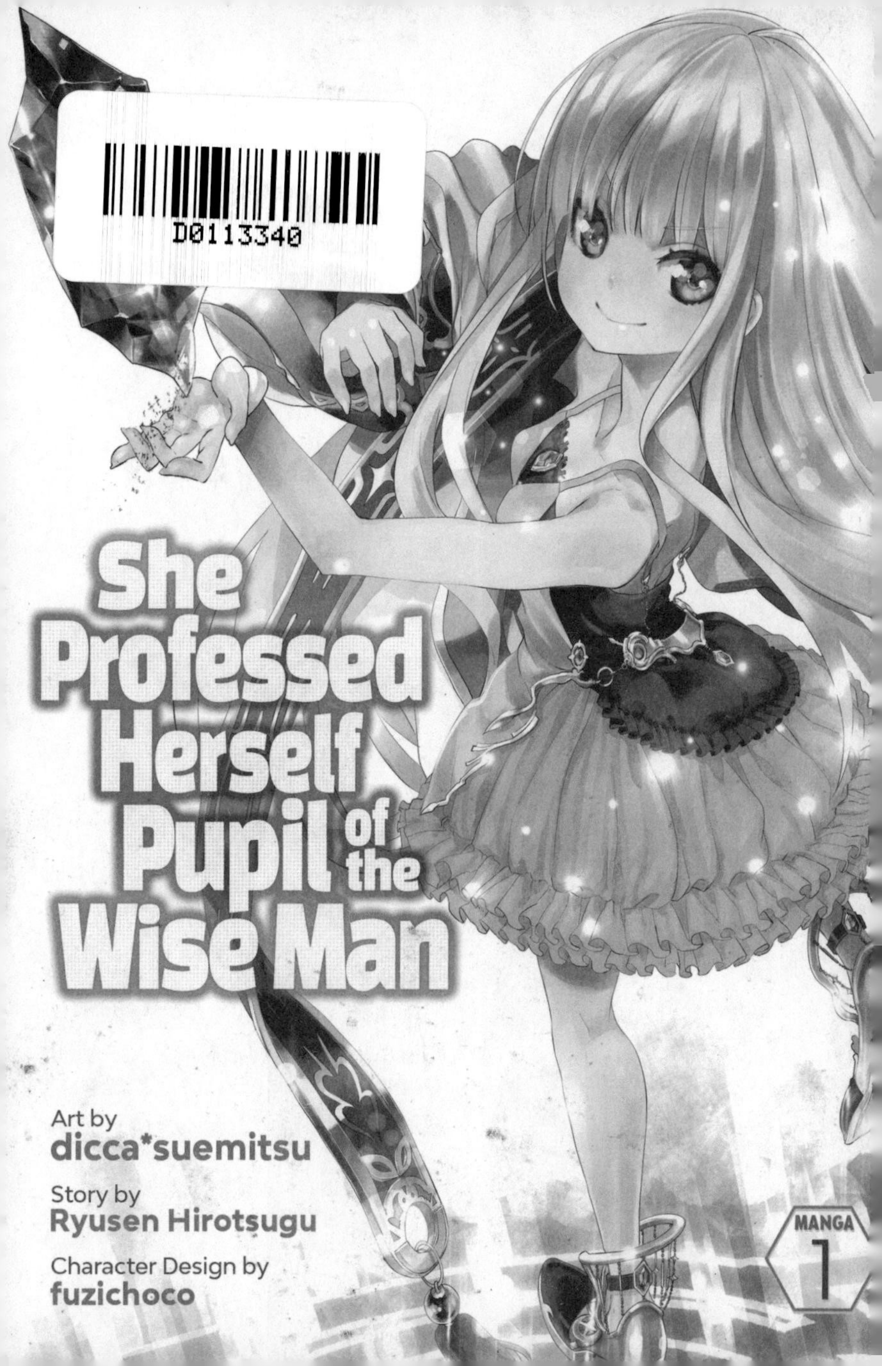
She Professed Herself Pupil of the Wise Man
Art by
dicca*suemitsu
Story by
Ryusen Hirotsugu
Character Design by
fuzichoco
MANGA
1

GN
Hirotsug

CONTENTS

She
Professed
Herself
Pupil of the
Wise Man

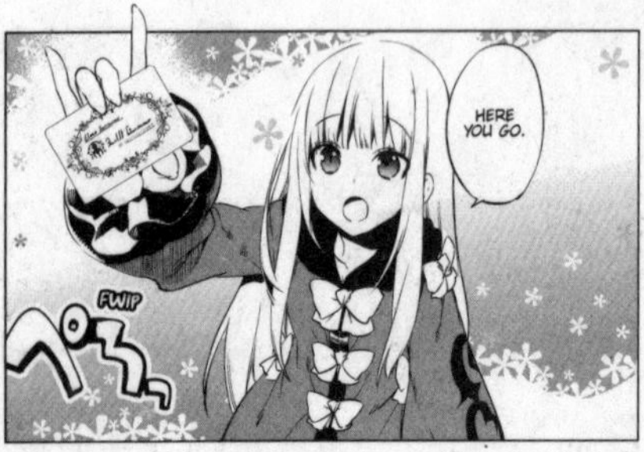
HERE YOU GO.
FWIP

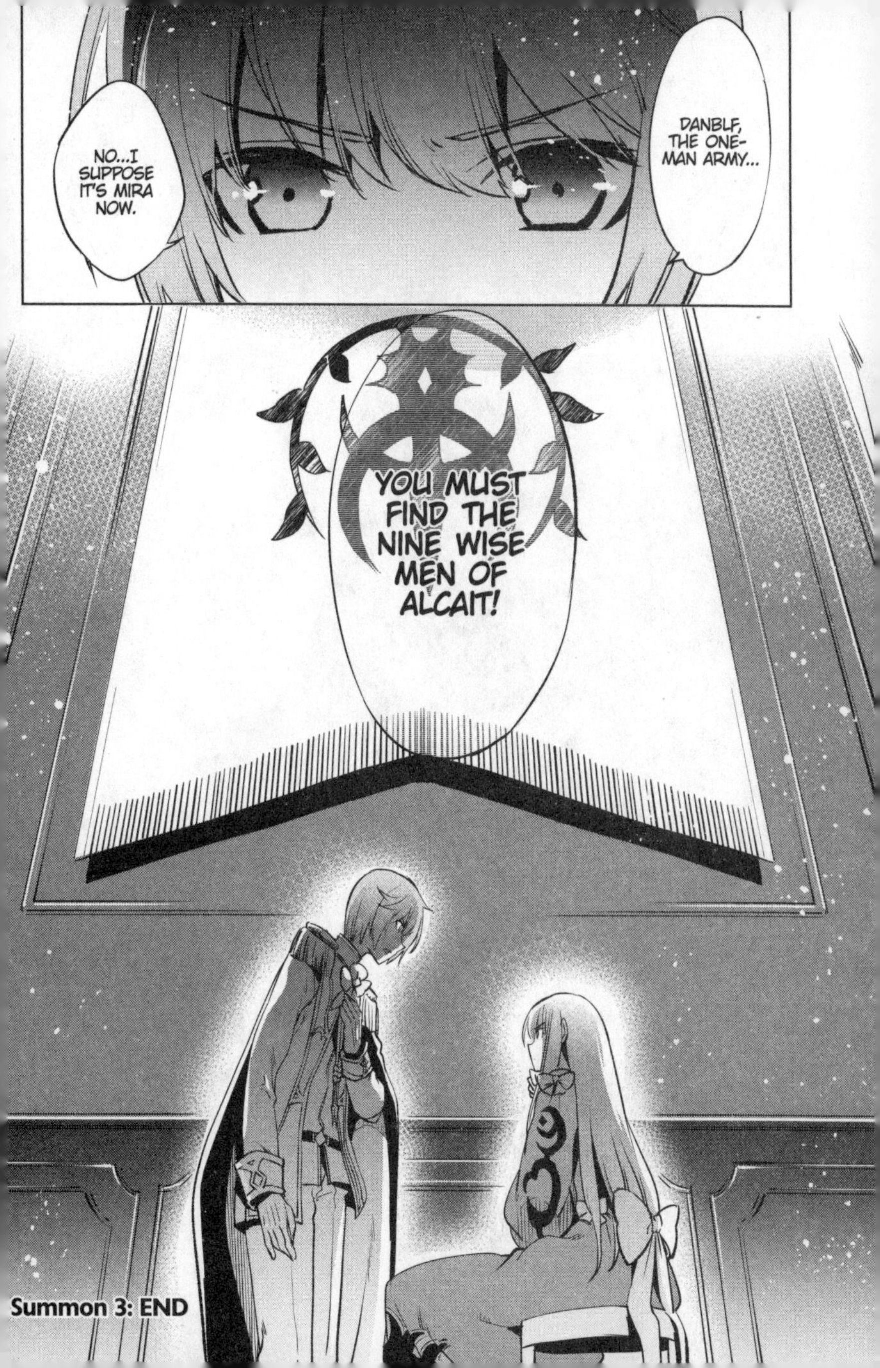
DANBLF, THE ONE-MAN ARMY...
NO...I SUPPOSE IT'S MIRA NOW.
YOU MUST FIND THE NINE WISE MEN OF ALCAIT!
Summon 3: END

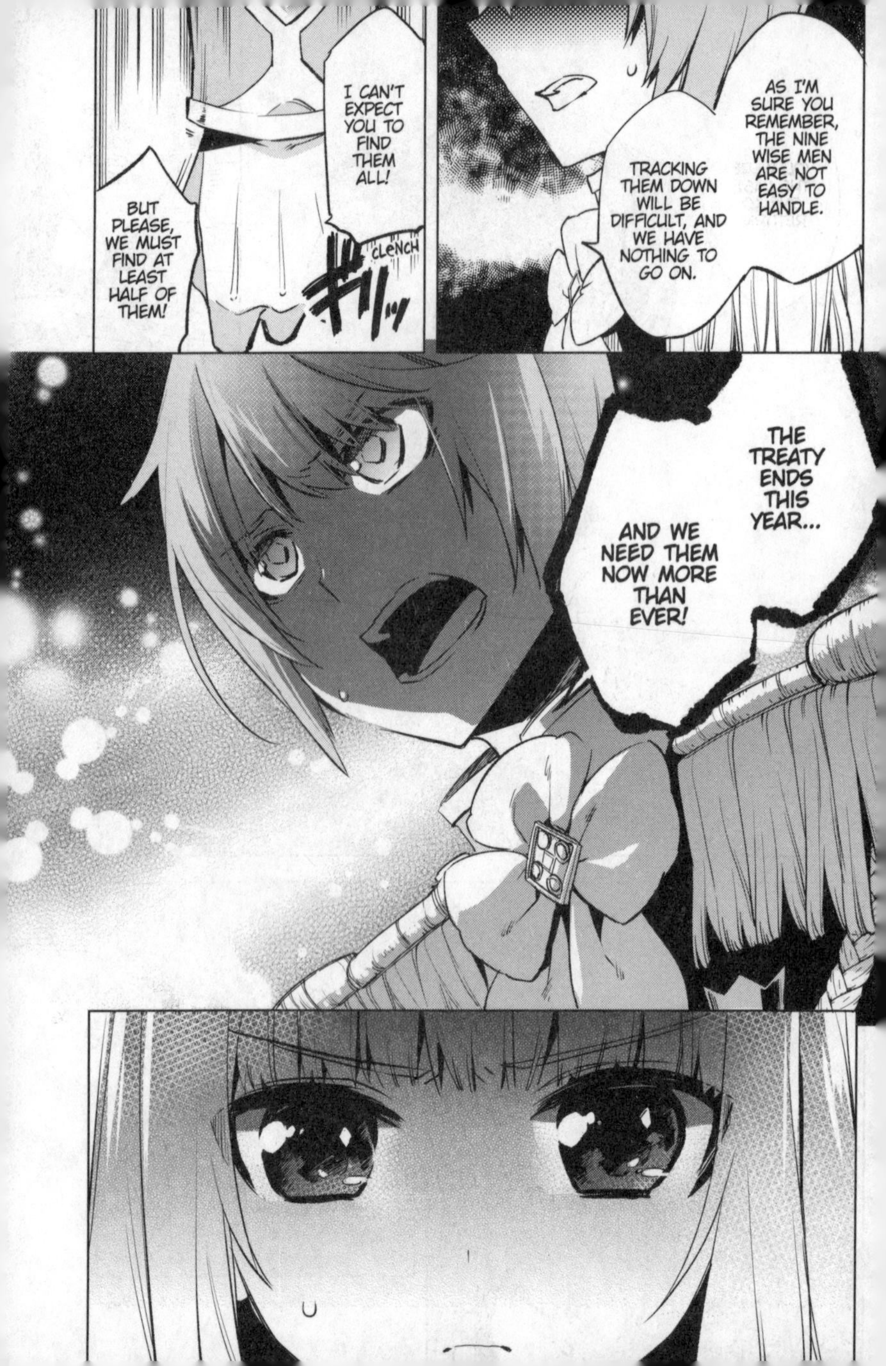
AS I'M SURE YOU REMEMBER, THE NINE WISE MEN ARE NOT EASY TO HANDLE.
TRACKING THEM DOWN WILL BE DIFFICULT, AND WE HAVE NOTHING TO GO ON.
I CAN'T EXPECT YOU TO FIND THEM ALL!
BUT PLEASE, WE MUST FIND AT LEAST HALF OF THEM!
CLENCH
THE TREATY ENDS THIS YEAR...
AND WE NEED THEM NOW MORE THAN EVER!

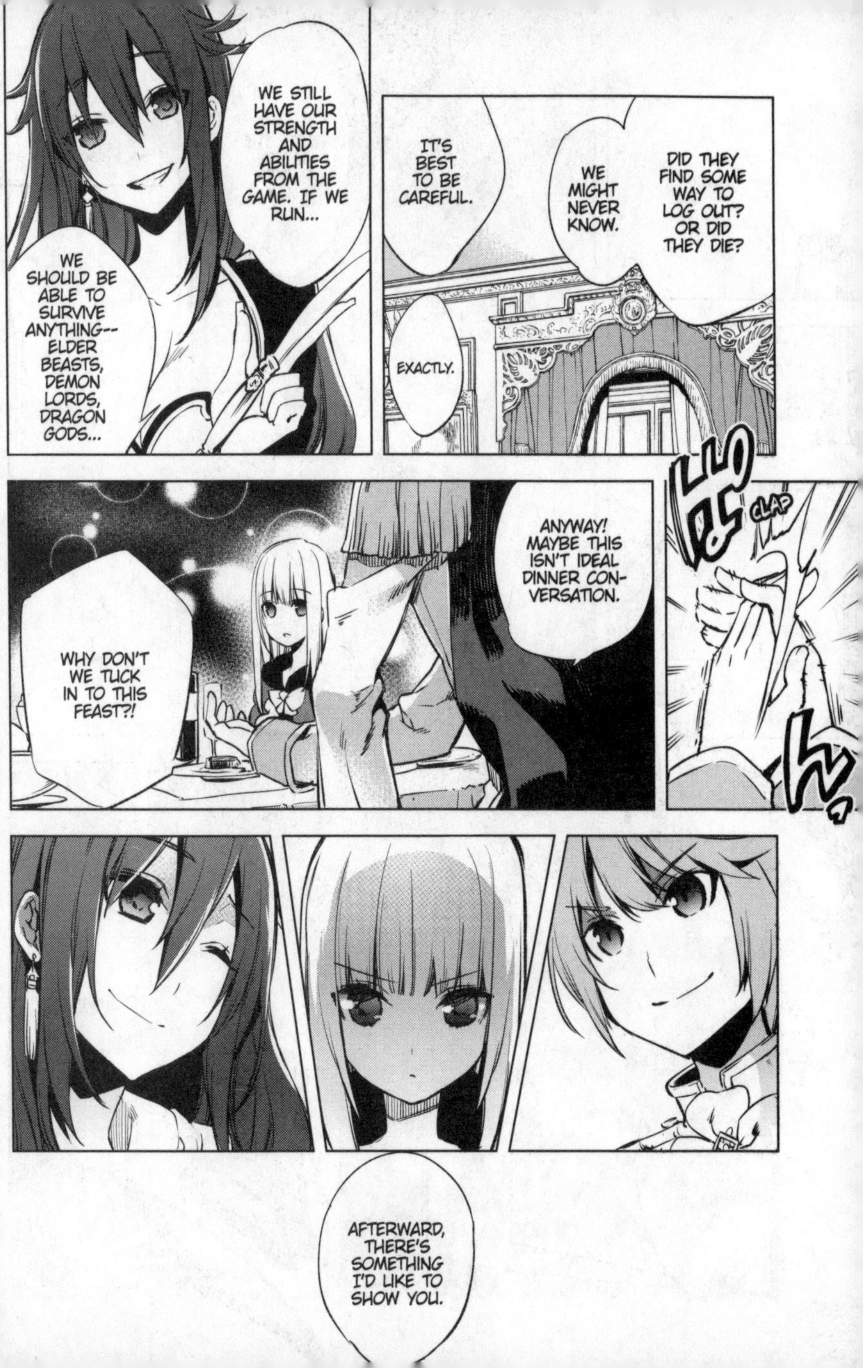
DID THEY FIND SOME WAY TO LOG OUT? OR DID THEY DIE?
WE MIGHT NEVER KNOW.
IT'S BEST TO BE CAREFUL.
EXACTLY.
WE STILL HAVE OUR STRENGTH AND ABILITIES FROM THE GAME. IF WE RUN...
WE SHOULD BE ABLE TO SURVIVE ANYTHING-- ELDER BEASTS, DEMON LORDS, DRAGON GODS...
CLAP
ANYWAY! MAYBE THIS ISN'T IDEAL DINNER CON-VERSATION.
WHY DON'T WE TUCK IN TO THIS FEAST?!
AFTERWARD, THERE'S SOMETHING I'D LIKE TO SHOW YOU.

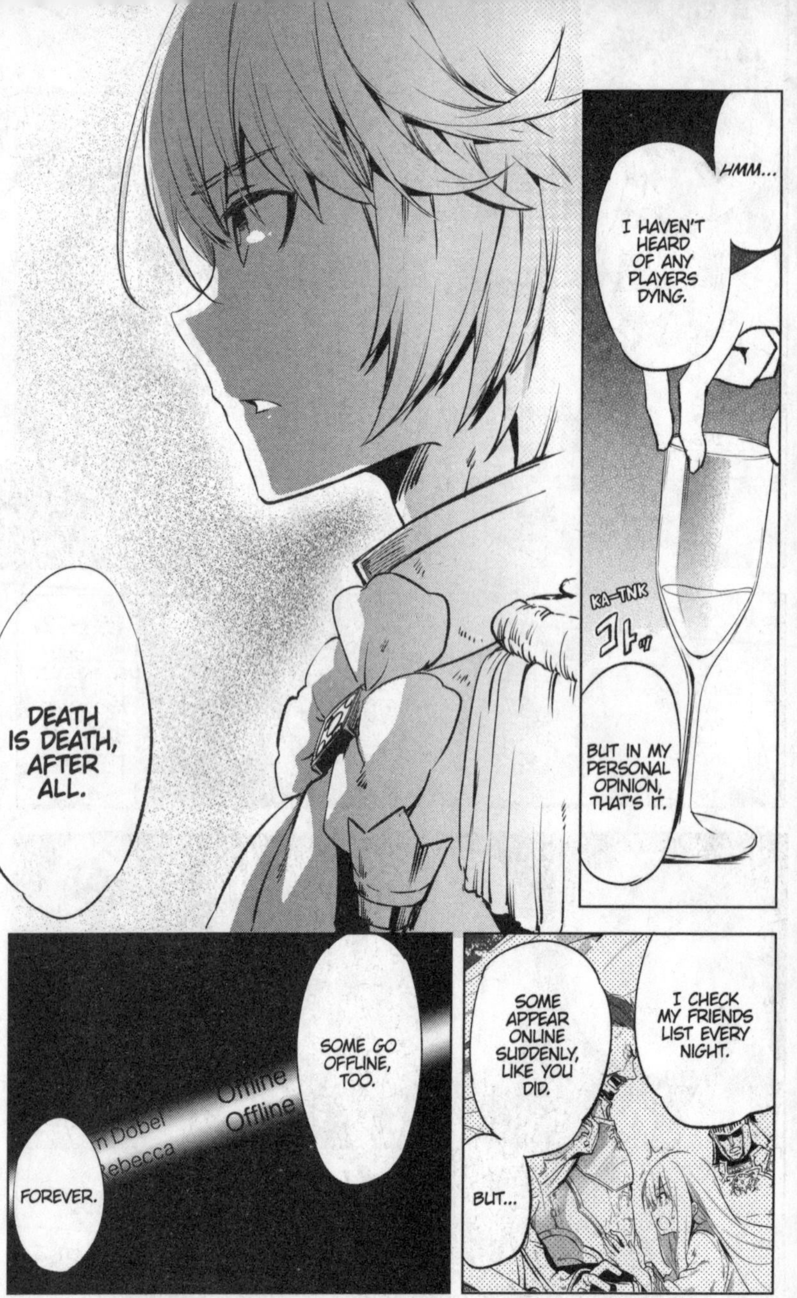
HMM...
I HAVEN'T HEARD OF ANY PLAYERS DYING.
KA-TNK
コトッ
BUT IN MY PERSONAL OPINION, THAT'S IT.
DEATH IS DEATH, AFTER ALL.
I CHECK MY FRIENDS LIST EVERY NIGHT.
SOME APPEAR ONLINE SUDDENLY, LIKE YOU DID.
BUT...
SOME GO OFFLINE, TOO.
Offline
Offline
Rebecca
FOREVER.

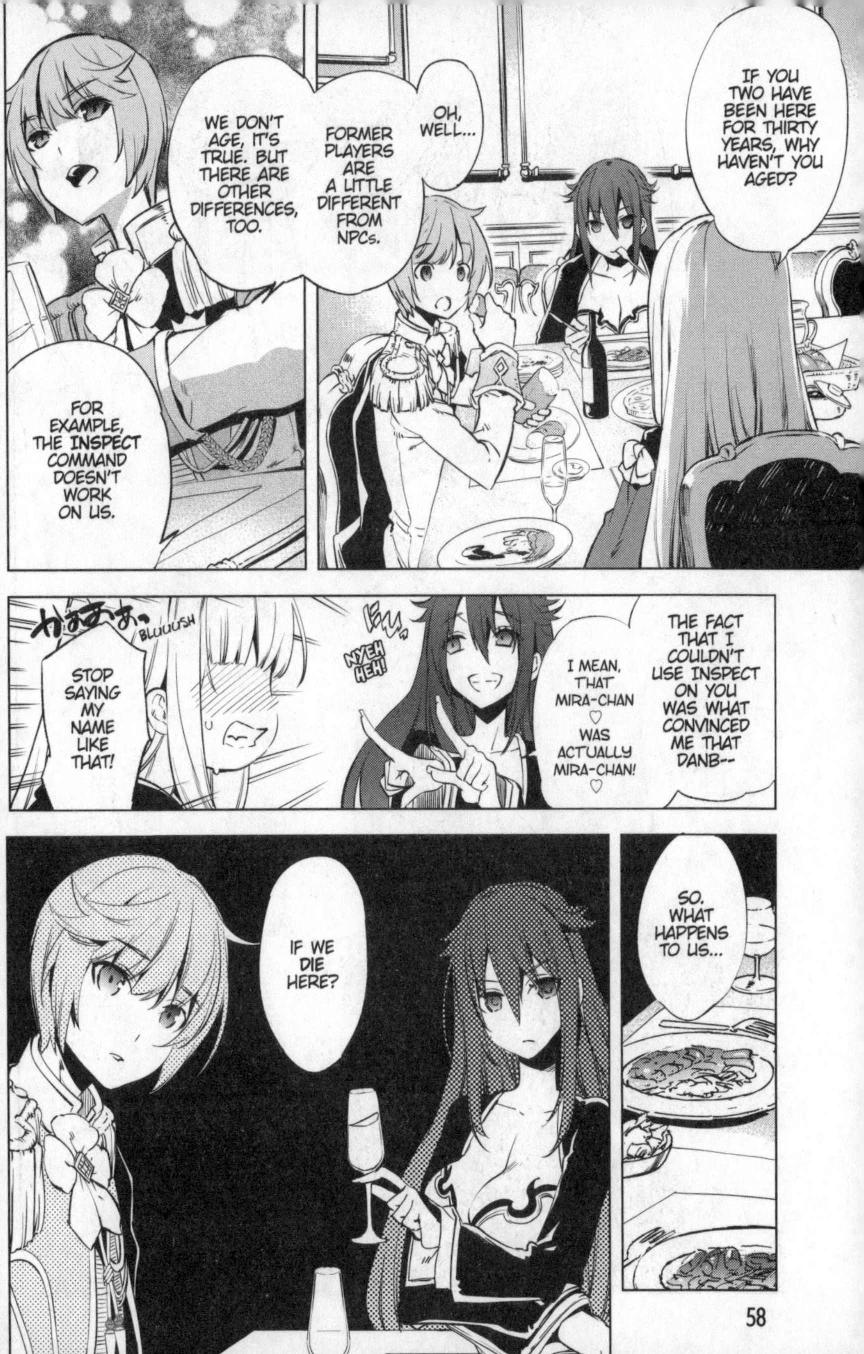
IF YOU TWO HAVE BEEN HERE FOR THIRTY YEARS, WHY HAVEN'T YOU AGED?
OH, WELL...
FORMER PLAYERS ARE A LITTLE DIFFERENT FROM NPCs.
WE DON'T AGE, IT'S TRUE. BUT THERE ARE OTHER DIFFERENCES, TOO.
FOR EXAMPLE, THE INSPECT COMMAND DOESN'T WORK ON US.
THE FACT THAT I COULDN'T USE INSPECT ON YOU WAS WHAT CONVINCED ME THAT DANB--
I MEAN, THAT MIRA-CHAN ♡ WAS ACTUALLY MIRA-CHAN! ♡
NYEH HEH!
BLUUUSH
STOP SAYING MY NAME LIKE THAT!
SO. WHAT HAPPENS TO US...
IF WE DIE HERE?

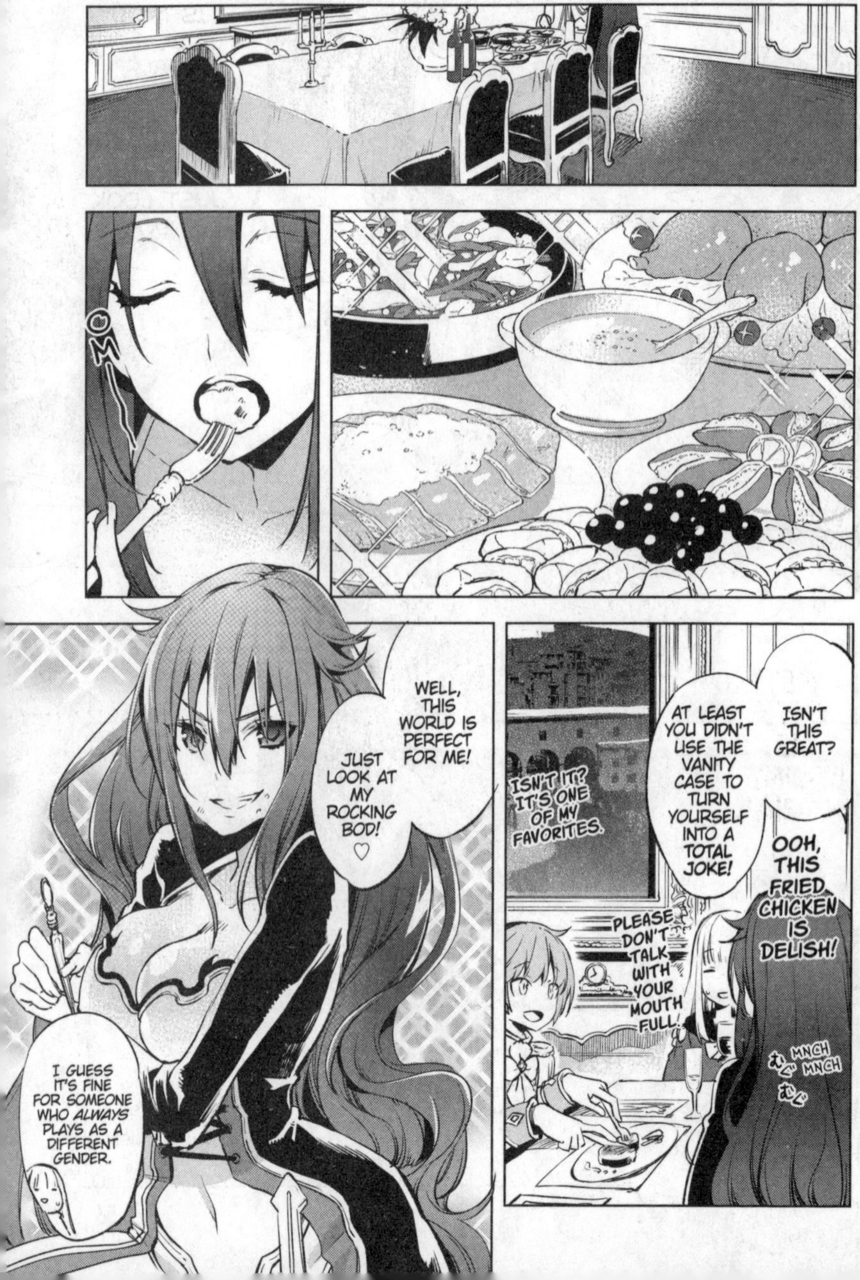
OM
ISN'T THIS GREAT?
AT LEAST YOU DIDN'T USE THE VANITY CASE TO TURN YOURSELF INTO A TOTAL JOKE!
ISN'T IT? IT'S ONE OF MY FAVORITES.
OOH, THIS FRIED CHICKEN IS DELISH!
PLEASE DON'T TALK WITH YOUR MOUTH FULL!
MNCH MNCH
WELL, THIS WORLD IS PERFECT FOR ME!
JUST LOOK AT MY ROCKING BOD! ♡
I GUESS IT'S FINE FOR SOMEONE WHO *ALWAYS* PLAYS AS A DIFFERENT GENDER.

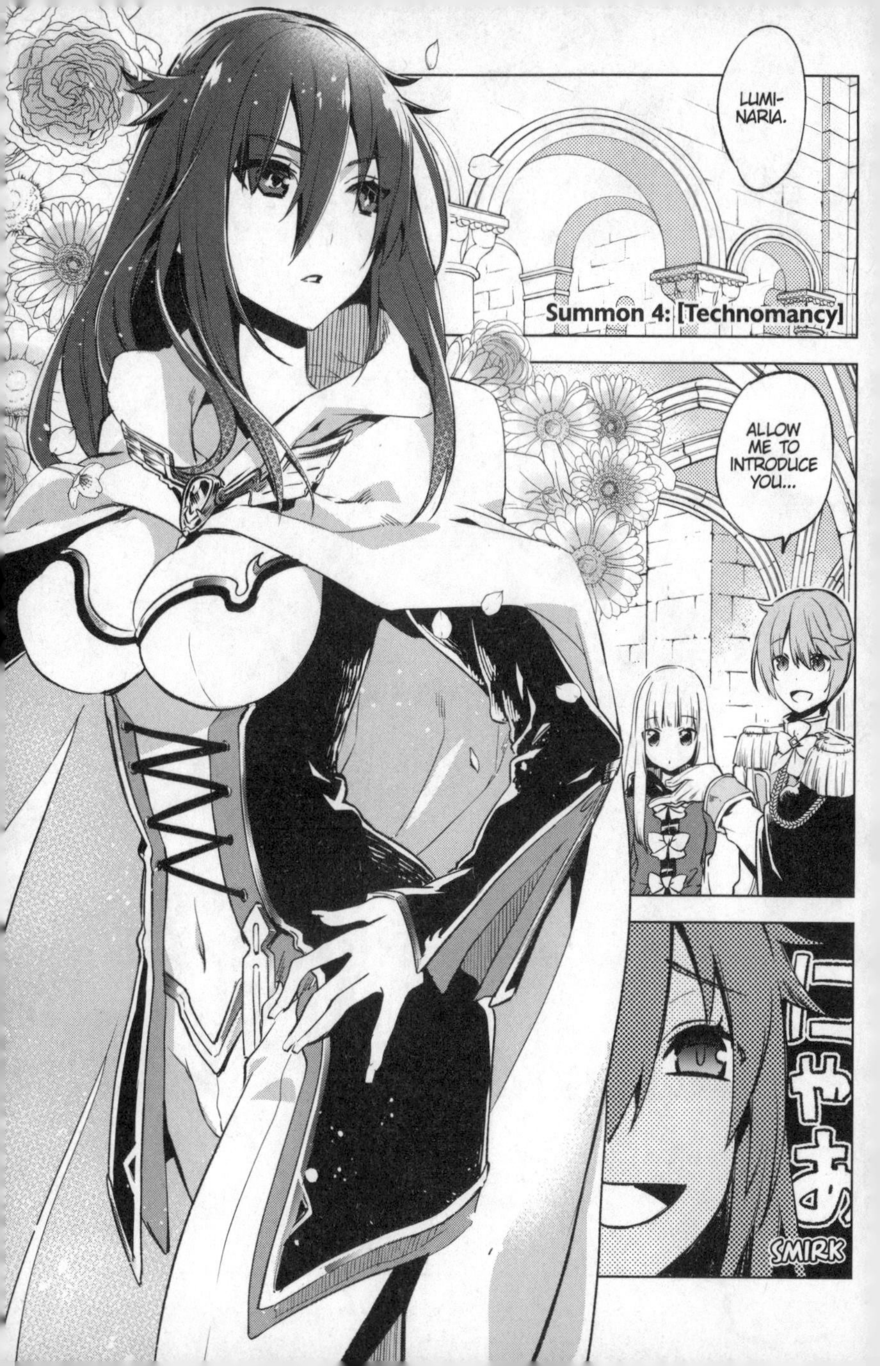
LUMI-
NARIA.
Summon 4: [Technomancy]
ALLOW ME TO INTRODUCE YOU...
にやぁ
SMIRK

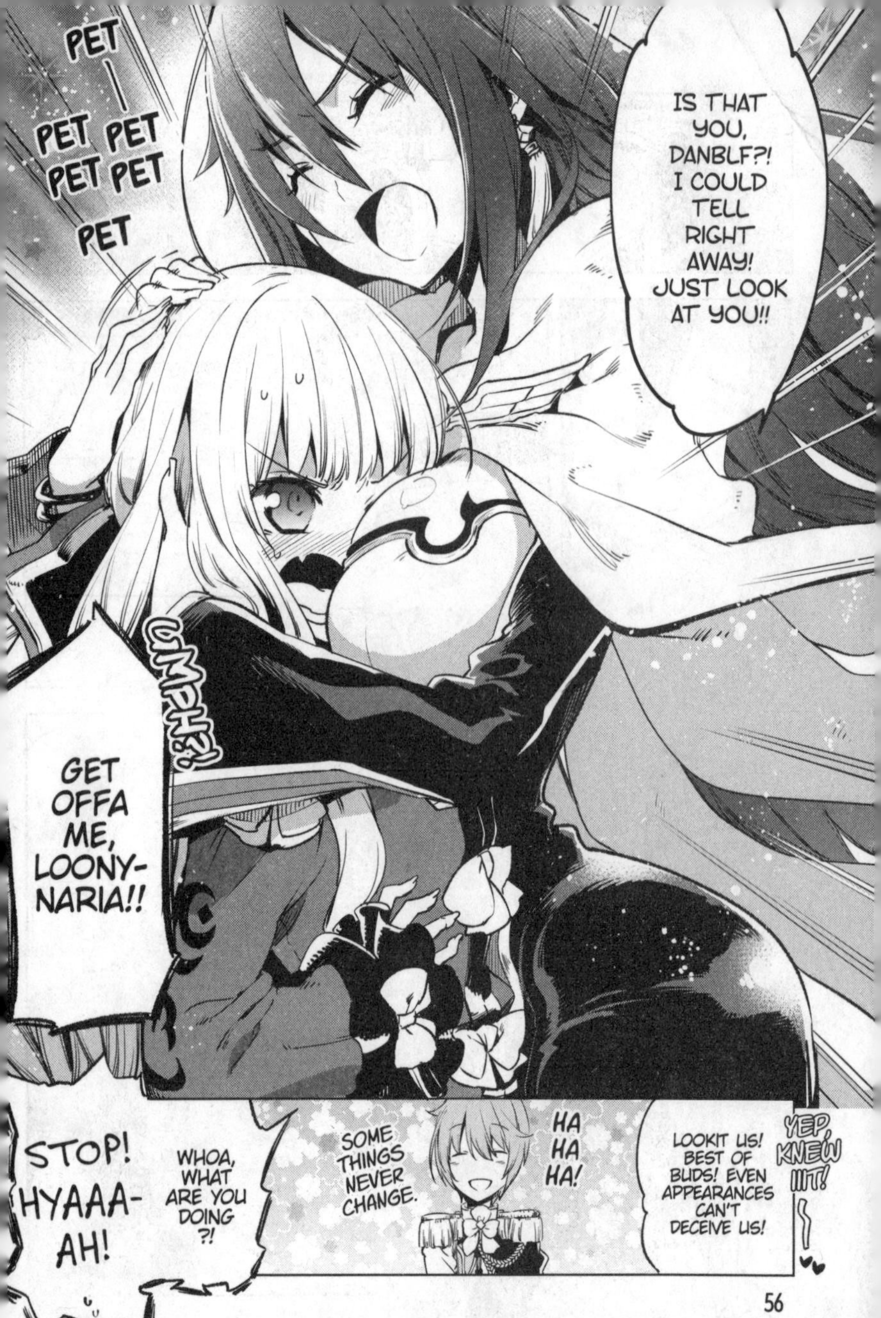
IS THAT YOU, DANBLF?! I COULD TELL RIGHT AWAY! JUST LOOK AT YOU!!
PET — PET PET PET PET PET
UMPH?!
GET OFFA ME, LOONY-NARIA!!
YEP, KNEW IIIT!
LOOKIT US! BEST OF BUDS! EVEN APPEARANCES CAN'T DECEIVE US!
HA HA HA!
SOME THINGS NEVER CHANGE.
WHOA, WHAT ARE YOU DOING ?!
STOP! HYAAAA-AH!

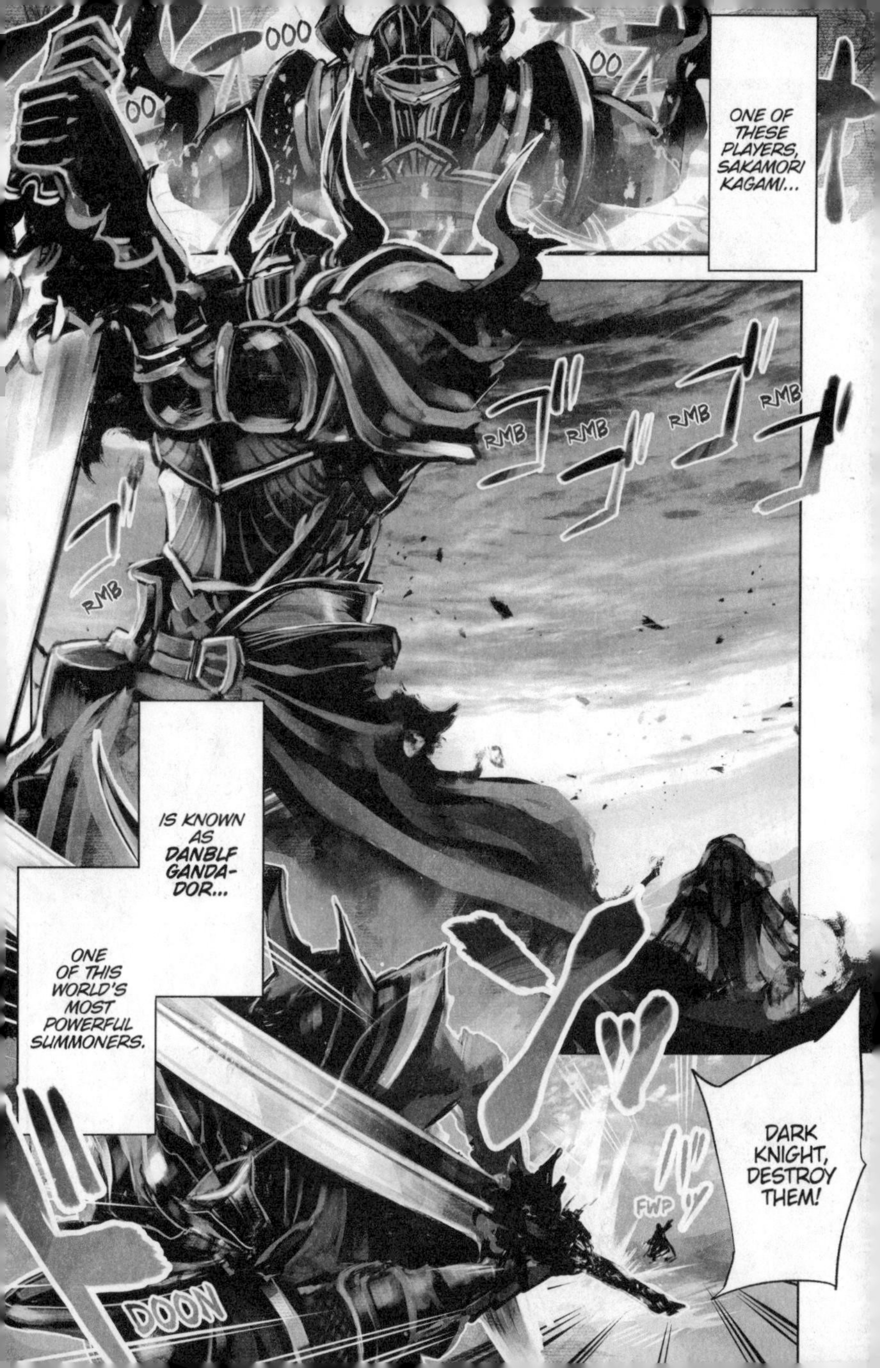
ONE OF THESE PLAYERS, SAKAMORI KAGAMI...
OO
OOO
OO
RMB RMB RMB RMB
RMB
IS KNOWN AS DANBLF GANDADOR...
ONE OF THIS WORLD'S MOST POWERFUL SUMMONERS.
DARK KNIGHT, DESTROY THEM!
FWP
DOON

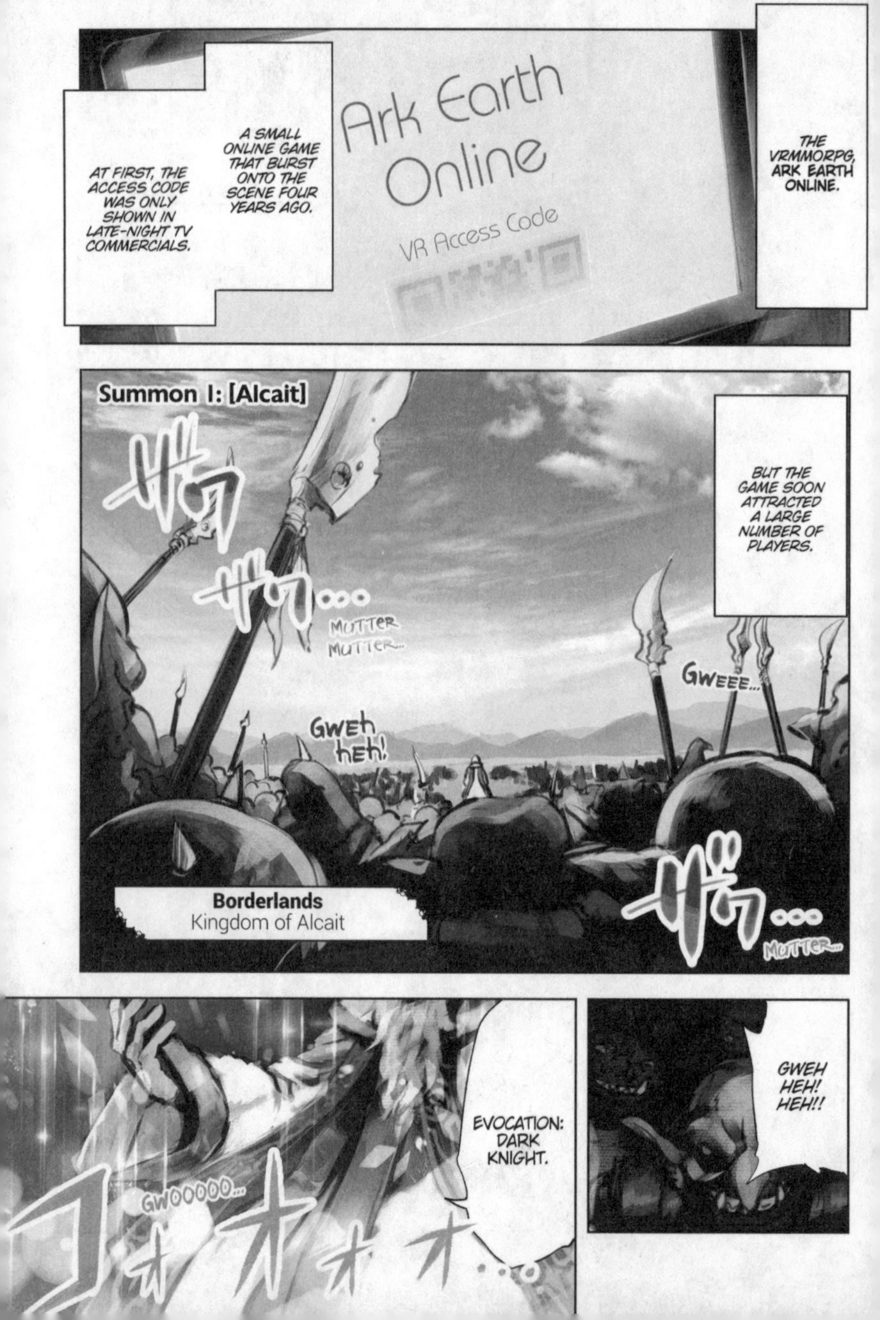

THE VRMMORPG, ARK EARTH ONLINE.
Ark Earth Online
VR Access Code
A SMALL ONLINE GAME THAT BURST ONTO THE SCENE FOUR YEARS AGO.
AT FIRST, THE ACCESS CODE WAS ONLY SHOWN IN LATE-NIGHT TV COMMERCIALS.
BUT THE GAME SOON ATTRACTED A LARGE NUMBER OF PLAYERS.
GWEEE...
Summon 1: [Alcait]
ザワ
ザワ…
MUTTER MUTTER...
Gweh heh!
Borderlands
Kingdom of Alcait
ザワ…
MUTTER...
GWEH HEH! HEH!!
EVOCATION: DARK KNIGHT.
GWOOOOO...

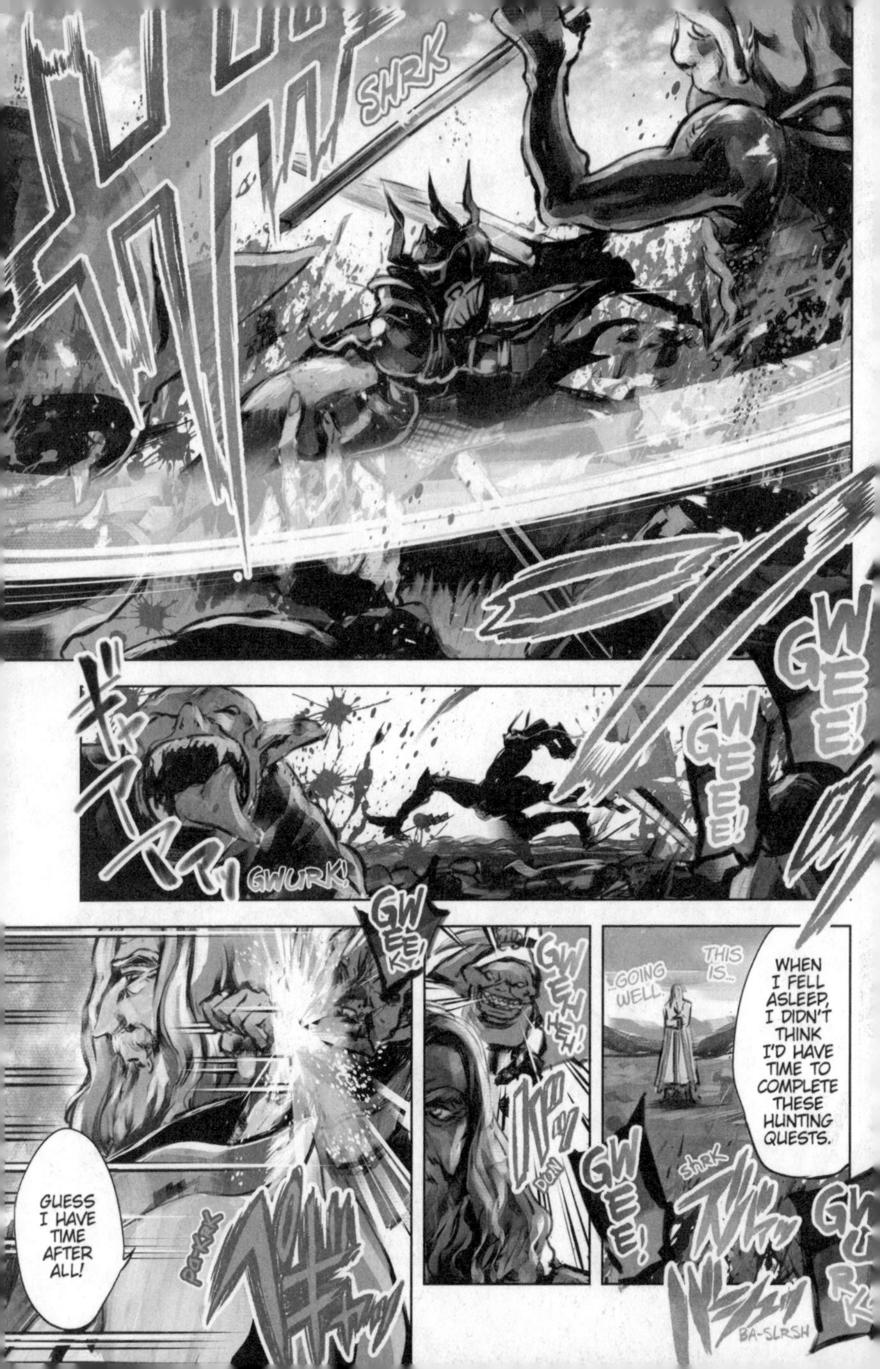
SHRK
GWEE!
GWEEEE!
GWURK!
WHEN I FELL ASLEEP, I DIDN'T THINK I'D HAVE TIME TO COMPLETE THESE HUNTING QUESTS.
THIS IS...
...GOING WELL.
shrk
GWURK
BA-SLRSH
GWEHHEH!
DON
GWEE!
GWEEK!
GUESS I HAVE TIME AFTER ALL!

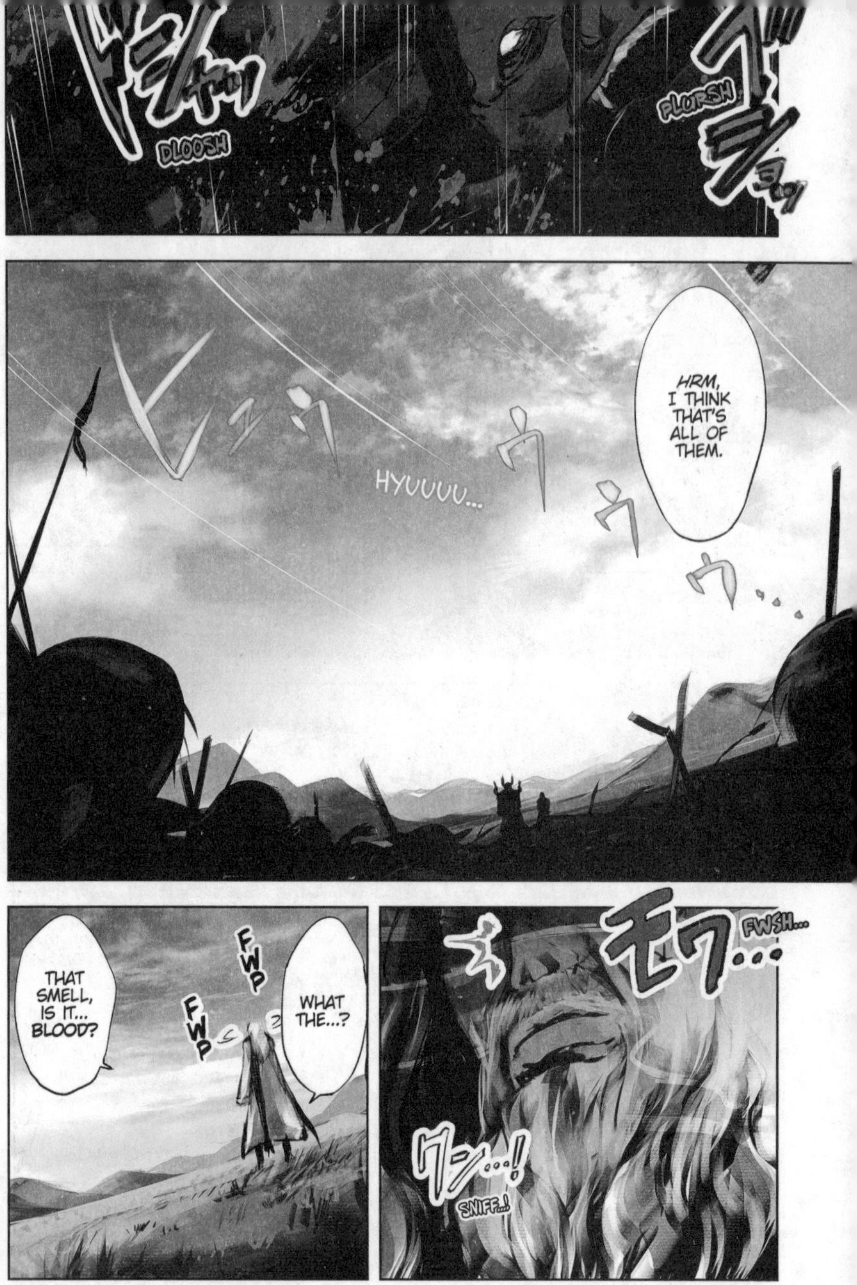
PLURSH
DLOOSH
HRM, I THINK THAT'S ALL OF THEM.
HYUUUU...
FWSH...
SNIFF...!
WHAT THE...?
FWP
FWP
THAT SMELL, IS IT... BLOOD?

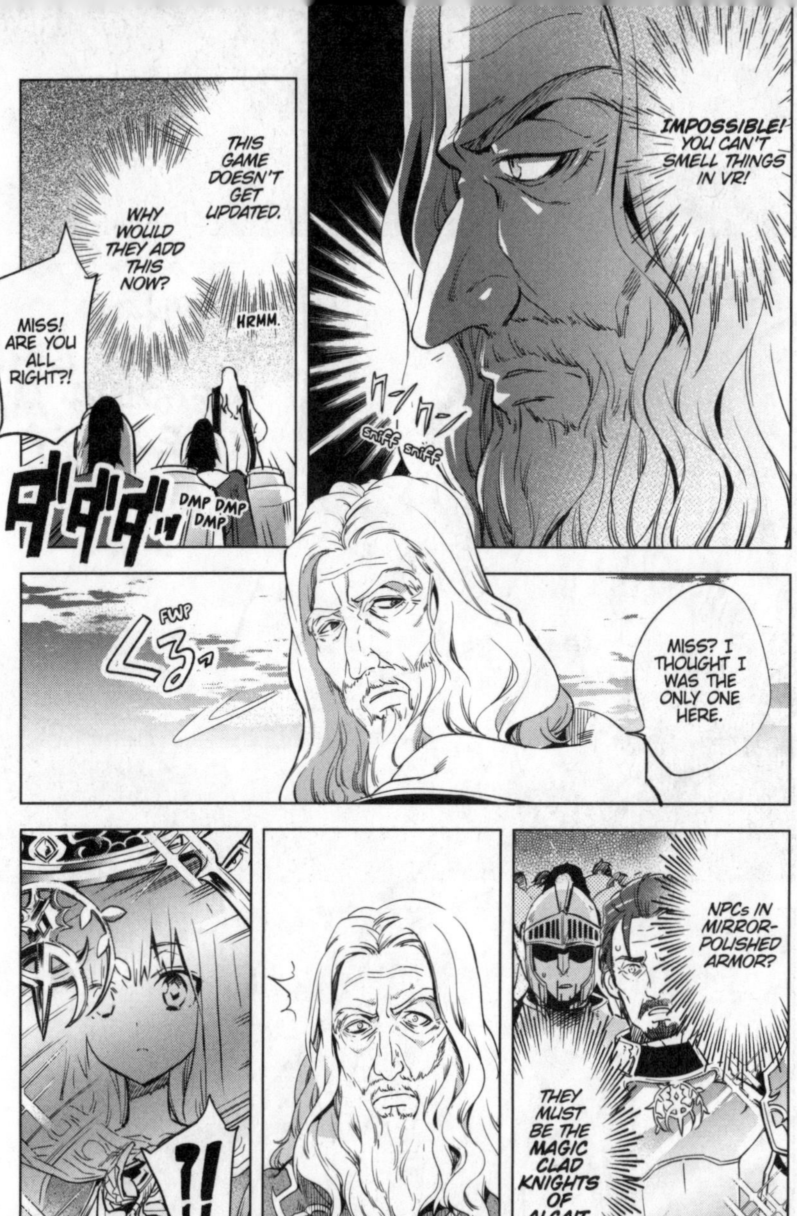
IMPOSSIBLE! YOU CAN'T SMELL THINGS IN VR!
sniff sniff
THIS GAME DOESN'T GET UPDATED.
WHY WOULD THEY ADD THIS NOW?
HRMM.
MISS! ARE YOU ALL RIGHT?!
DMP DMP DMP
MISS? I THOUGHT I WAS THE ONLY ONE HERE.
FWP
NPCs IN MIRROR-POLISHED ARMOR?
THEY MUST BE THE MAGIC CLAD KNIGHTS OF ALCAIT.
?!

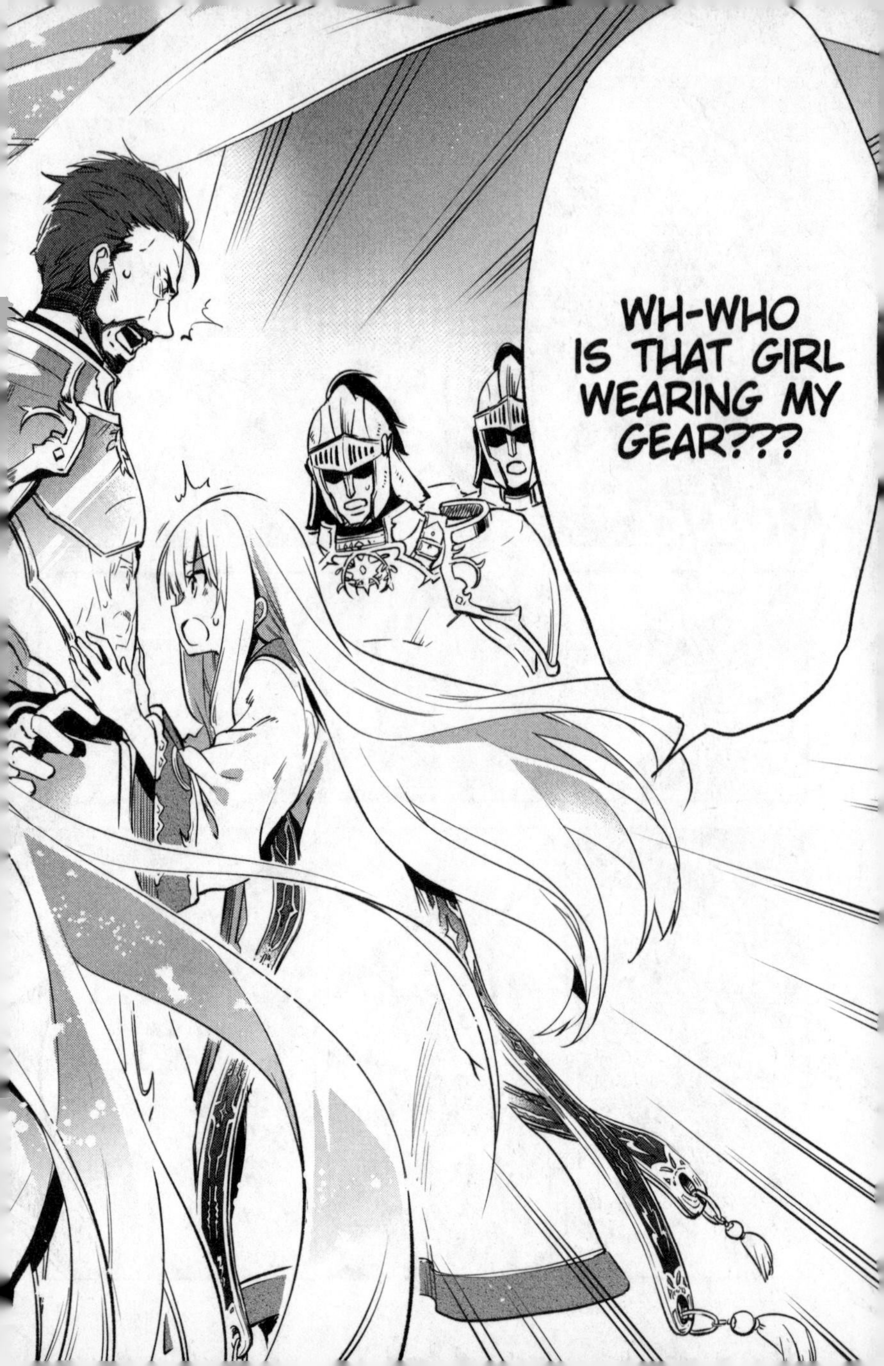
WH-WHO IS THAT GIRL WEARING MY GEAR???

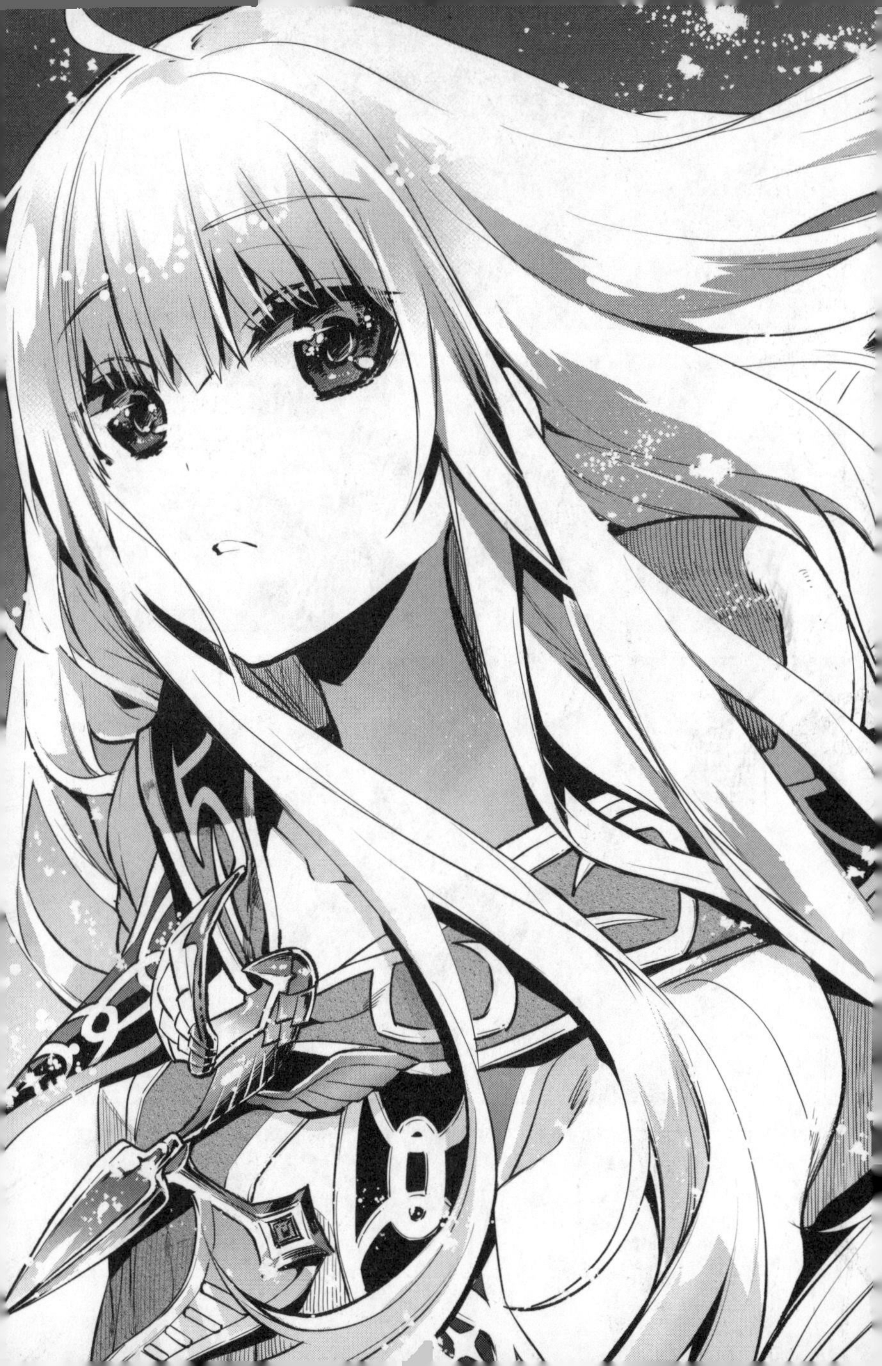

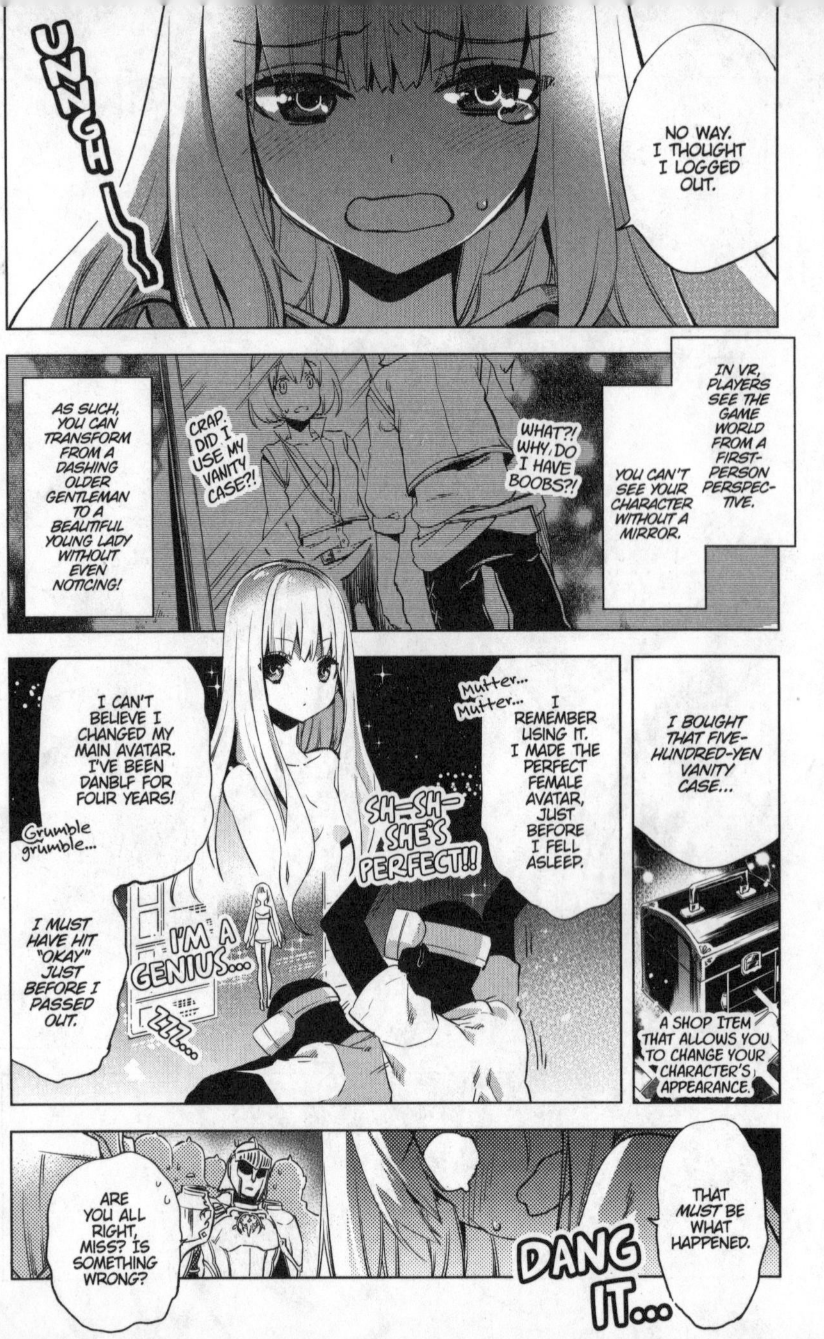
NO WAY. I THOUGHT I LOGGED OUT.
UNNGH
IN VR, PLAYERS SEE THE GAME WORLD FROM A FIRST-PERSON PERSPECTIVE.
YOU CAN'T SEE YOUR CHARACTER WITHOUT A MIRROR.
WHAT?! WHY DO I HAVE BOOBS?!
CRAP. DID I USE MY VANITY CASE?!
AS SUCH, YOU CAN TRANSFORM FROM A DASHING OLDER GENTLEMAN TO A BEAUTIFUL YOUNG LADY WITHOUT EVEN NOTICING!
I BOUGHT THAT FIVE-HUNDRED-YEN VANITY CASE...
A SHOP ITEM THAT ALLOWS YOU TO CHANGE YOUR CHARACTER'S APPEARANCE.
Mutter... Mutter...
I REMEMBER USING IT. I MADE THE PERFECT FEMALE AVATAR, JUST BEFORE I FELL ASLEEP.
SH-SH-SHE'S PERFECT!!
I CAN'T BELIEVE I CHANGED MY MAIN AVATAR. I'VE BEEN DANBLF FOR FOUR YEARS!
Grumble grumble...
I'M A GENIUS...
ZZZ...
I MUST HAVE HIT "OKAY" JUST BEFORE I PASSED OUT.
THAT MUST BE WHAT HAPPENED.
DANG IT...
ARE YOU ALL RIGHT, MISS? IS SOMETHING WRONG?

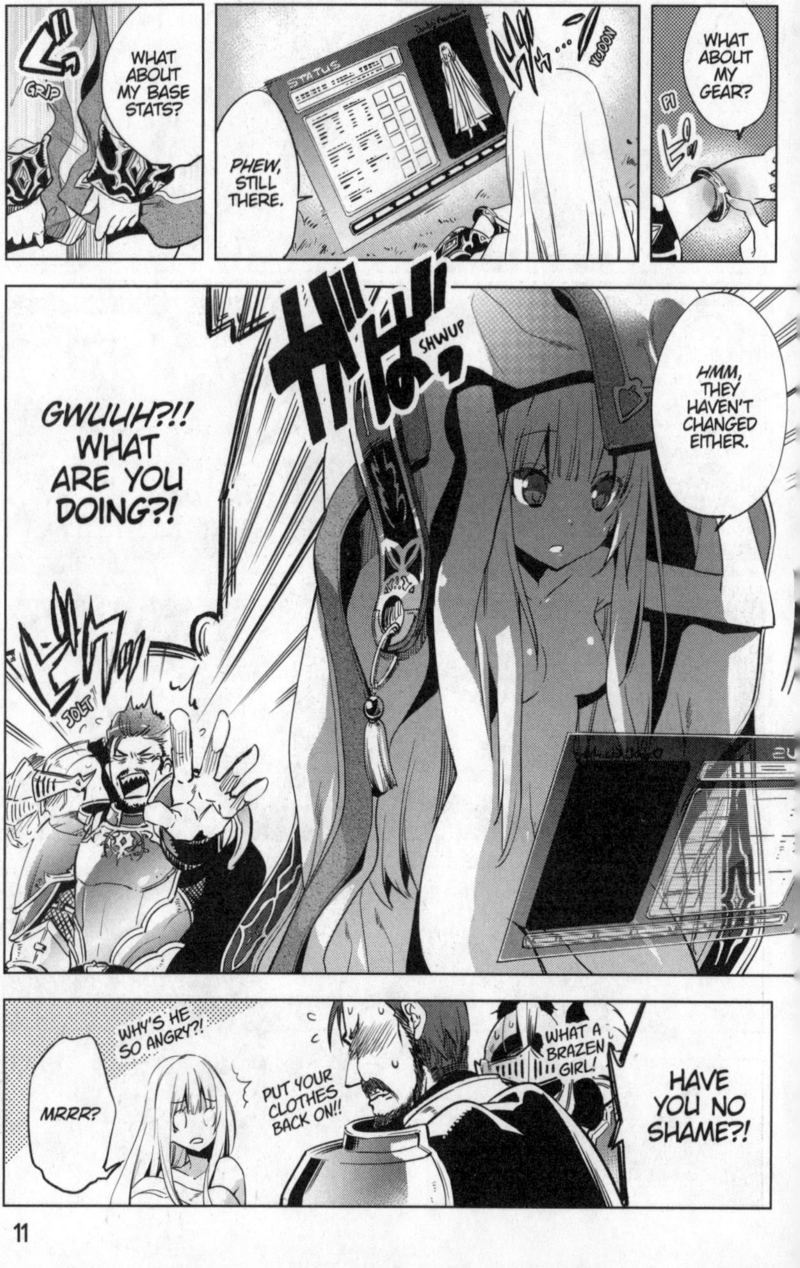
WHAT ABOUT MY GEAR?
PI
YOOON
STATUS
PHEW, STILL THERE.
WHAT ABOUT MY BASE STATS?
GRIP
SHWUP
HMM, THEY HAVEN'T CHANGED EITHER.
GWUUH?!! WHAT ARE YOU DOING?!
JOLT
HAVE YOU NO SHAME?!
WHAT A BRAZEN GIRL!
PUT YOUR CLOTHES BACK ON!!
WHY'S HE SO ANGRY?!
MRRR?

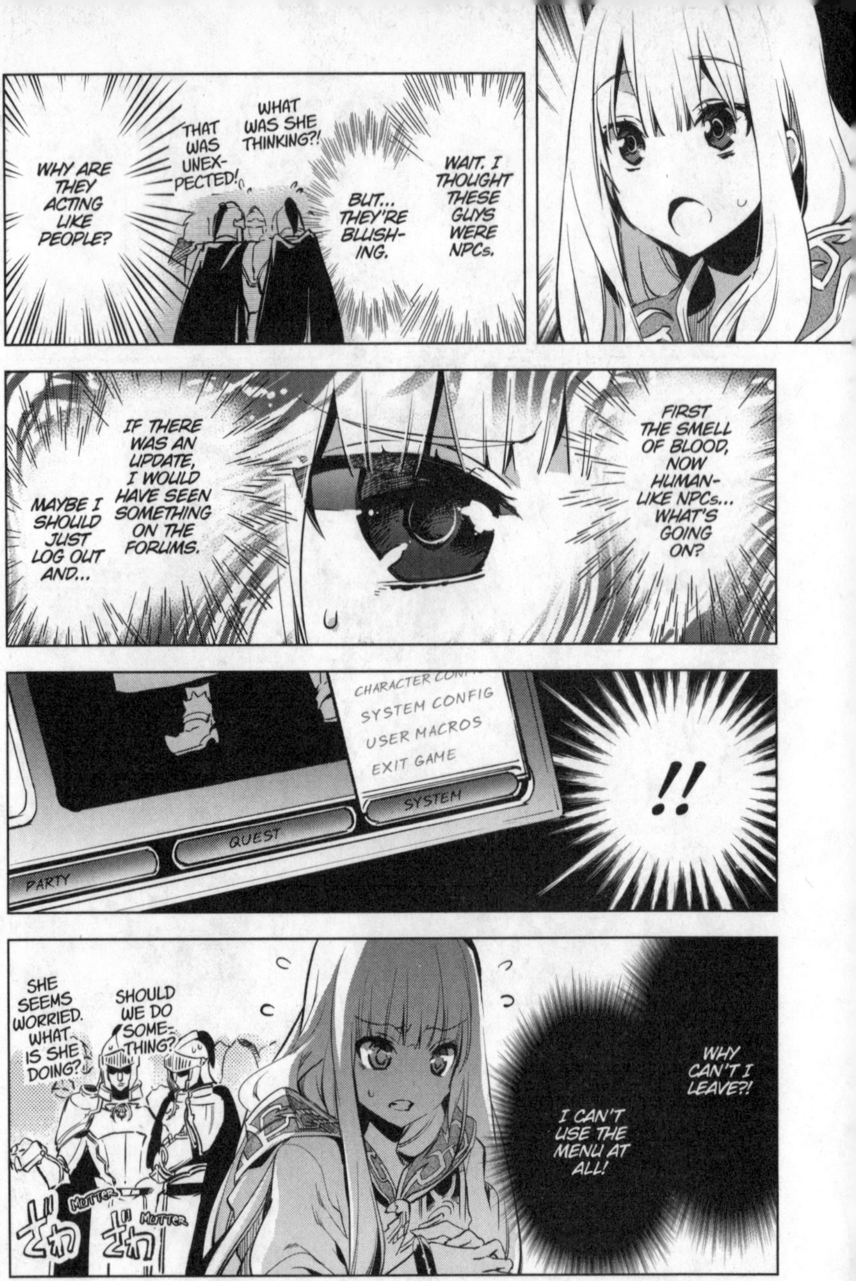
WAIT. I THOUGHT THESE GUYS WERE NPCs.
BUT... THEY'RE BLUSH-ING.
WHAT WAS SHE THINKING?!
THAT WAS UNEX-PECTED!
WHY ARE THEY ACTING LIKE PEOPLE?
FIRST THE SMELL OF BLOOD, NOW HUMAN-LIKE NPCs... WHAT'S GOING ON?
IF THERE WAS AN UPDATE, I WOULD HAVE SEEN SOMETHING ON THE FORUMS.
MAYBE I SHOULD JUST LOG OUT AND...
!!
SYSTEM CONFIG
USER MACROS
EXIT GAME
SYSTEM
QUEST
PARTY
WHY CAN'T I LEAVE?!
I CAN'T USE THE MENU AT ALL!
SHOULD WE DO SOME-THING?
SHE SEEMS WORRIED. WHAT IS SHE DOING?
ざわ MUTTER
ざわ MUTTER

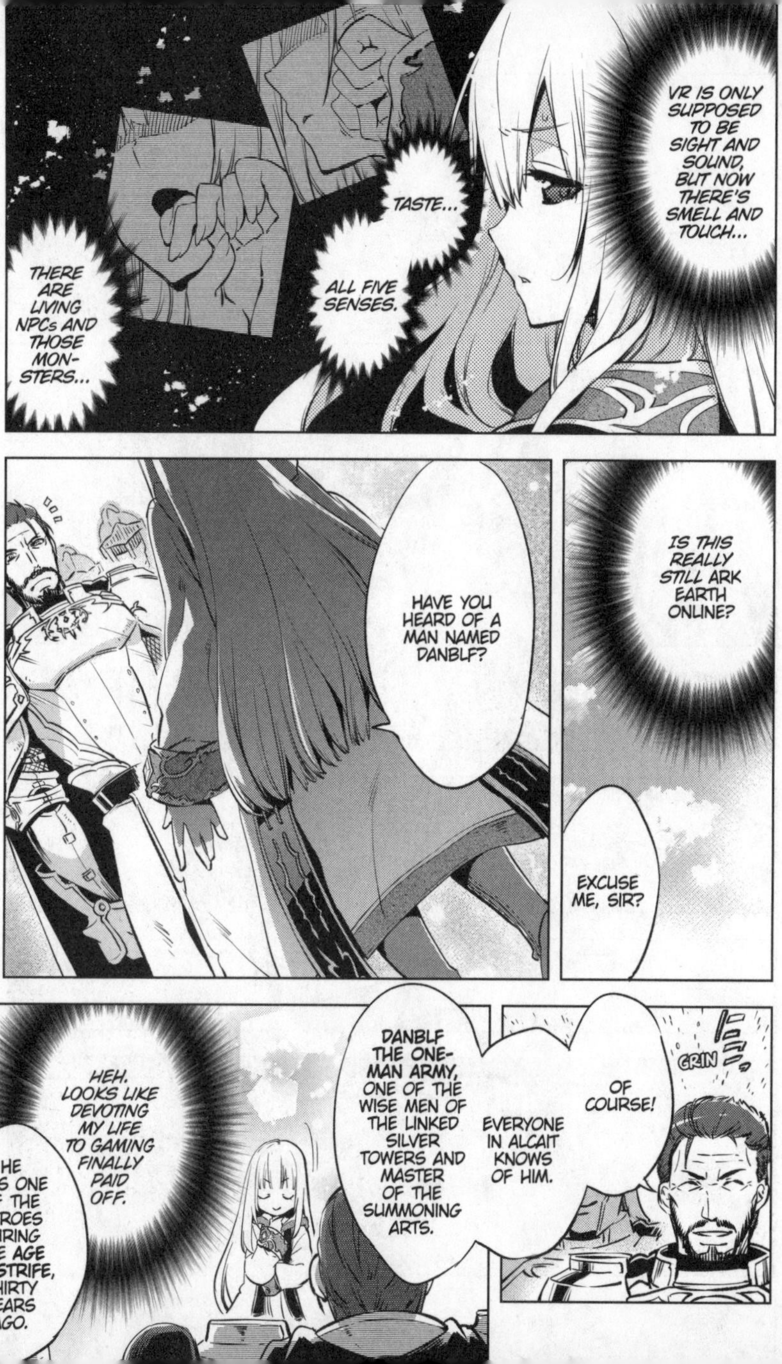
VR IS ONLY SUPPOSED TO BE SIGHT AND SOUND, BUT NOW THERE'S SMELL AND TOUCH...
TASTE...
ALL FIVE SENSES.
THERE ARE LIVING NPCs AND THOSE MON-STERS...
IS THIS REALLY STILL ARK EARTH ONLINE?
EXCUSE ME, SIR?
HAVE YOU HEARD OF A MAN NAMED DANBLF?
GRIN
OF COURSE!
EVERYONE IN ALCAIT KNOWS OF HIM.
DANBLF THE ONE-MAN ARMY, ONE OF THE WISE MEN OF THE LINKED SILVER TOWERS AND MASTER OF THE SUMMONING ARTS.
HE WAS ONE OF THE HEROES DURING THE AGE OF STRIFE, THIRTY YEARS AGO.
HEH. LOOKS LIKE DEVOTING MY LIFE TO GAMING FINALLY PAID OFF.

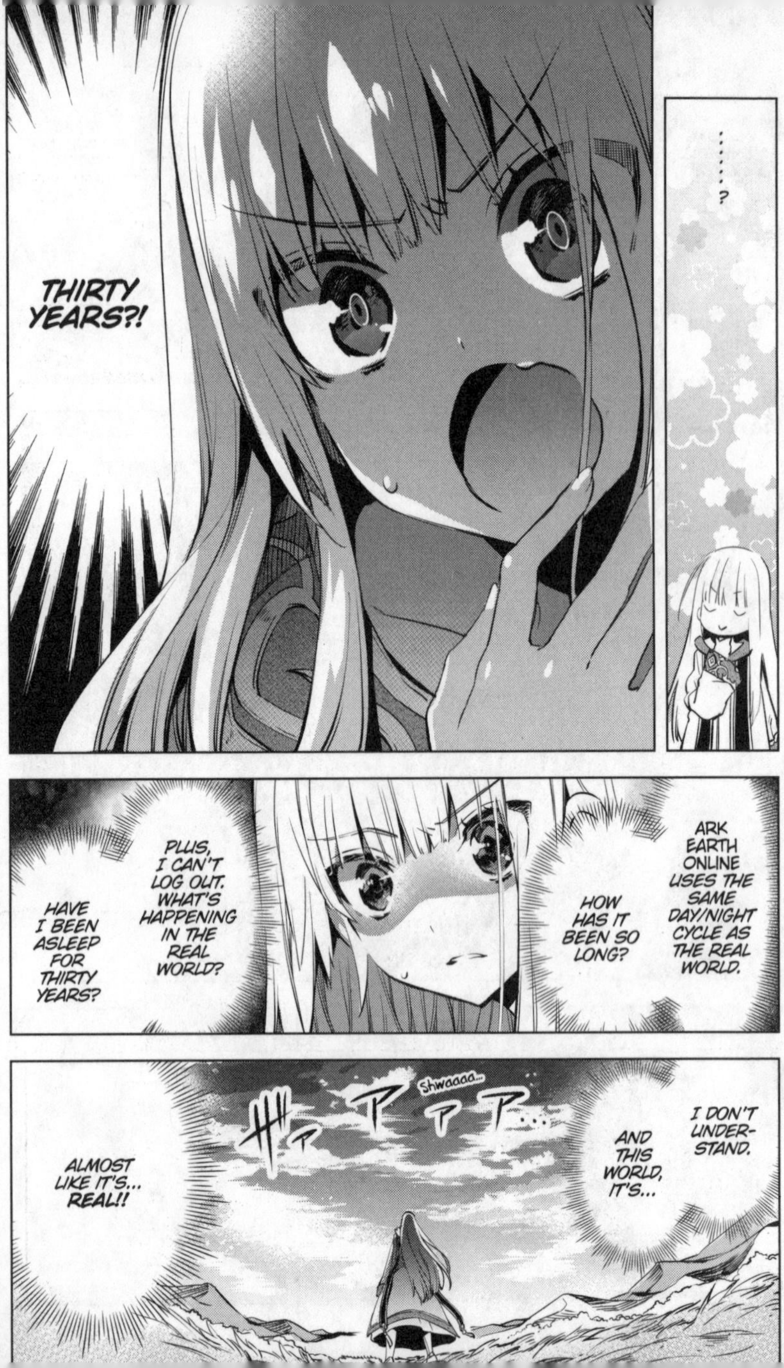
......?
THIRTY YEARS?!
ARK EARTH ONLINE USES THE SAME DAY/NIGHT CYCLE AS THE REAL WORLD.
HOW HAS IT BEEN SO LONG?
PLUS, I CAN'T LOG OUT. WHAT'S HAPPENING IN THE REAL WORLD?
HAVE I BEEN ASLEEP FOR THIRTY YEARS?
I DON'T UNDER-STAND.
AND THIS WORLD, IT'S...
Shwaaaa...
ALMOST LIKE IT'S... REAL!!

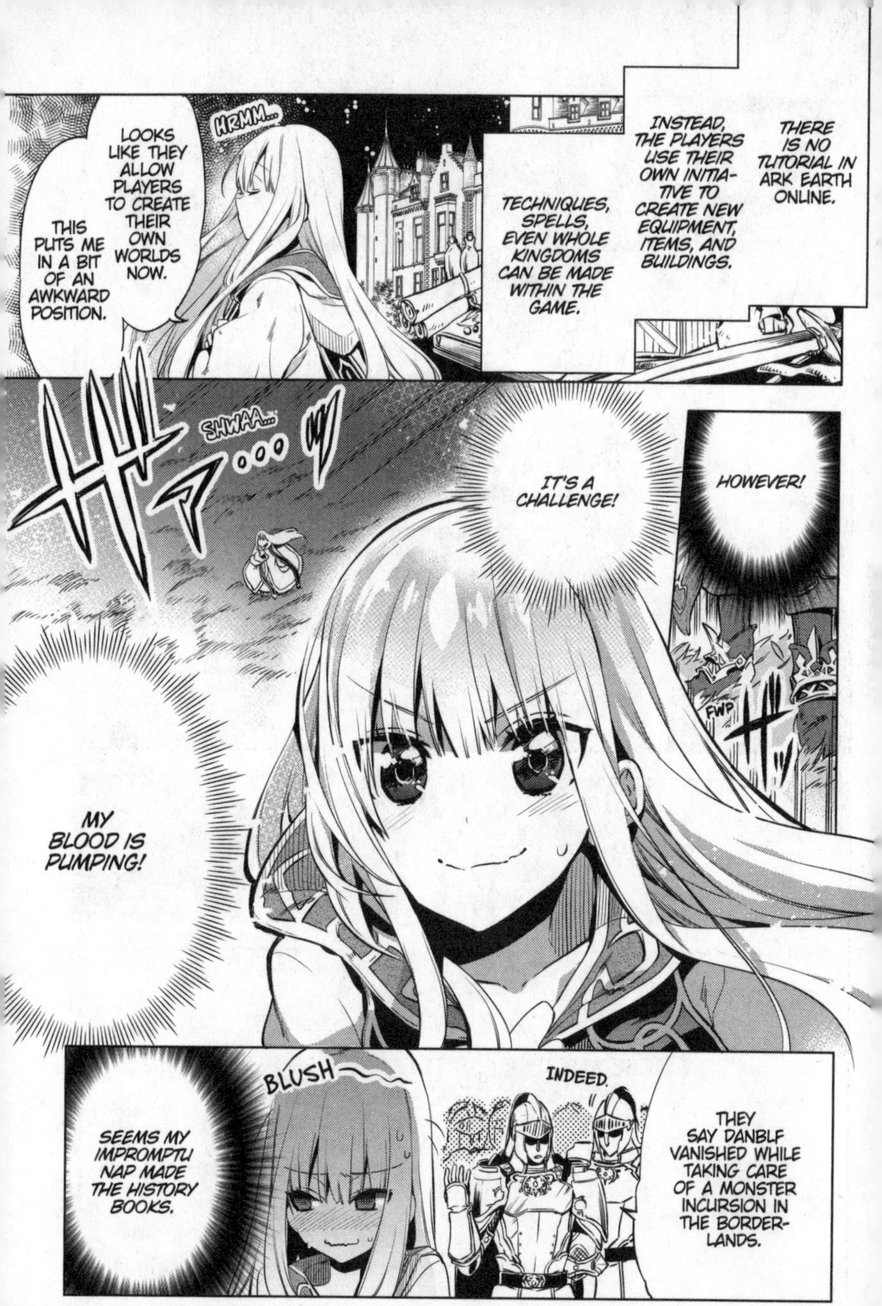
THERE IS NO TUTORIAL IN ARK EARTH ONLINE.
INSTEAD, THE PLAYERS USE THEIR OWN INITIA-TIVE TO CREATE NEW EQUIPMENT, ITEMS, AND BUILDINGS.
TECHNIQUES, SPELLS, EVEN WHOLE KINGDOMS CAN BE MADE WITHIN THE GAME.
HRMM...
LOOKS LIKE THEY ALLOW PLAYERS TO CREATE THEIR OWN WORLDS NOW.
THIS PUTS ME IN A BIT OF AN AWKWARD POSITION.
HOWEVER!
FWP
IT'S A CHALLENGE!
SHWAA...
MY BLOOD IS PUMPING!
THEY SAY DANBLF VANISHED WHILE TAKING CARE OF A MONSTER INCURSION IN THE BORDER-LANDS.
INDEED.
BLUSH
SEEMS MY IMPROMPTU NAP MADE THE HISTORY BOOKS.

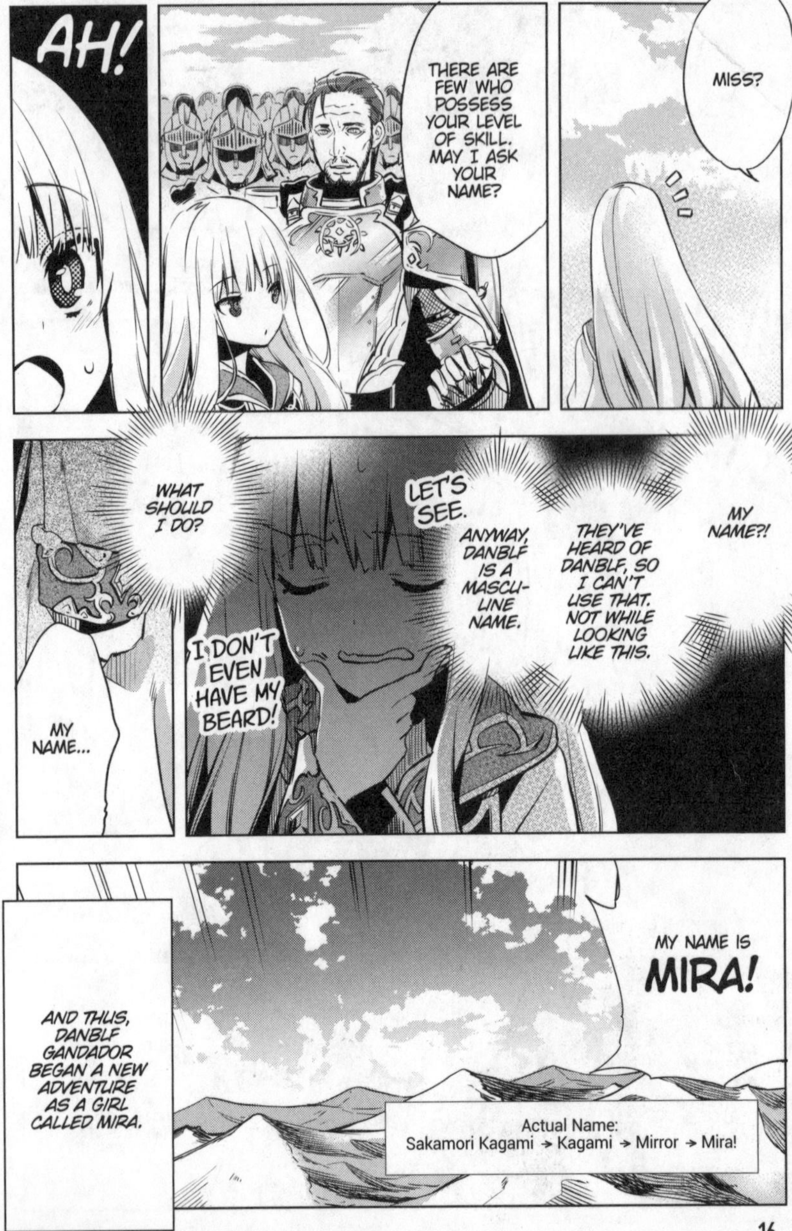
MISS?
THERE ARE FEW WHO POSSESS YOUR LEVEL OF SKILL. MAY I ASK YOUR NAME?
AH!
MY NAME?!
THEY'VE HEARD OF DANBLF, SO I CAN'T USE THAT. NOT WHILE LOOKING LIKE THIS.
ANYWAY, DANBLF IS A MASCU-LINE NAME.
LET'S SEE.
WHAT SHOULD I DO?
I DON'T EVEN HAVE MY BEARD!
MY NAME...
MY NAME IS MIRA!
Actual Name:
Sakamori Kagami → Kagami → Mirror → Mira!
AND THUS, DANBLF GANDADOR BEGAN A NEW ADVENTURE AS A GIRL CALLED MIRA.

Summon 1: END

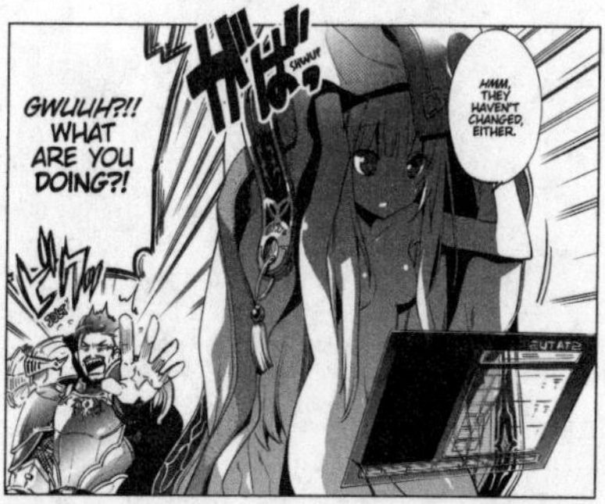
HMM, THEY HAVEN'T CHANGED, EITHER.
SHWUP
GWUUH?!! WHAT ARE YOU DOING?!

She
Professed
Herself
Pupil of
the
Wise Man

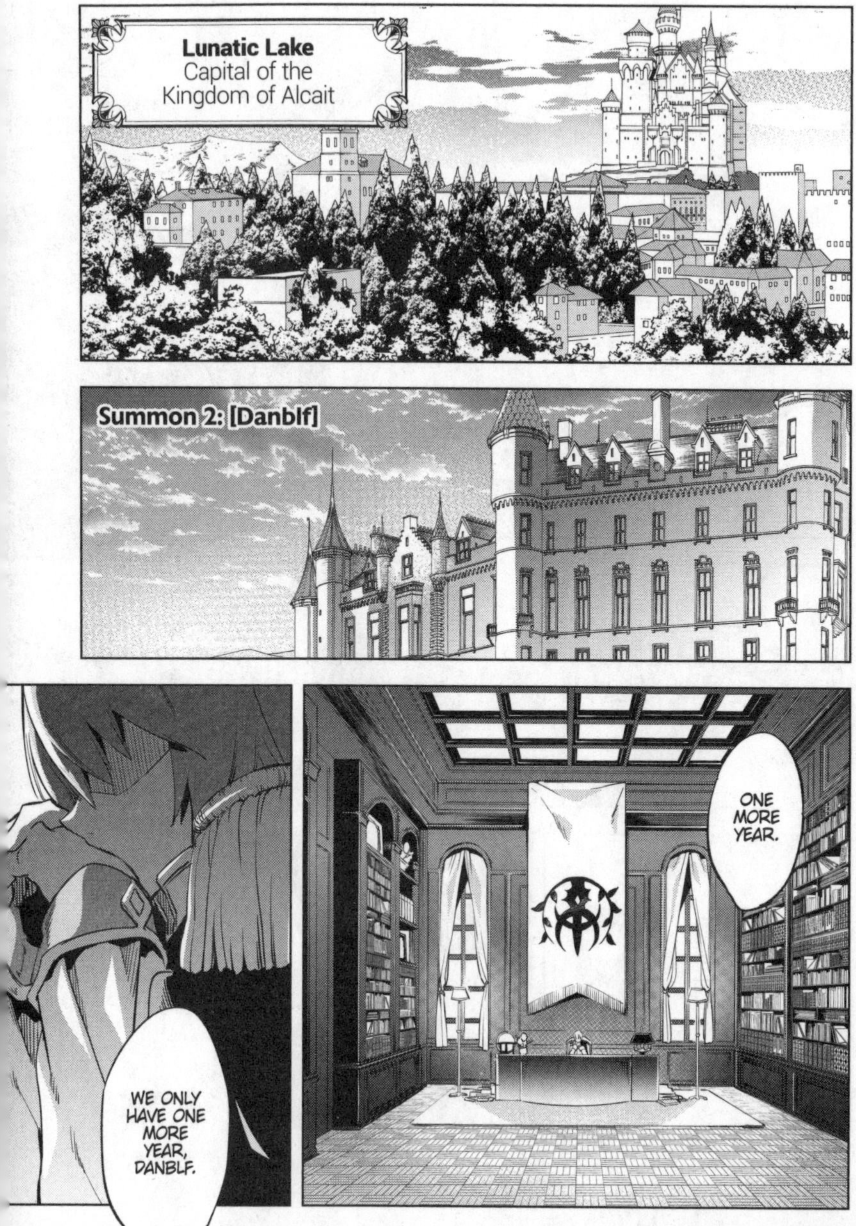
Lunatic Lake
Capital of the Kingdom of Alcait
Summon 2: [Danblf]
ONE MORE YEAR.
WE ONLY HAVE ONE MORE YEAR, DANBLF.

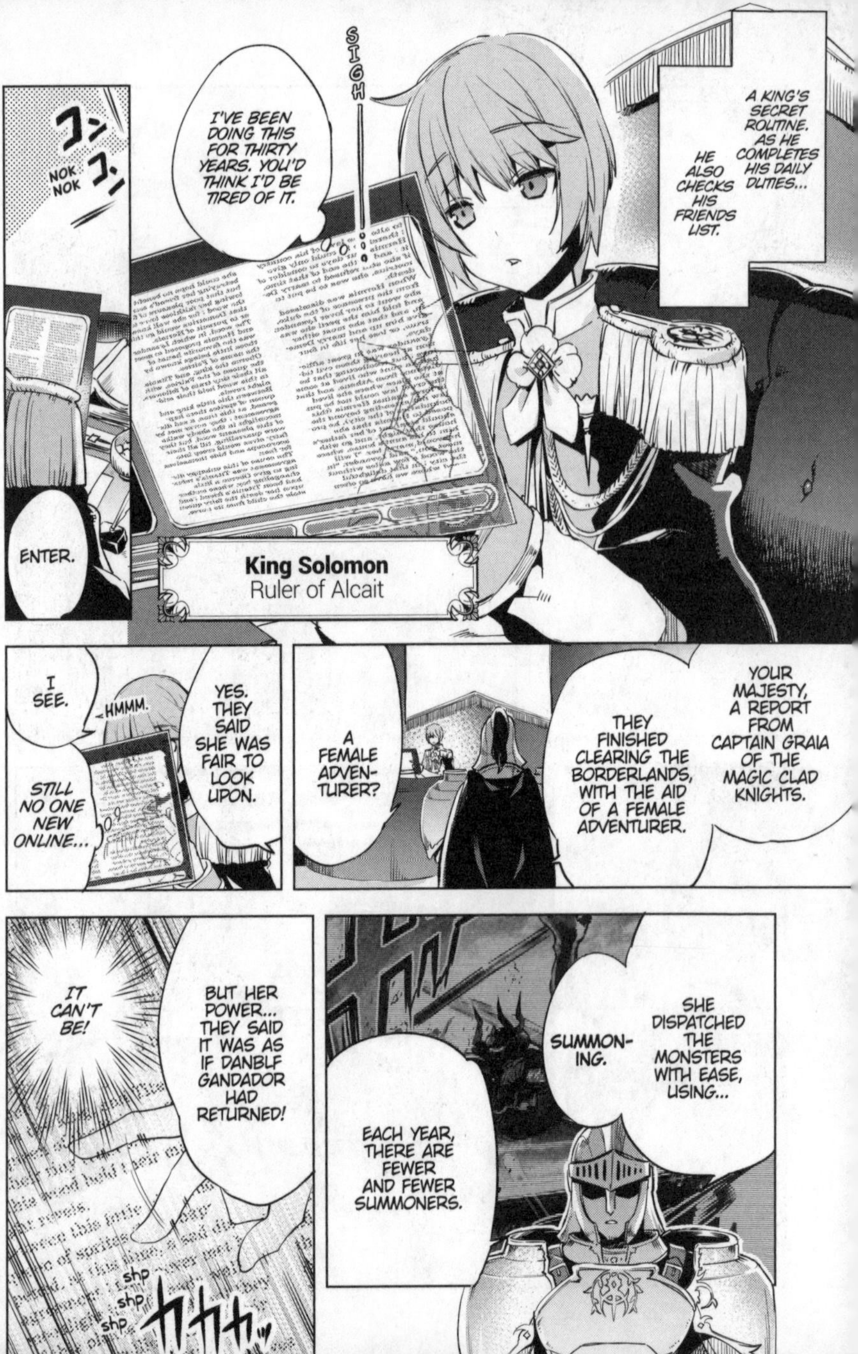
A KING'S SECRET ROUTINE. AS HE COMPLETES HIS DAILY DUTIES...
HE ALSO CHECKS HIS FRIENDS LIST.
SIGH
I'VE BEEN DOING THIS FOR THIRTY YEARS. YOU'D THINK I'D BE TIRED OF IT.
コンコン
NOK NOK
ENTER.
King Solomon
Ruler of Alcait
YOUR MAJESTY, A REPORT FROM CAPTAIN GRAIA OF THE MAGIC CLAD KNIGHTS.
THEY FINISHED CLEARING THE BORDERLANDS, WITH THE AID OF A FEMALE ADVENTURER.
A FEMALE ADVENTURER?
YES. THEY SAID SHE WAS FAIR TO LOOK UPON.
HMMM.
I SEE.
STILL NO ONE NEW ONLINE...
SHE DISPATCHED THE MONSTERS WITH EASE, USING...
SUMMONING.
EACH YEAR, THERE ARE FEWER AND FEWER SUMMONERS.
BUT HER POWER... THEY SAID IT WAS AS IF DANBLF GANDADOR HAD RETURNED!
IT CAN'T BE!
shp
shp
shp

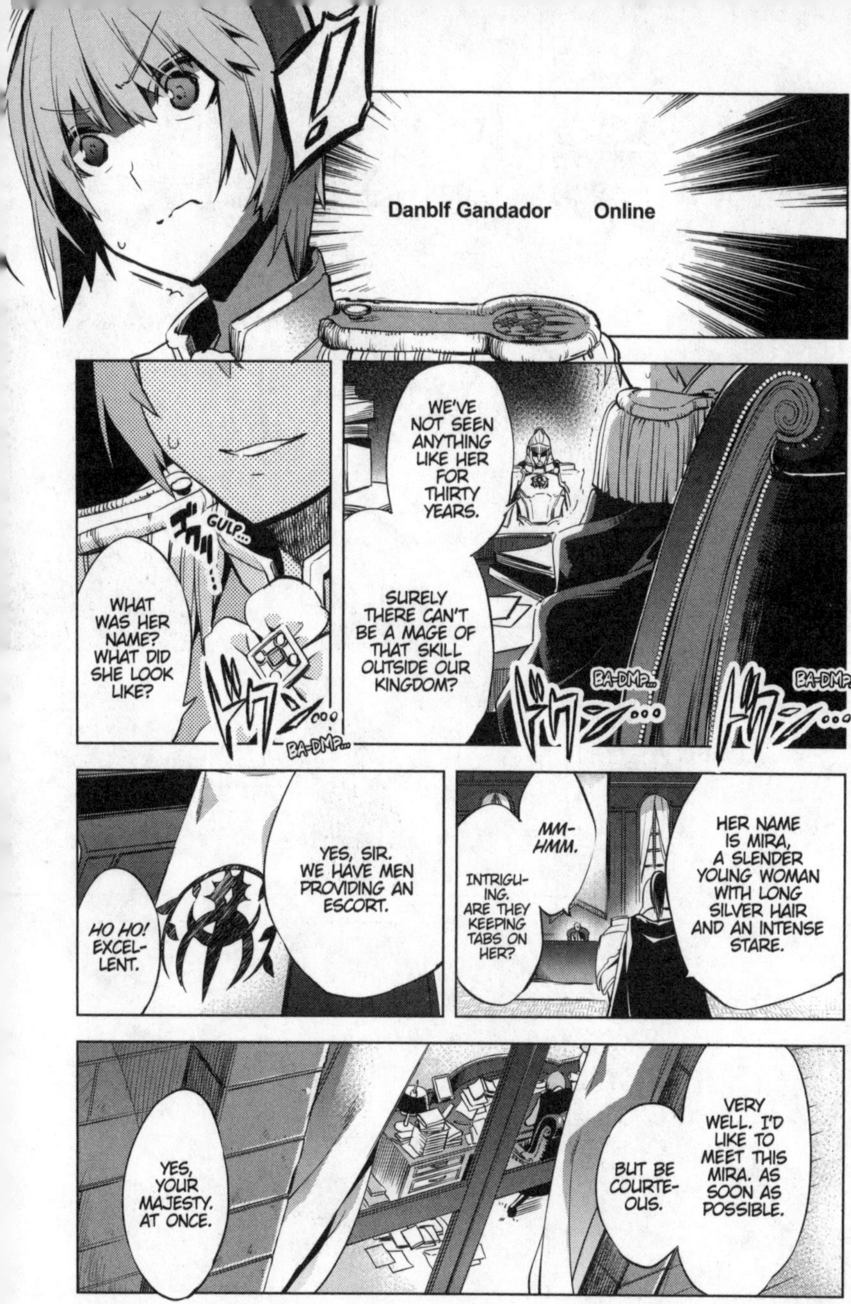
Danblf Gandador Online
WE'VE NOT SEEN ANYTHING LIKE HER FOR THIRTY YEARS.
SURELY THERE CAN'T BE A MAGE OF THAT SKILL OUTSIDE OUR KINGDOM?
BA-DMP...
BA-DMP...
GULP...
WHAT WAS HER NAME? WHAT DID SHE LOOK LIKE?
BA-DMP...
HER NAME IS MIRA, A SLENDER YOUNG WOMAN WITH LONG SILVER HAIR AND AN INTENSE STARE.
MM-HMM.
INTRIGUING. ARE THEY KEEPING TABS ON HER?
YES, SIR. WE HAVE MEN PROVIDING AN ESCORT.
HO HO! EXCELLENT.
VERY WELL. I'D LIKE TO MEET THIS MIRA. AS SOON AS POSSIBLE.
BUT BE COURTEOUS.
YES, YOUR MAJESTY. AT ONCE.

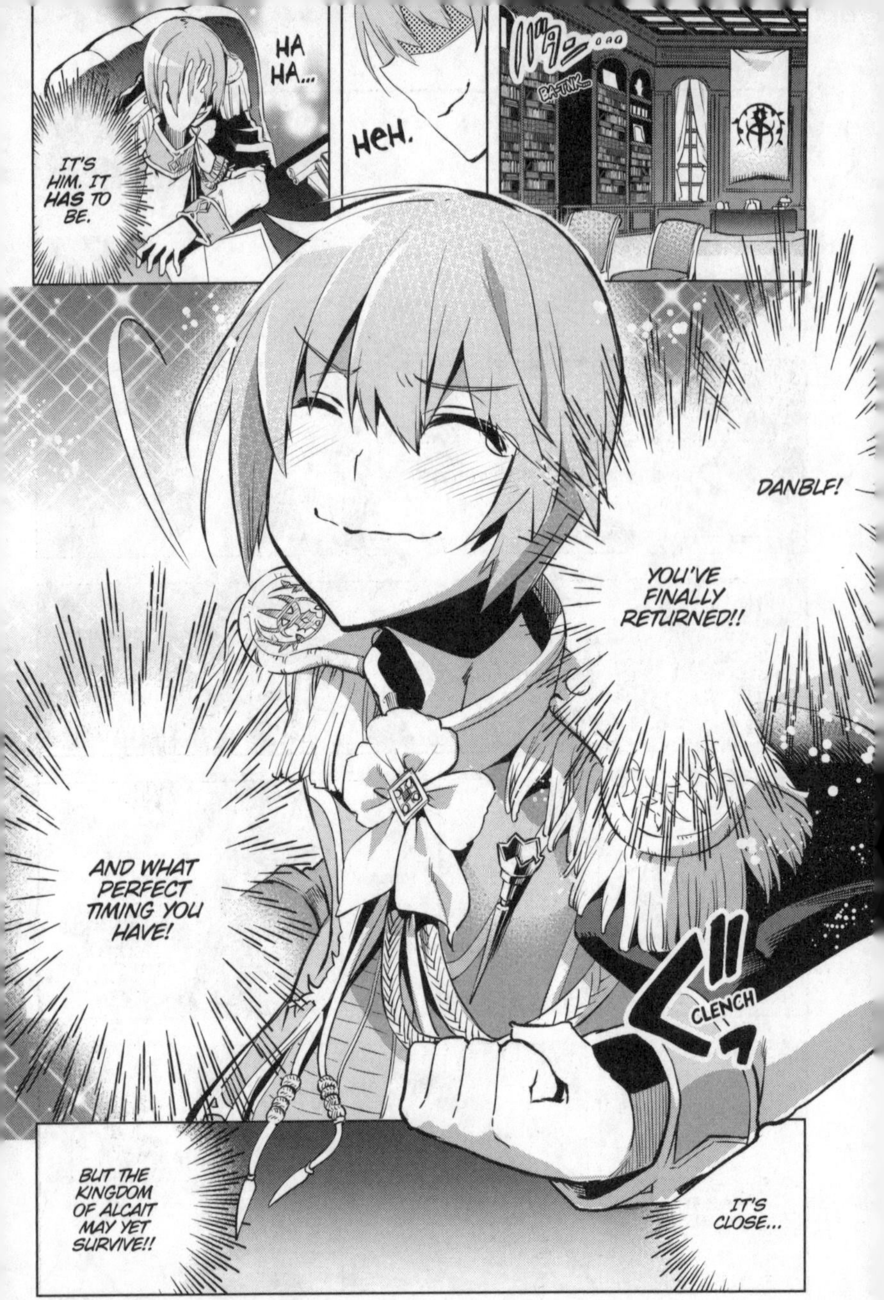
BA-TINK...
HEH.
HA HA...
IT'S HIM. IT HAS TO BE.
DANBLF!
YOU'VE FINALLY RETURNED!!
AND WHAT PERFECT TIMING YOU HAVE!
CLENCH
IT'S CLOSE...
BUT THE KINGDOM OF ALCAIT MAY YET SURVIVE!!

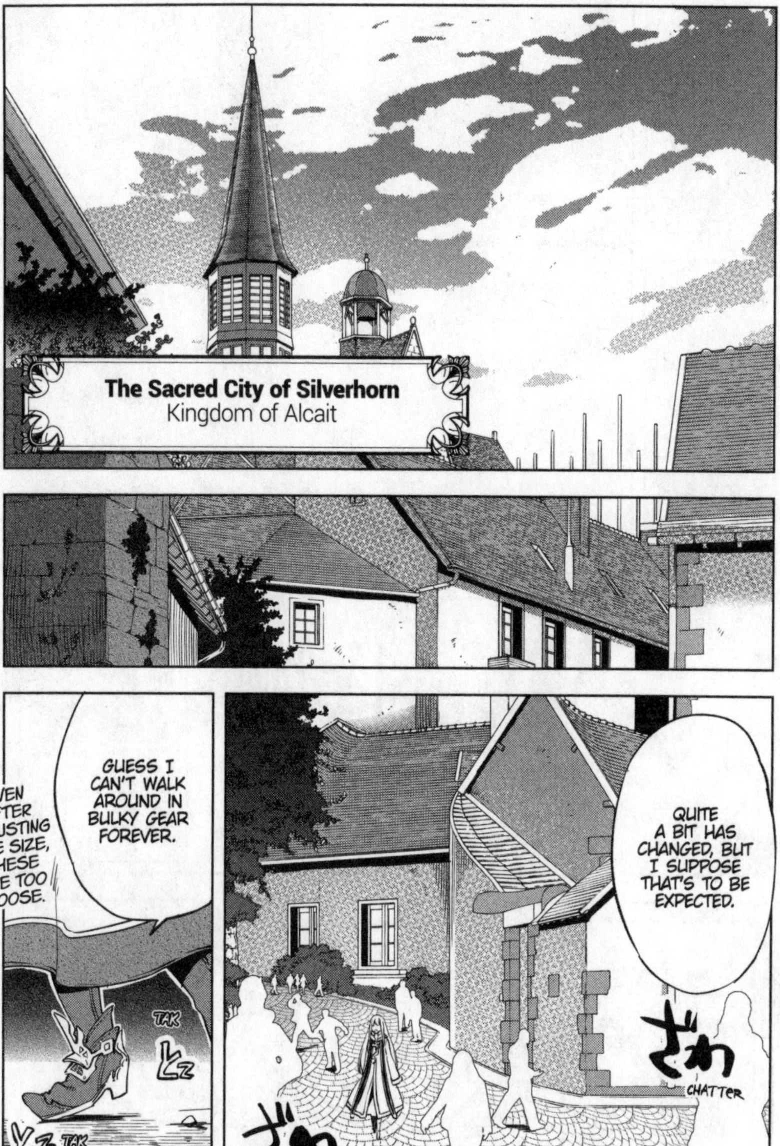
The Sacred City of Silverhorn
Kingdom of Alcait
QUITE A BIT HAS CHANGED, BUT I SUPPOSE THAT'S TO BE EXPECTED.
ざわ
CHATTER
ざわ
CHATTER
GUESS I CAN'T WALK AROUND IN BULKY GEAR FOREVER.
EVEN AFTER ADJUSTING THE SIZE, THESE ARE TOO LOOSE.
TAK
TAK

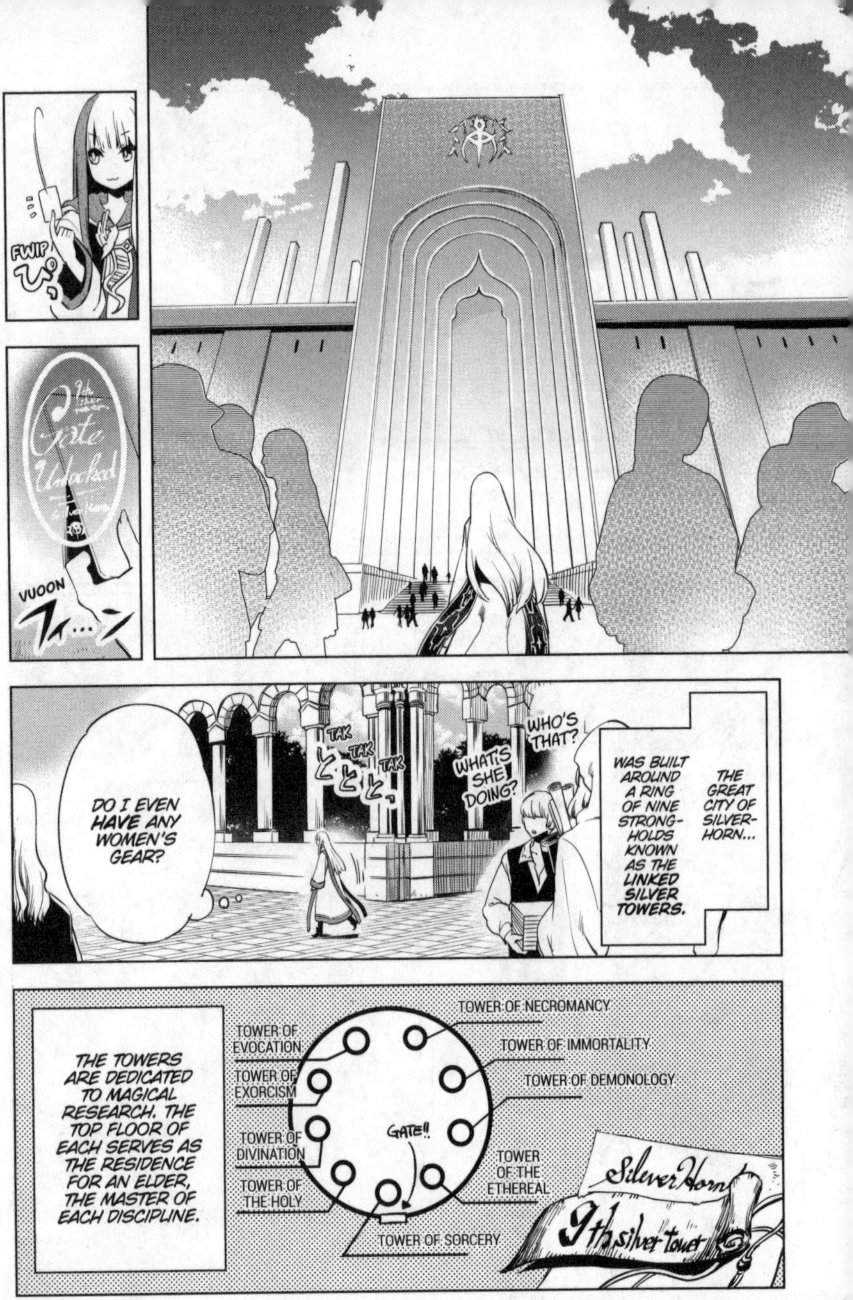
FWIP
Gate Unlocked
VUOON
THE GREAT CITY OF SILVER-HORN...
WAS BUILT AROUND A RING OF NINE STRONG-HOLDS KNOWN AS THE LINKED SILVER TOWERS.
WHO'S THAT?
WHAT'S SHE DOING?
TAK TAK TAK
DO I EVEN HAVE ANY WOMEN'S GEAR?
THE TOWERS ARE DEDICATED TO MAGICAL RESEARCH. THE TOP FLOOR OF EACH SERVES AS THE RESIDENCE FOR AN ELDER, THE MASTER OF EACH DISCIPLINE.
TOWER OF NECROMANCY
TOWER OF IMMORTALITY
TOWER OF DEMONOLOGY
TOWER OF THE ETHEREAL
TOWER OF SORCERY
TOWER OF THE HOLY
TOWER OF DIVINATION
TOWER OF EXORCISM
TOWER OF EVOCATION
GATE!!
Silever Horn

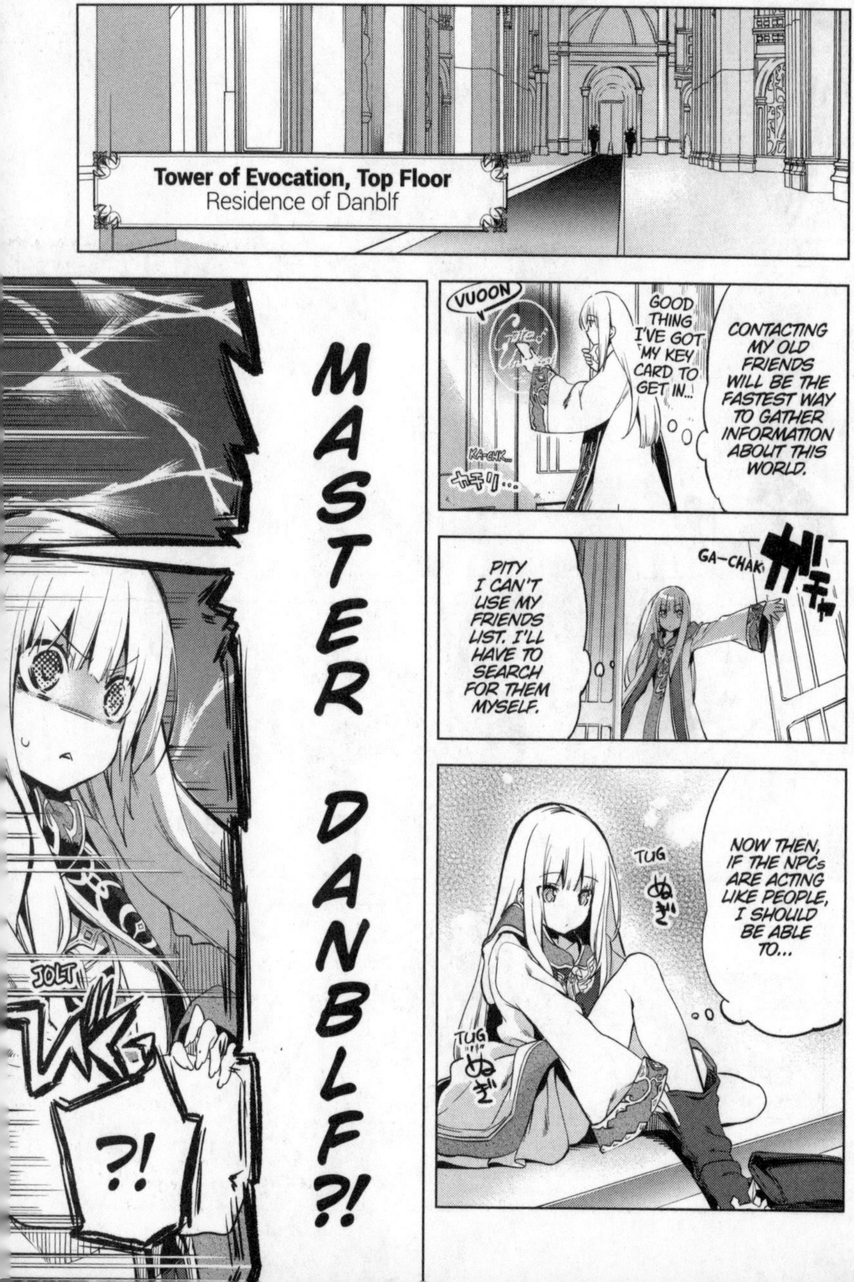
Tower of Evocation, Top Floor
Residence of Danblf
CONTACTING MY OLD FRIENDS WILL BE THE FASTEST WAY TO GATHER INFORMATION ABOUT THIS WORLD.
GOOD THING I'VE GOT MY KEY CARD TO GET IN...
VUOON
KA-CHK...
カチリ...
GA-CHAK
ガチャ
PITY I CAN'T USE MY FRIENDS LIST. I'LL HAVE TO SEARCH FOR THEM MYSELF.
NOW THEN, IF THE NPCs ARE ACTING LIKE PEOPLE, I SHOULD BE ABLE TO...
TUG
ぬぎ
TUG
ぬぎ
MASTER DANBLF?!
JOLT
?!

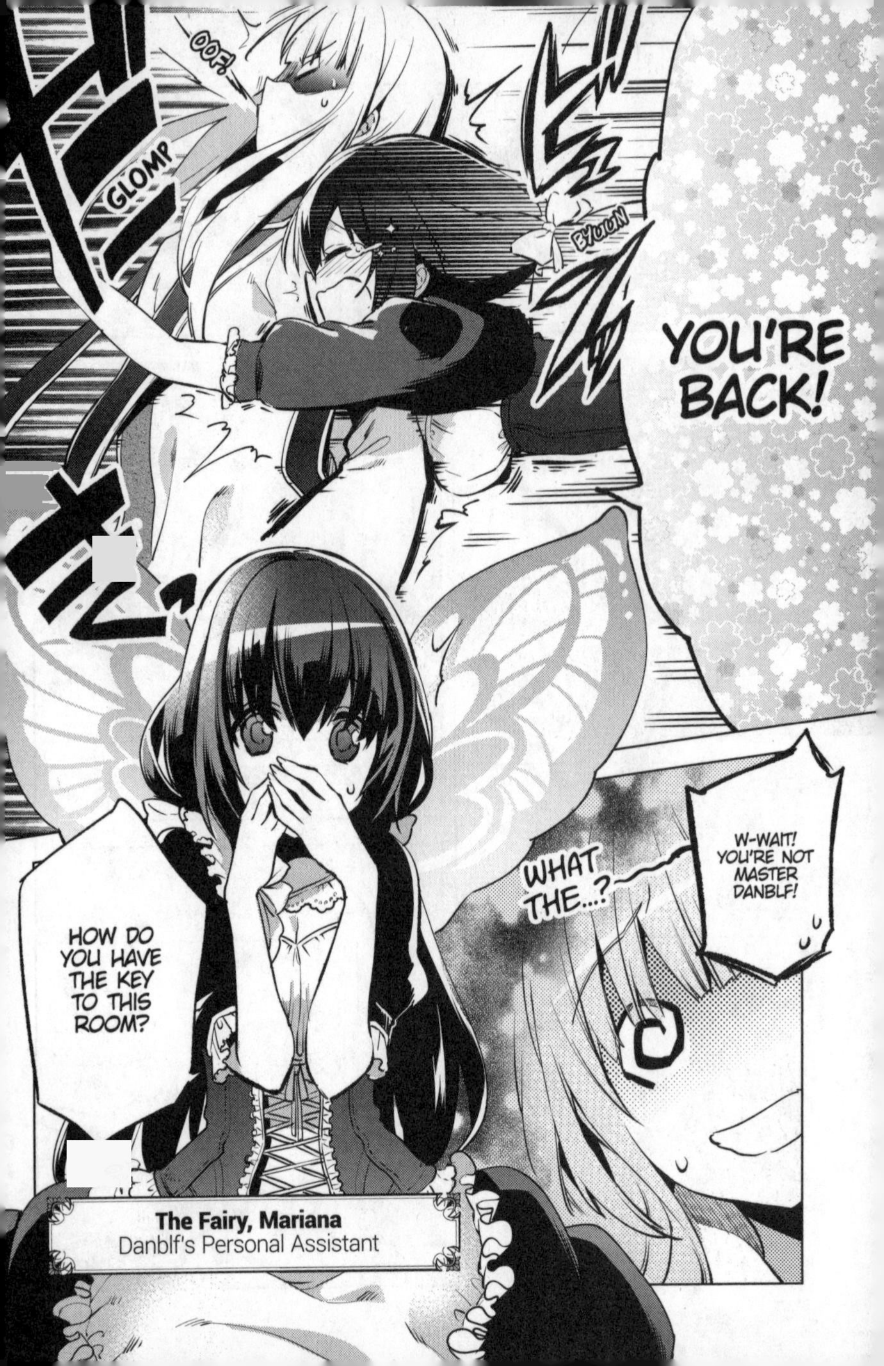
OOF
BYUUN
YOU'RE BACK!
GLOMP
W-WAIT! YOU'RE NOT MASTER DANBLF!
WHAT THE...?
HOW DO YOU HAVE THE KEY TO THIS ROOM?
The Fairy, Mariana
Danblf's Personal Assistant

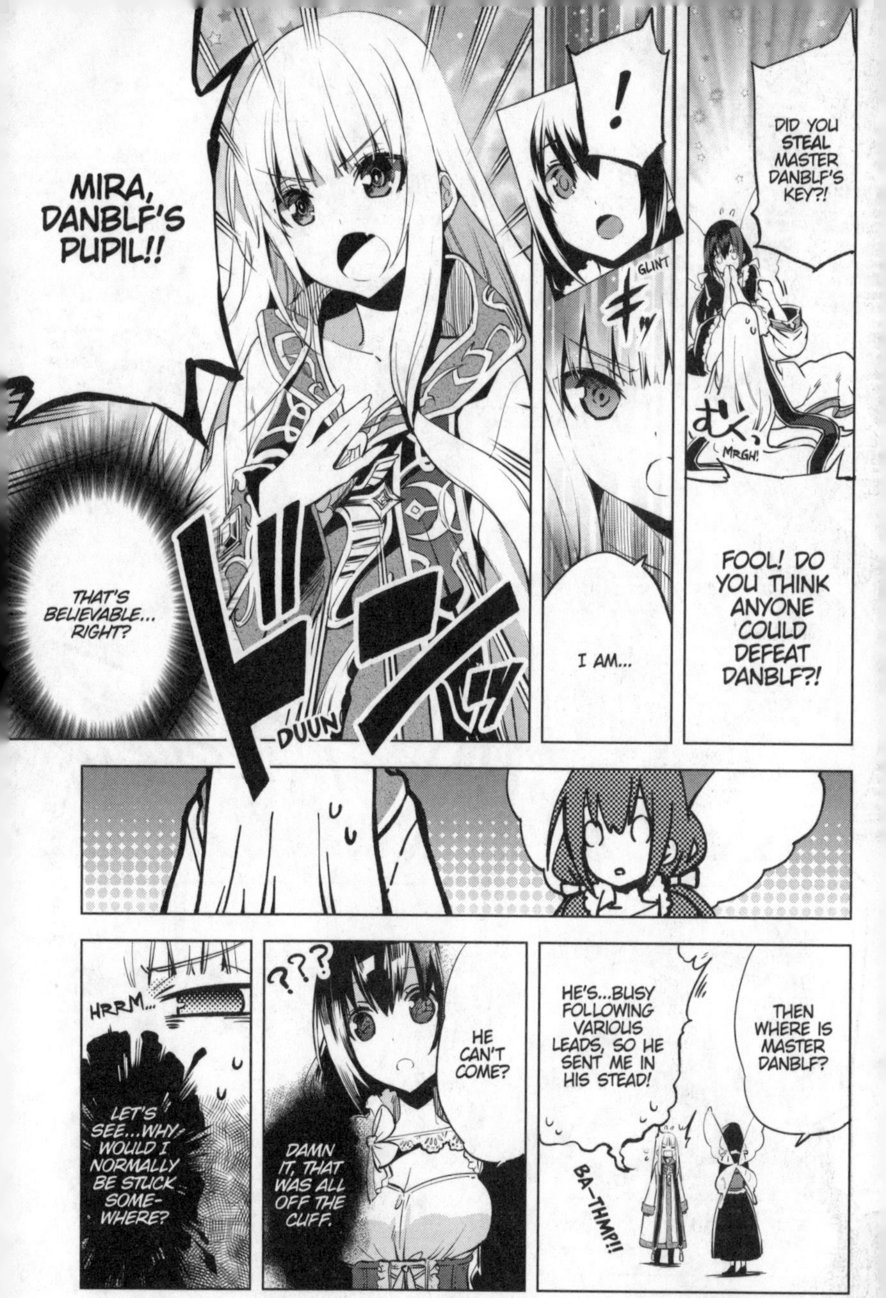
DID YOU STEAL MASTER DANBLF'S KEY?!
むく
MRGH!
FOOL! DO YOU THINK ANYONE COULD DEFEAT DANBLF?!
!
GLINT
キッ
I AM...
MIRA, DANBLF'S PUPIL!!
DUUN
THAT'S BELIEVABLE... RIGHT?
THEN WHERE IS MASTER DANBLF?
HE'S...BUSY FOLLOWING VARIOUS LEADS, SO HE SENT ME IN HIS STEAD!
BA-THMP!!
???
HE CAN'T COME?
DAMN IT, THAT WAS ALL OFF THE CUFF.
HRRM...
LET'S SEE...WHY WOULD I NORMALLY BE STUCK SOME-WHERE?

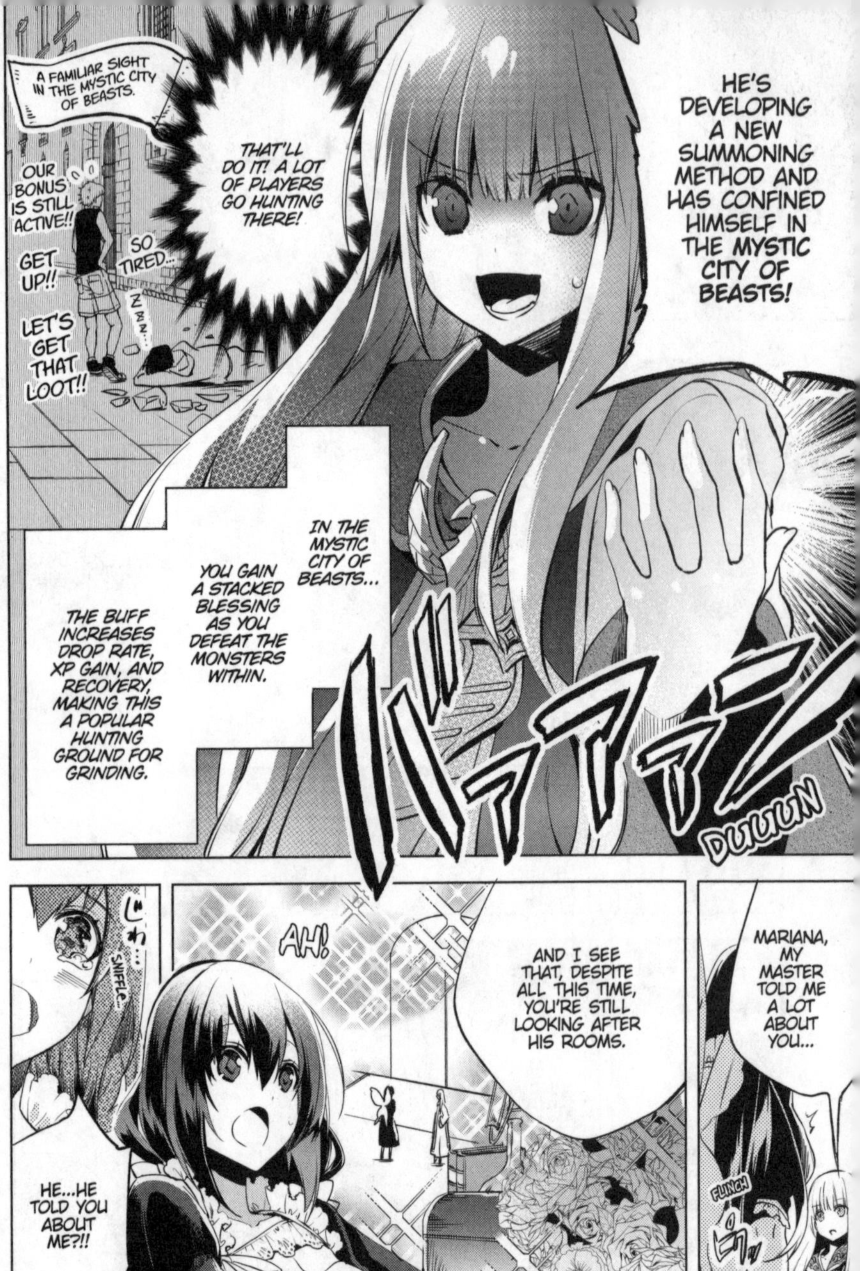
HE'S DEVELOPING A NEW SUMMONING METHOD AND HAS CONFINED HIMSELF IN THE MYSTIC CITY OF BEASTS!
THAT'LL DO IT! A LOT OF PLAYERS GO HUNTING THERE!
A FAMILIAR SIGHT IN THE MYSTIC CITY OF BEASTS.
OUR BONUS IS STILL ACTIVE!!
SO TIRED...
GET UP!!
LET'S GET THAT LOOT!!
IN THE MYSTIC CITY OF BEASTS...
YOU GAIN A STACKED BLESSING AS YOU DEFEAT THE MONSTERS WITHIN.
THE BUFF INCREASES DROP RATE, XP GAIN, AND RECOVERY, MAKING THIS A POPULAR HUNTING GROUND FOR GRINDING.
DUUUN
MARIANA, MY MASTER TOLD ME A LOT ABOUT YOU...
FLINCH
AND I SEE THAT, DESPITE ALL THIS TIME, YOU'RE STILL LOOKING AFTER HIS ROOMS.
AH!
SNIFFLE...
HE...HE TOLD YOU ABOUT ME?!!

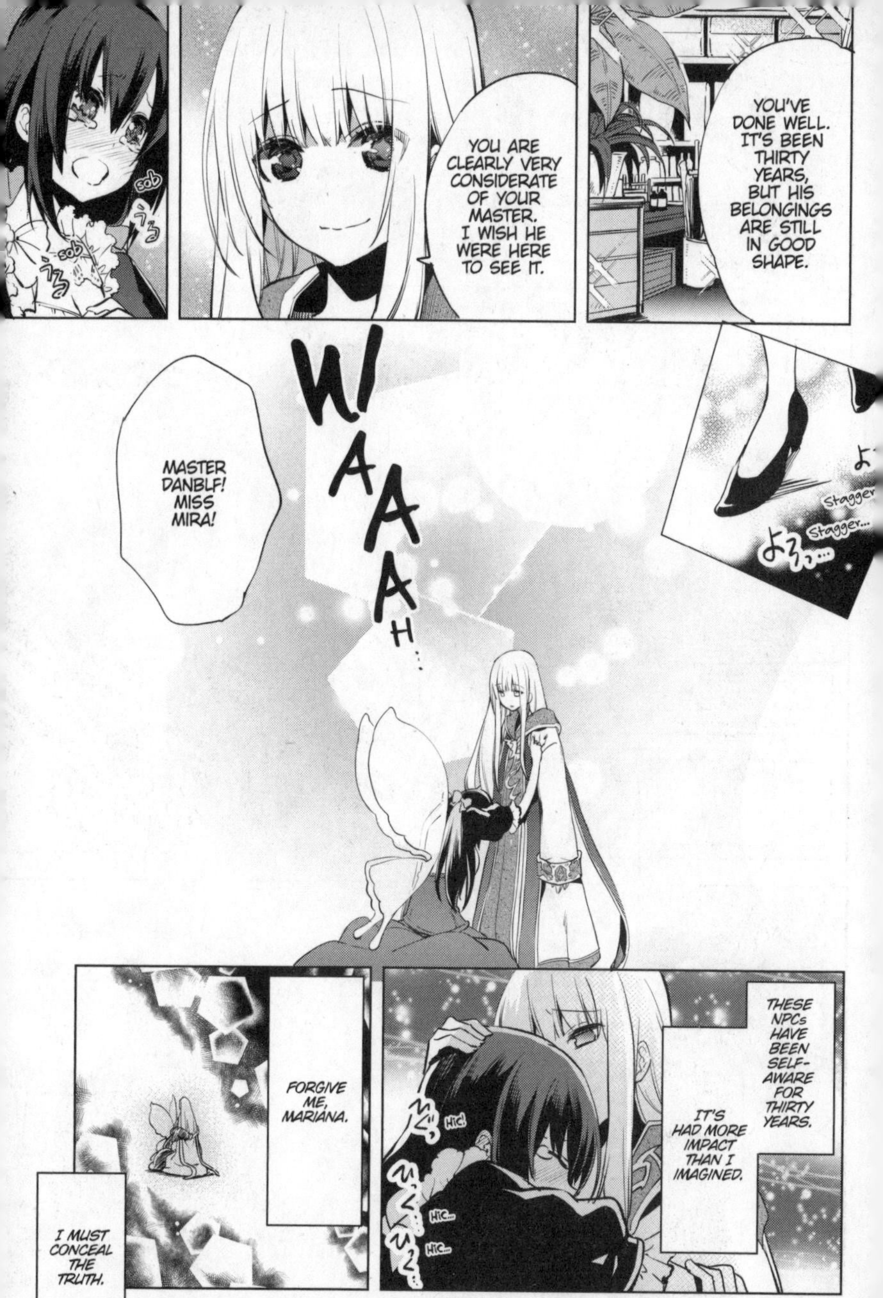
YOU'VE DONE WELL. IT'S BEEN THIRTY YEARS, BUT HIS BELONGINGS ARE STILL IN GOOD SHAPE.
YOU ARE CLEARLY VERY CONSIDERATE OF YOUR MASTER. I WISH HE WERE HERE TO SEE IT.
sob
うる
sob
うる
よ
Stagger...
Stagger...
よろっ...
WAAAAH...
MASTER DANBLF! MISS MIRA!
THESE NPCs HAVE BEEN SELF-AWARE FOR THIRTY YEARS.
IT'S HAD MORE IMPACT THAN I IMAGINED.
Hic!
Hic...
Hic...
FORGIVE ME, MARIANA.
I MUST CONCEAL THE TRUTH.

Summon 2: END

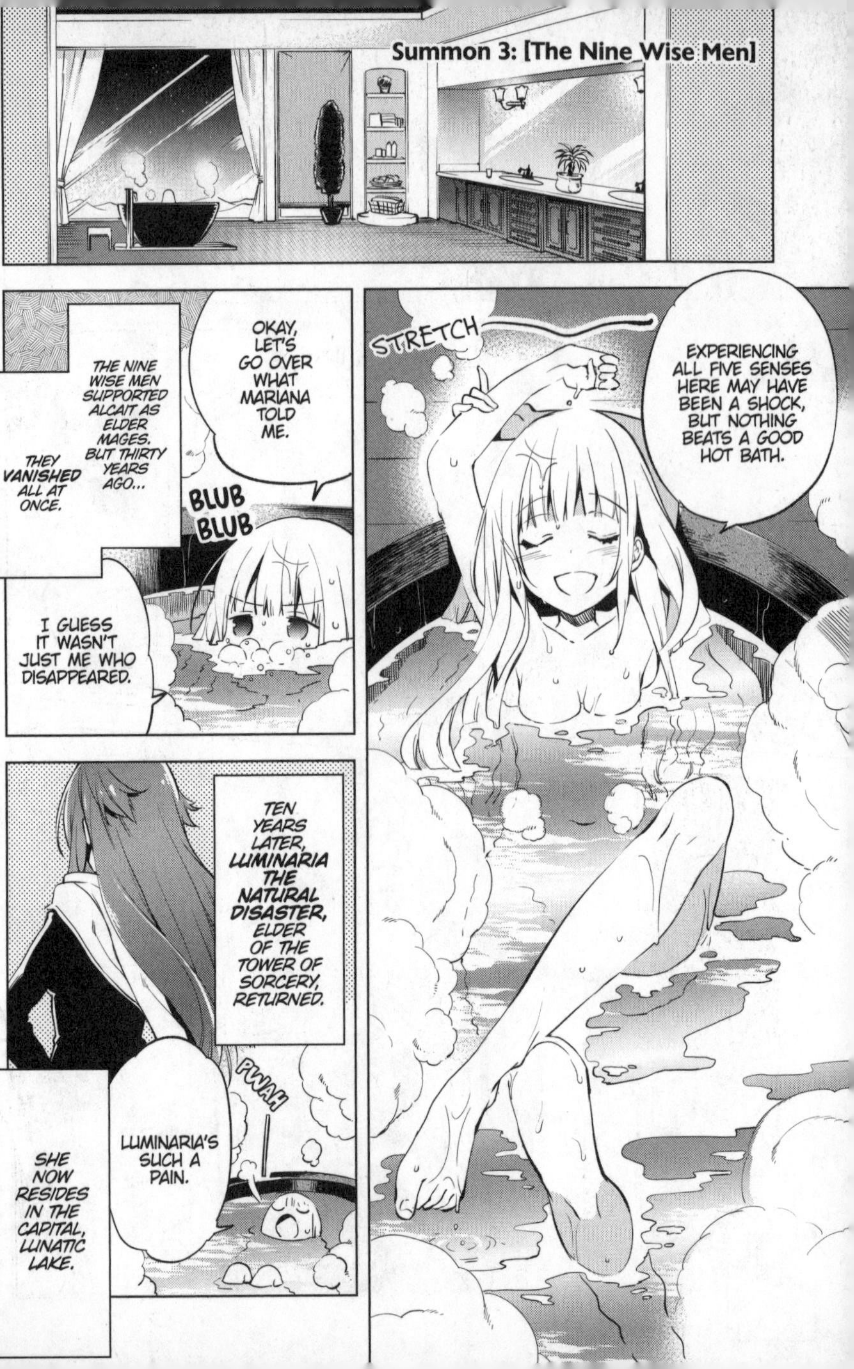
Summon 3: [The Nine Wise Men]
STRETCH
EXPERIENCING ALL FIVE SENSES HERE MAY HAVE BEEN A SHOCK, BUT NOTHING BEATS A GOOD HOT BATH.
OKAY, LET'S GO OVER WHAT MARIANA TOLD ME.
THE NINE WISE MEN SUPPORTED ALCAIT AS ELDER MAGES. BUT THIRTY YEARS AGO...
THEY VANISHED ALL AT ONCE.
BLUB BLUB
I GUESS IT WASN'T JUST ME WHO DISAPPEARED.
TEN YEARS LATER, LUMINARIA THE NATURAL DISASTER, ELDER OF THE TOWER OF SORCERY, RETURNED.
PWAH
LUMINARIA'S SUCH A PAIN.
SHE NOW RESIDES IN THE CAPITAL, LUNATIC LAKE.

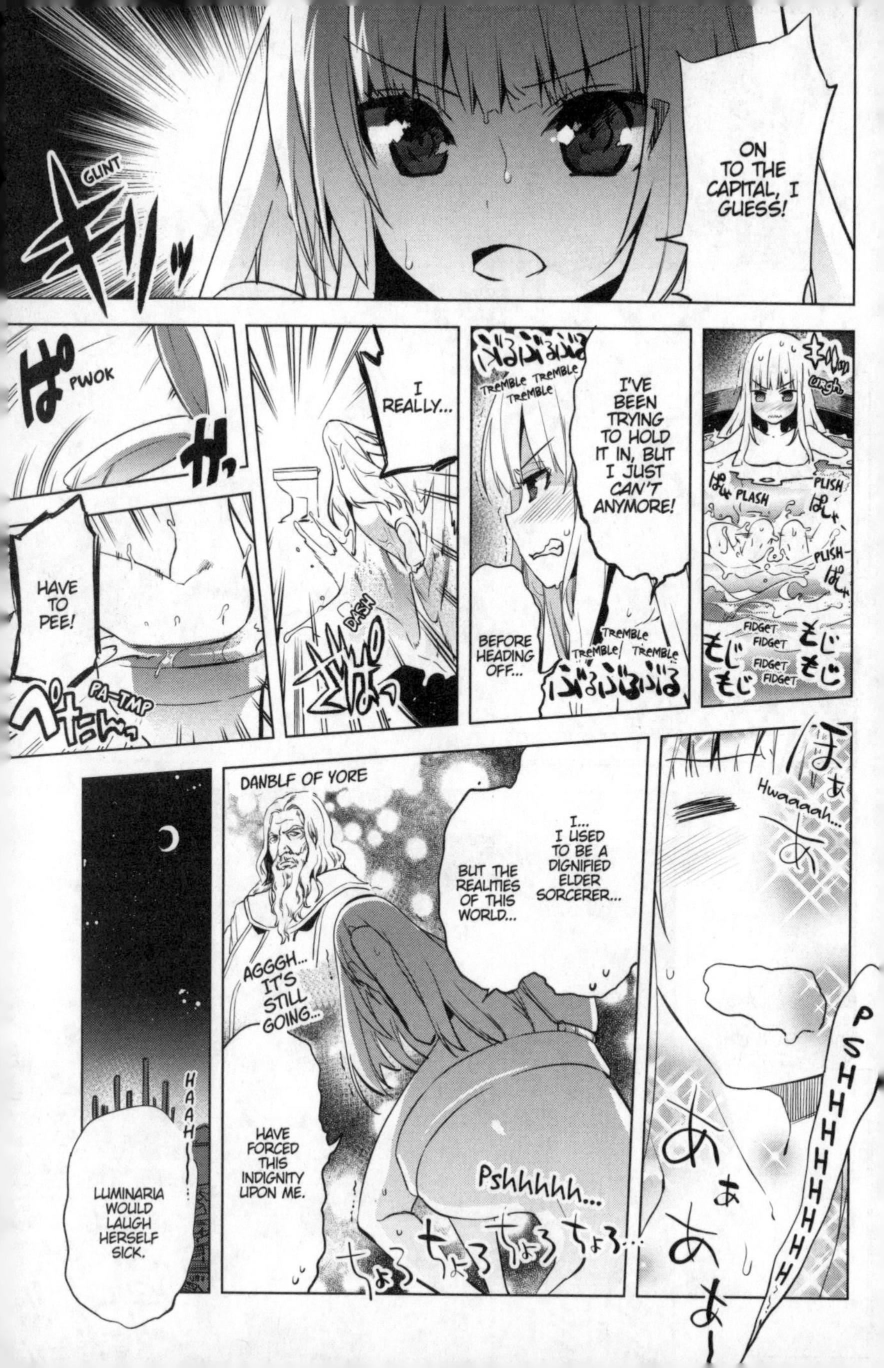
GLINT
ON TO THE CAPITAL, I GUESS!
ORGH
PLISH
PLASH
PLISH
FIDGET FIDGET
FIDGET FIDGET
TREMBLE TREMBLE TREMBLE
I'VE BEEN TRYING TO HOLD IT IN, BUT I JUST CAN'T ANYMORE!
BEFORE HEADING OFF...
TREMBLE TREMBLE TREMBLE
I REALLY...
DASH
PWOK
HAVE TO PEE!
PA-TMP
Hwaaaah...
DANBLF OF YORE
I... I USED TO BE A DIGNIFIED ELDER SORCERER...
BUT THE REALITIES OF THIS WORLD...
HAVE FORCED THIS INDIGNITY UPON ME.
AGGGH... IT'S STILL GOING...
Pshhhhh...
LUMINARIA WOULD LAUGH HERSELF SICK.

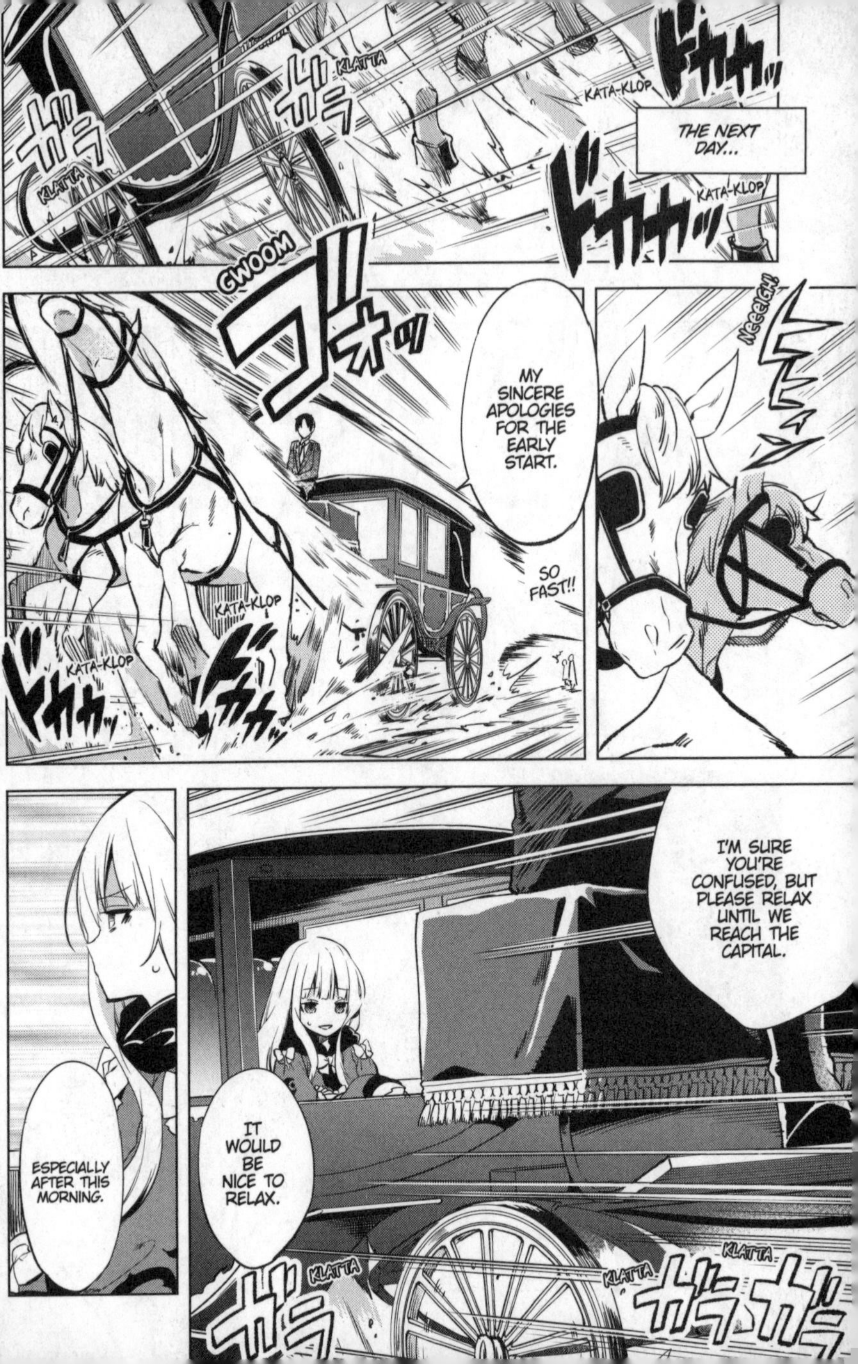
THE NEXT DAY...
KATA-KLOP
KATA-KLOP
KLATTA
KLATTA
NEEEIGH!
GWOOM
MY SINCERE APOLOGIES FOR THE EARLY START.
SO FAST!!
KATA-KLOP
KATA-KLOP
I'M SURE YOU'RE CONFUSED, BUT PLEASE RELAX UNTIL WE REACH THE CAPITAL.
IT WOULD BE NICE TO RELAX.
KLATTA
KLATTA
KLATTA
ESPECIALLY AFTER THIS MORNING.

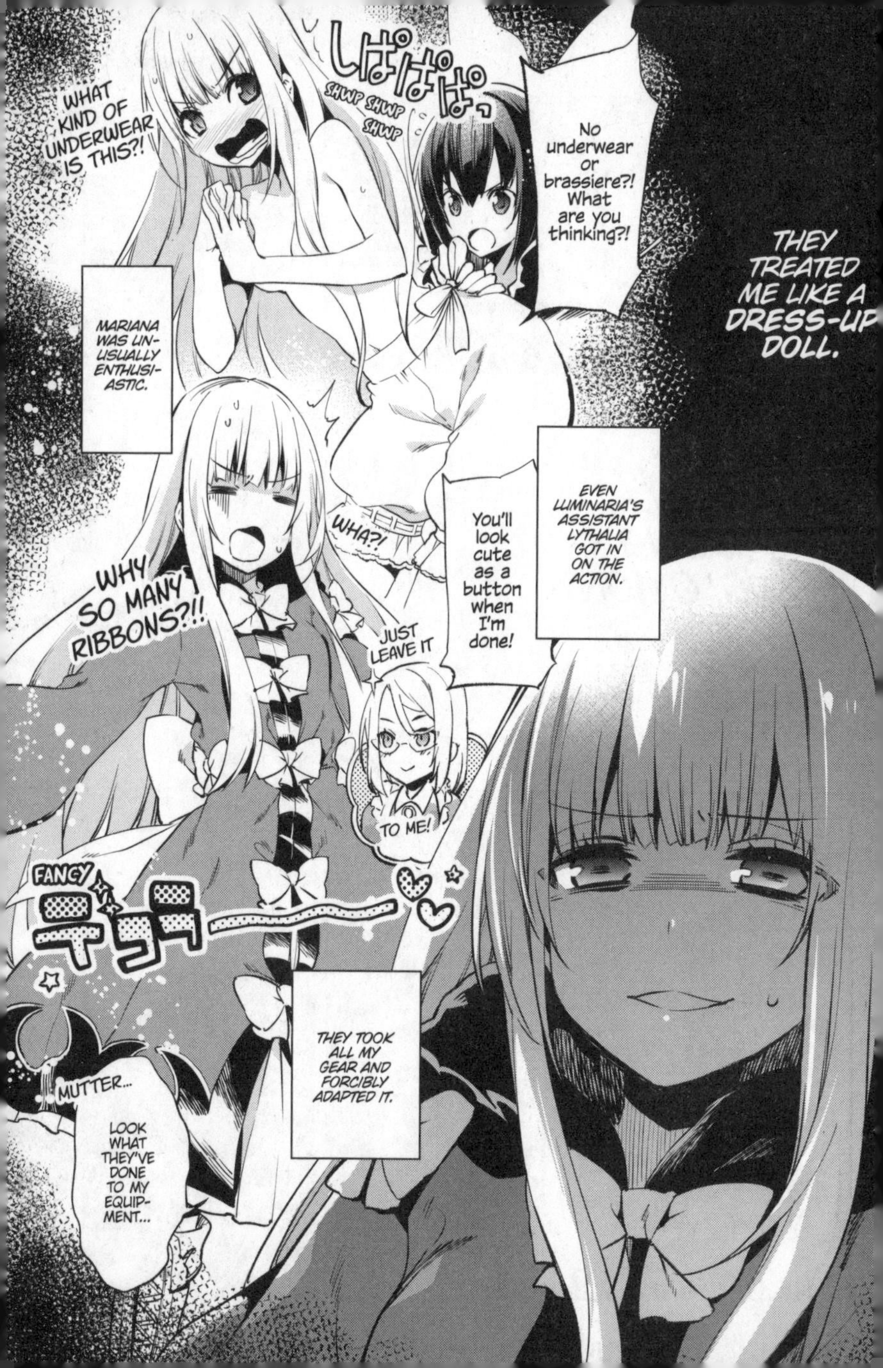
THEY TREATED ME LIKE A DRESS-UP DOLL.
No underwear or brassiere?! What are you thinking?!
しぱぱっ
SHWP SHWP SHWP
WHAT KIND OF UNDERWEAR IS THIS?!
MARIANA WAS UN-USUALLY ENTHUSI-ASTIC.
EVEN LUMINARIA'S ASSISTANT LYTHALIA GOT IN ON THE ACTION.
You'll look cute as a button when I'm done!
WHA?!
JUST LEAVE IT TO ME!
WHY SO MANY RIBBONS?!!
FANCY
THEY TOOK ALL MY GEAR AND FORCIBLY ADAPTED IT.
MUTTER...
LOOK WHAT THEY'VE DONE TO MY EQUIP-MENT...

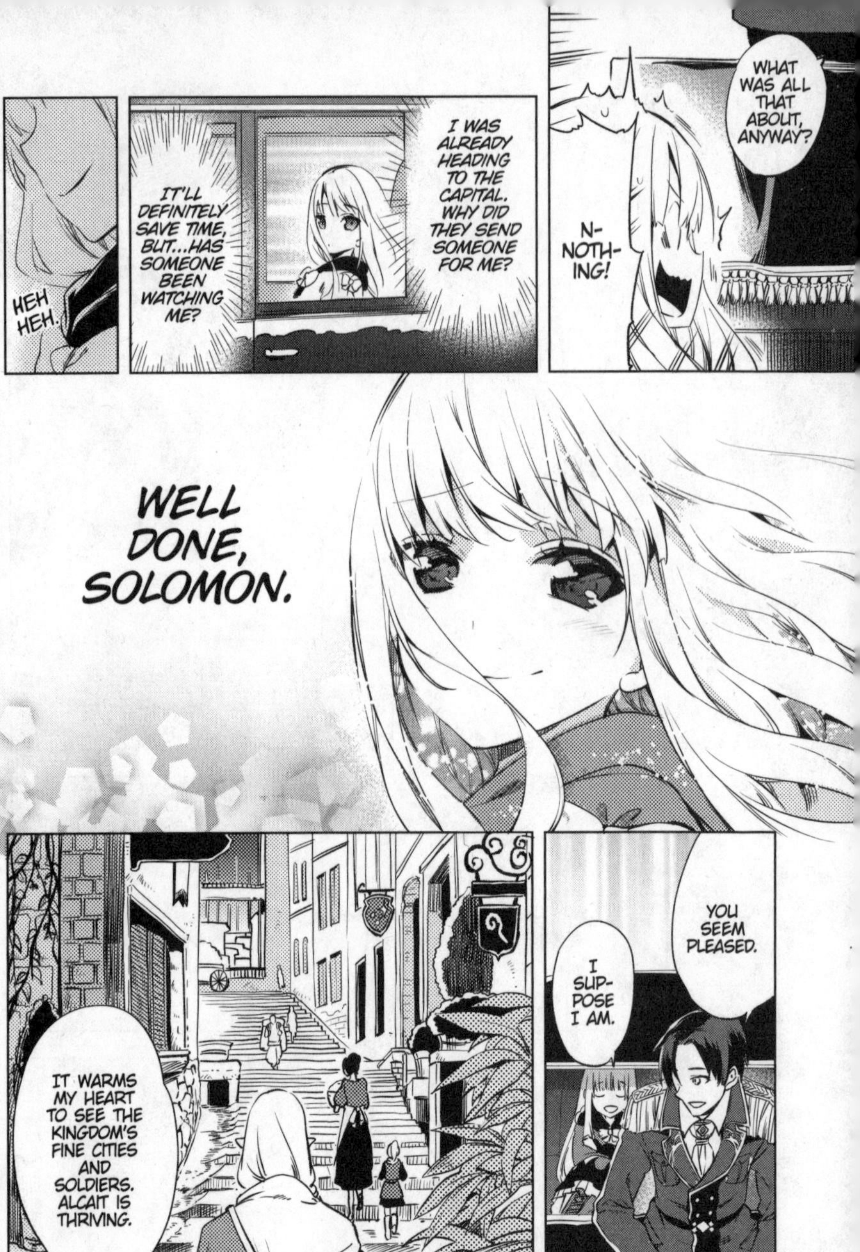
WHAT WAS ALL THAT ABOUT, ANYWAY?
N-NOTH-ING!
I WAS ALREADY HEADING TO THE CAPITAL. WHY DID THEY SEND SOMEONE FOR ME?
IT'LL DEFINITELY SAVE TIME, BUT...HAS SOMEONE BEEN WATCHING ME?
HEH HEH.
WELL DONE, SOLOMON.
YOU SEEM PLEASED.
I SUPPOSE I AM.
IT WARMS MY HEART TO SEE THE KINGDOM'S FINE CITIES AND SOLDIERS. ALCAIT IS THRIVING.

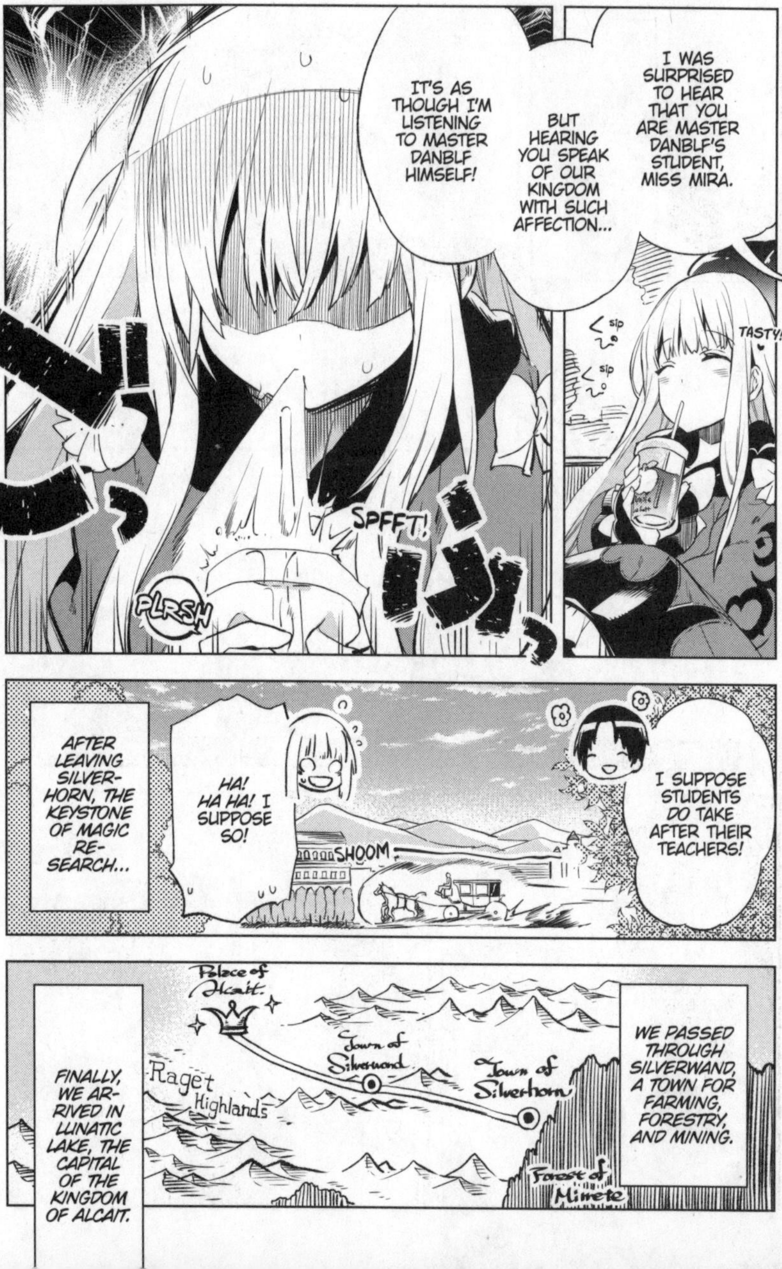
I WAS SURPRISED TO HEAR THAT YOU ARE MASTER DANBLF'S STUDENT, MISS MIRA.
sip
sip
TASTY!
BUT HEARING YOU SPEAK OF OUR KINGDOM WITH SUCH AFFECTION...
IT'S AS THOUGH I'M LISTENING TO MASTER DANBLF HIMSELF!
SPFFT!
PLRSH
I SUPPOSE STUDENTS DO TAKE AFTER THEIR TEACHERS!
HA! HA HA! I SUPPOSE SO!
SHOOM
AFTER LEAVING SILVER-HORN, THE KEYSTONE OF MAGIC RE-SEARCH...
WE PASSED THROUGH SILVERWAND, A TOWN FOR FARMING, FORESTRY, AND MINING.
Palace of Alcait
Town of Silverwand
Town of Silverhorn
Raget Highlands
Forest of Mirrete
FINALLY, WE AR-RIVED IN LUNATIC LAKE, THE CAPITAL OF THE KINGDOM OF ALCAIT.

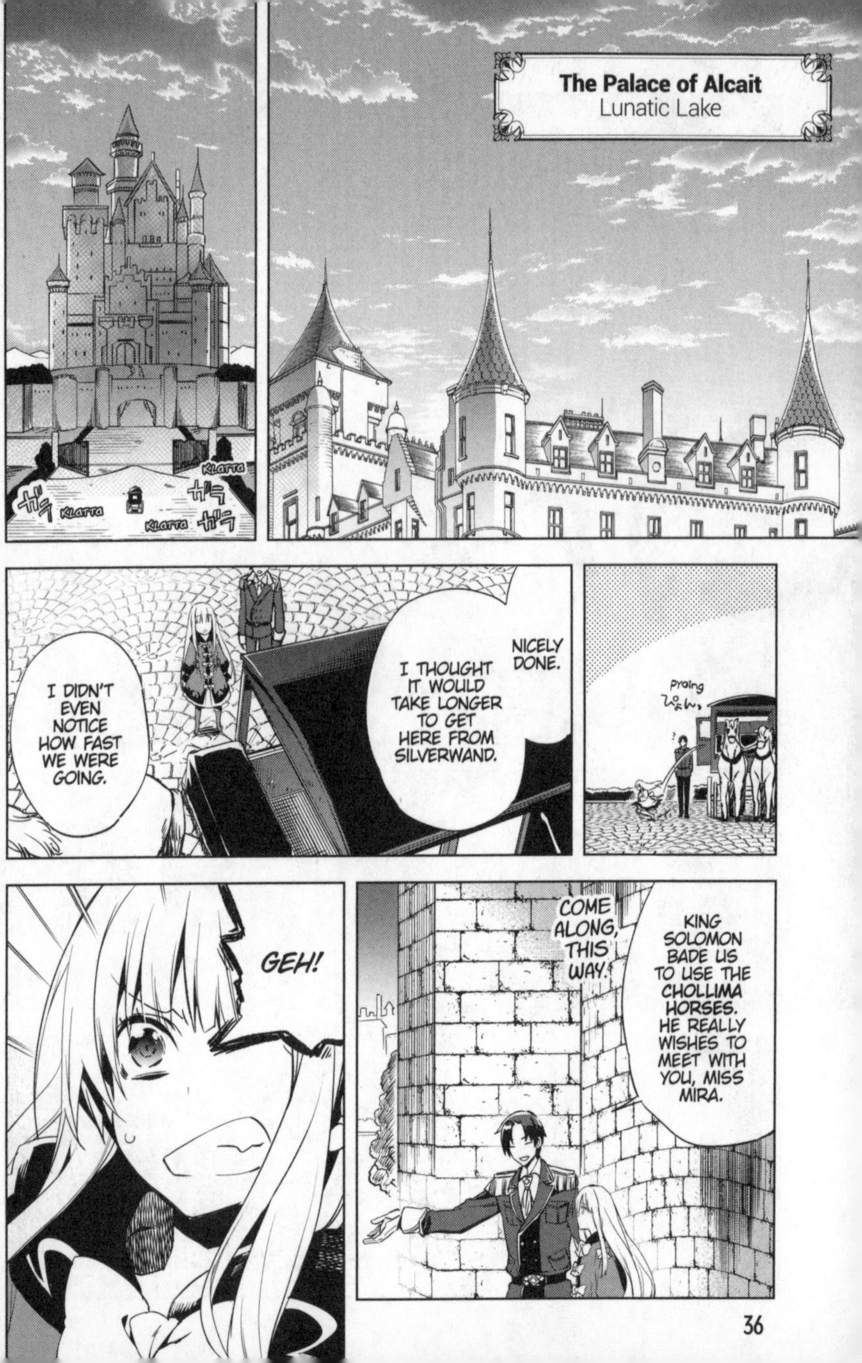

The Palace of Alcait
Lunatic Lake
KLATTA ガラ
KLATTA ガラ
KLATTA ガラ
Praing ぴょん
NICELY DONE.
I THOUGHT IT WOULD TAKE LONGER TO GET HERE FROM SILVERWAND.
I DIDN'T EVEN NOTICE HOW FAST WE WERE GOING.
KING SOLOMON BADE US TO USE THE CHOLLIMA HORSES. HE REALLY WISHES TO MEET WITH YOU, MISS MIRA.
COME ALONG, THIS WAY.
GEH!

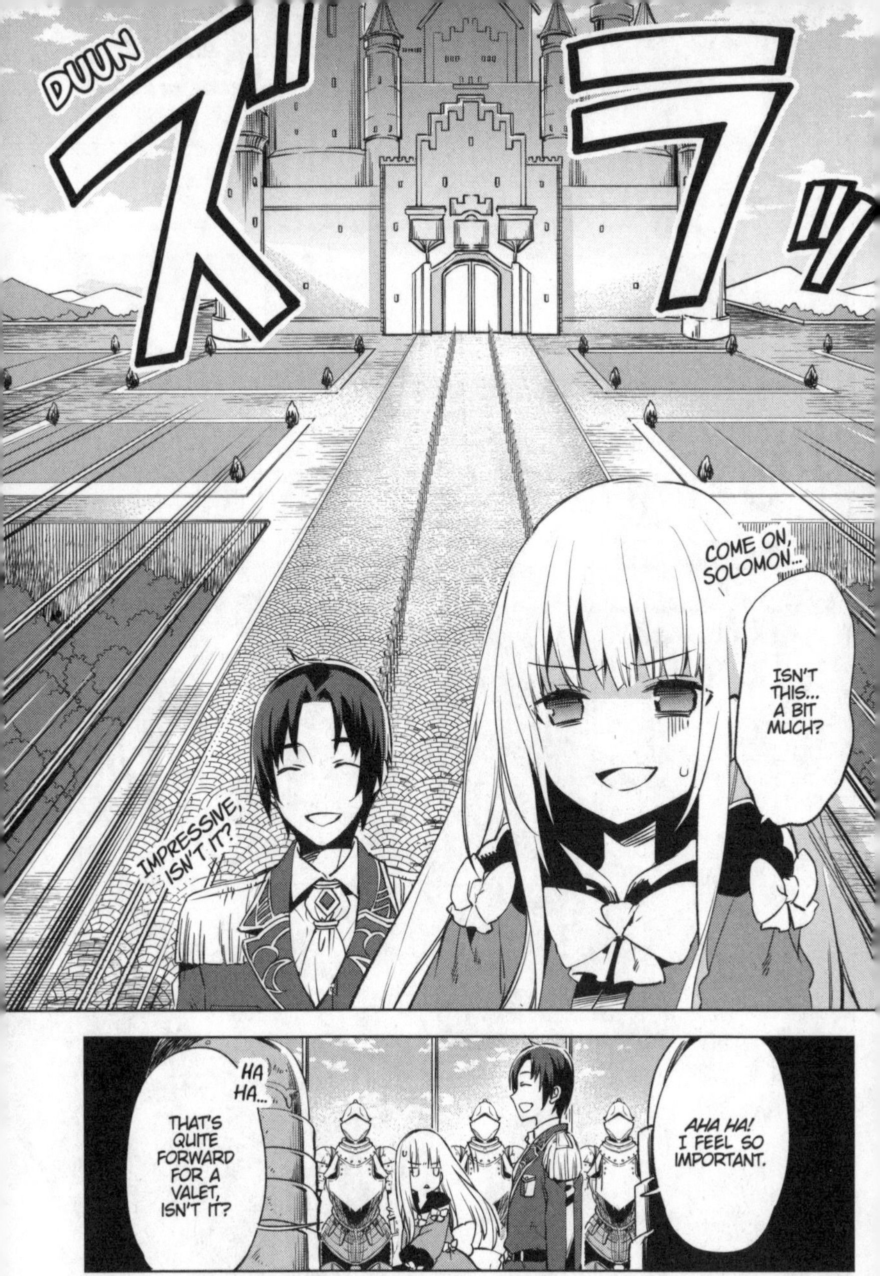
DUUN
ズラッ
COME ON, SOLOMON...
ISN'T THIS... A BIT MUCH?
IMPRESSIVE, ISN'T IT?
AHA HA! I FEEL SO IMPORTANT.
HA HA...
THAT'S QUITE FORWARD FOR A VALET, ISN'T IT?

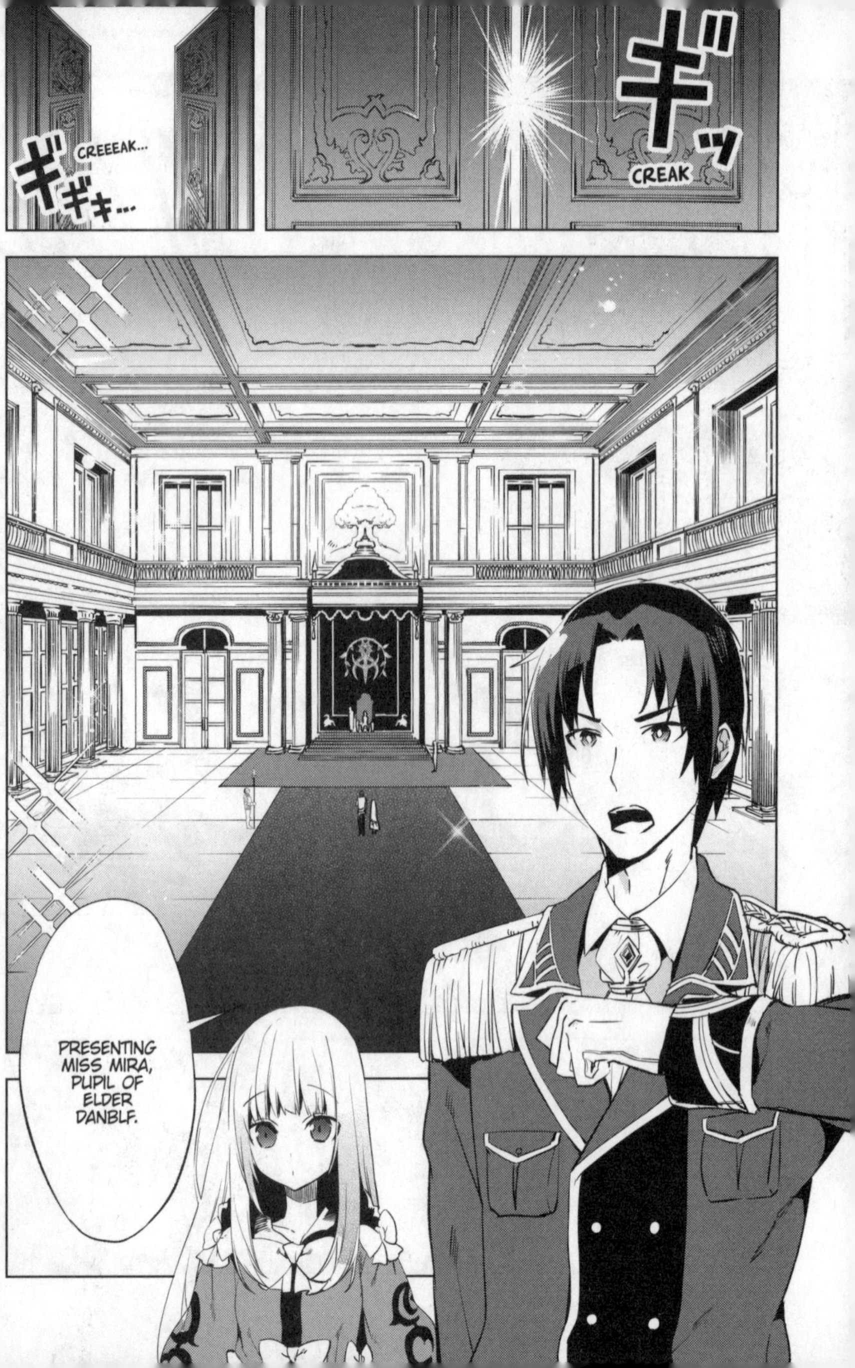
ギッ
CREAK
ギギキ...
CREEEAK...
PRESENTING MISS MIRA, PUPIL OF ELDER DANBLF.

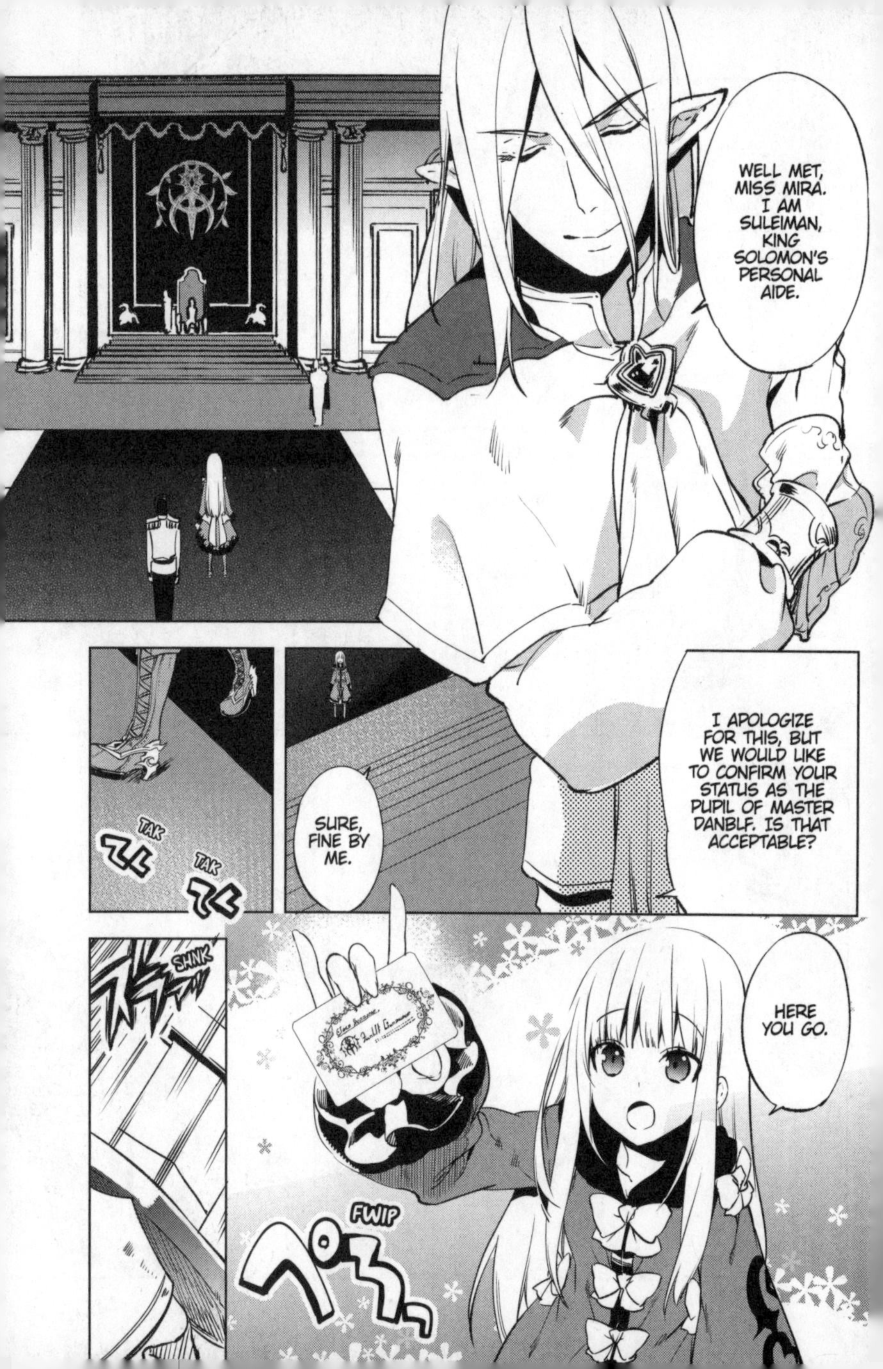
WELL MET, MISS MIRA. I AM SULEIMAN, KING SOLOMON'S PERSONAL AIDE.
I APOLOGIZE FOR THIS, BUT WE WOULD LIKE TO CONFIRM YOUR STATUS AS THE PUPIL OF MASTER DANBLF. IS THAT ACCEPTABLE?
SURE, FINE BY ME.
TAK
TAK
HERE YOU GO.
FWIP
SHNK

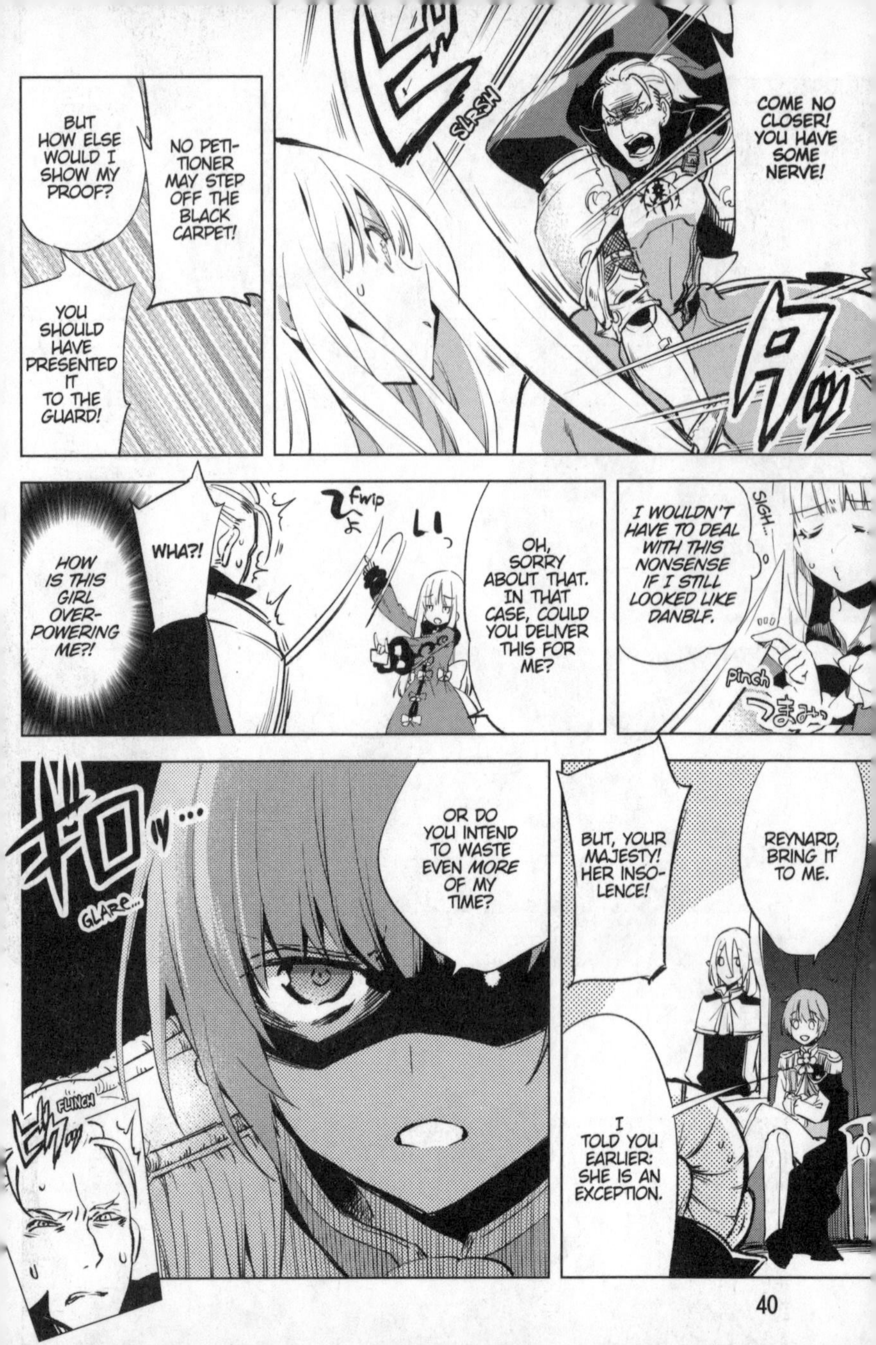
SLRSH
COME NO CLOSER! YOU HAVE SOME NERVE!
NO PETITIONER MAY STEP OFF THE BLACK CARPET!
BUT HOW ELSE WOULD I SHOW MY PROOF?
YOU SHOULD HAVE PRESENTED IT TO THE GUARD!
SIGH...
I WOULDN'T HAVE TO DEAL WITH THIS NONSENSE IF I STILL LOOKED LIKE DANBLF.
pinch
fwip
OH, SORRY ABOUT THAT. IN THAT CASE, COULD YOU DELIVER THIS FOR ME?
WHA?!
HOW IS THIS GIRL OVER-POWERING ME?!
REYNARD, BRING IT TO ME.
BUT, YOUR MAJESTY! HER INSOLENCE!
I TOLD YOU EARLIER: SHE IS AN EXCEPTION.
OR DO YOU INTEND TO WASTE EVEN MORE OF MY TIME?
GLARE...
FLINCH

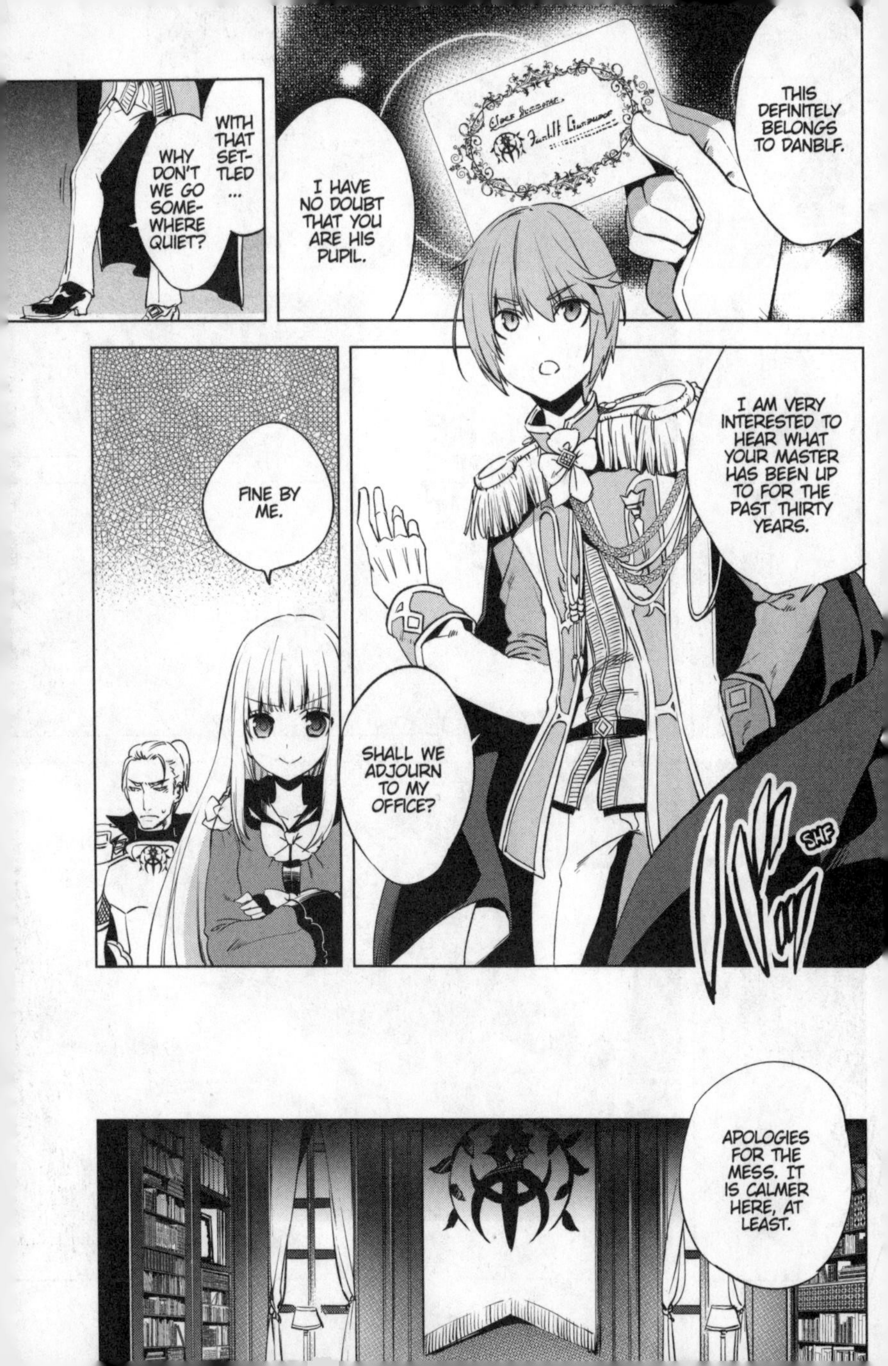
THIS DEFINITELY BELONGS TO DANBLF.
I HAVE NO DOUBT THAT YOU ARE HIS PUPIL.
WITH THAT SETTLED ...
WHY DON'T WE GO SOMEWHERE QUIET?
I AM VERY INTERESTED TO HEAR WHAT YOUR MASTER HAS BEEN UP TO FOR THE PAST THIRTY YEARS.
SHALL WE ADJOURN TO MY OFFICE?
SHF
FINE BY ME.
APOLOGIES FOR THE MESS. IT IS CALMER HERE, AT LEAST.

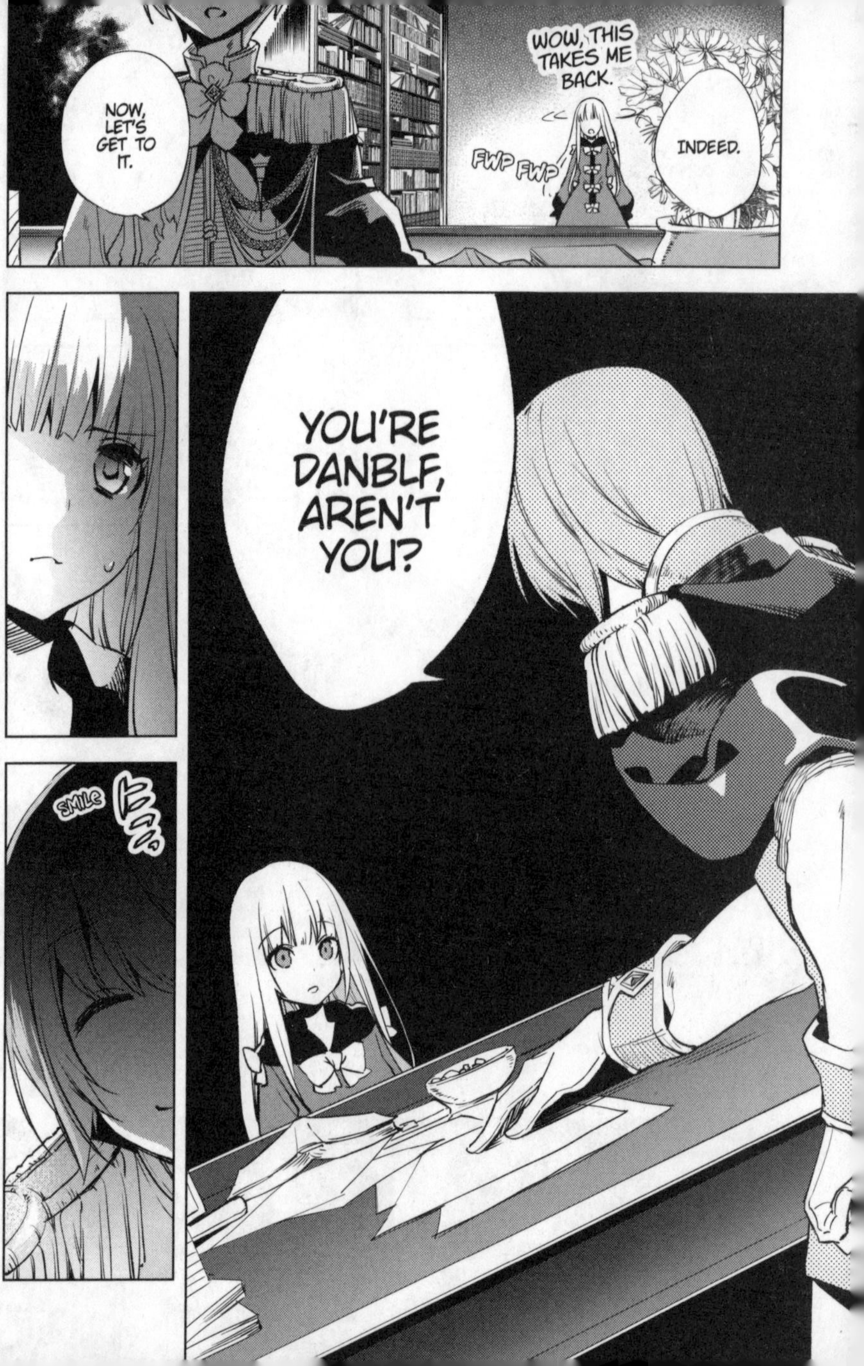
WOW, THIS TAKES ME BACK.
INDEED.
FWP FWP
NOW, LET'S GET TO IT.
YOU'RE DANBLF, AREN'T YOU?
SMILE

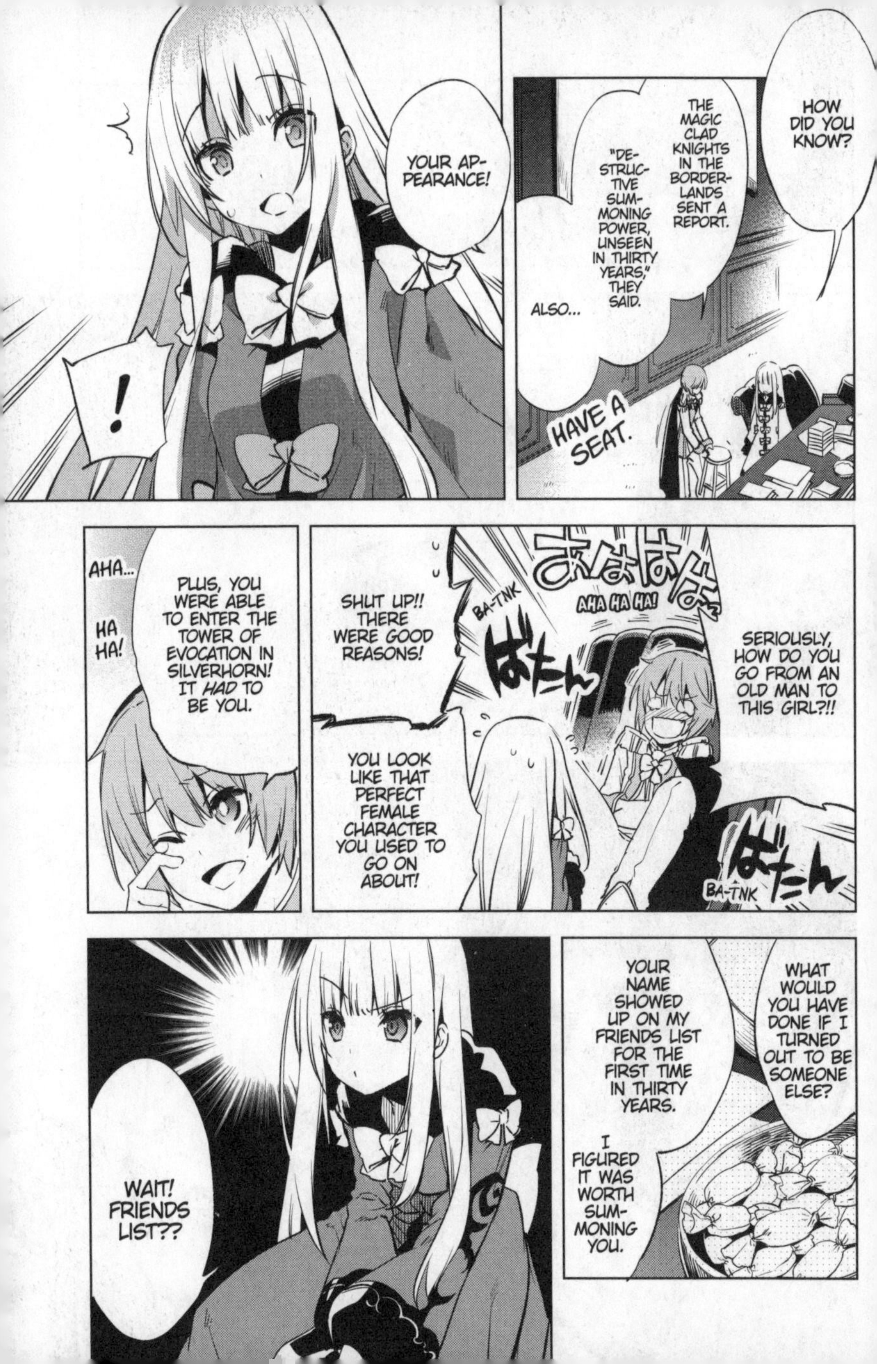
HOW DID YOU KNOW?
THE MAGIC CLAD KNIGHTS IN THE BORDERLANDS SENT A REPORT.
"DESTRUCTIVE SUMMONING POWER, UNSEEN IN THIRTY YEARS," THEY SAID.
ALSO...
HAVE A SEAT.
...
YOUR APPEARANCE!
!
あははは
AHA HA HA!
SERIOUSLY, HOW DO YOU GO FROM AN OLD MAN TO THIS GIRL?!!
BA-TNK
ばたん
SHUT UP!! THERE WERE GOOD REASONS!
YOU LOOK LIKE THAT PERFECT FEMALE CHARACTER YOU USED TO GO ON ABOUT!
ばたん
BA-TNK
AHA...
HA HA!
PLUS, YOU WERE ABLE TO ENTER THE TOWER OF EVOCATION IN SILVERHORN! IT *HAD* TO BE YOU.
WHAT WOULD YOU HAVE DONE IF I TURNED OUT TO BE SOMEONE ELSE?
YOUR NAME SHOWED UP ON MY FRIENDS LIST FOR THE FIRST TIME IN THIRTY YEARS.
I FIGURED IT WAS WORTH SUMMONING YOU.
WAIT! FRIENDS LIST??

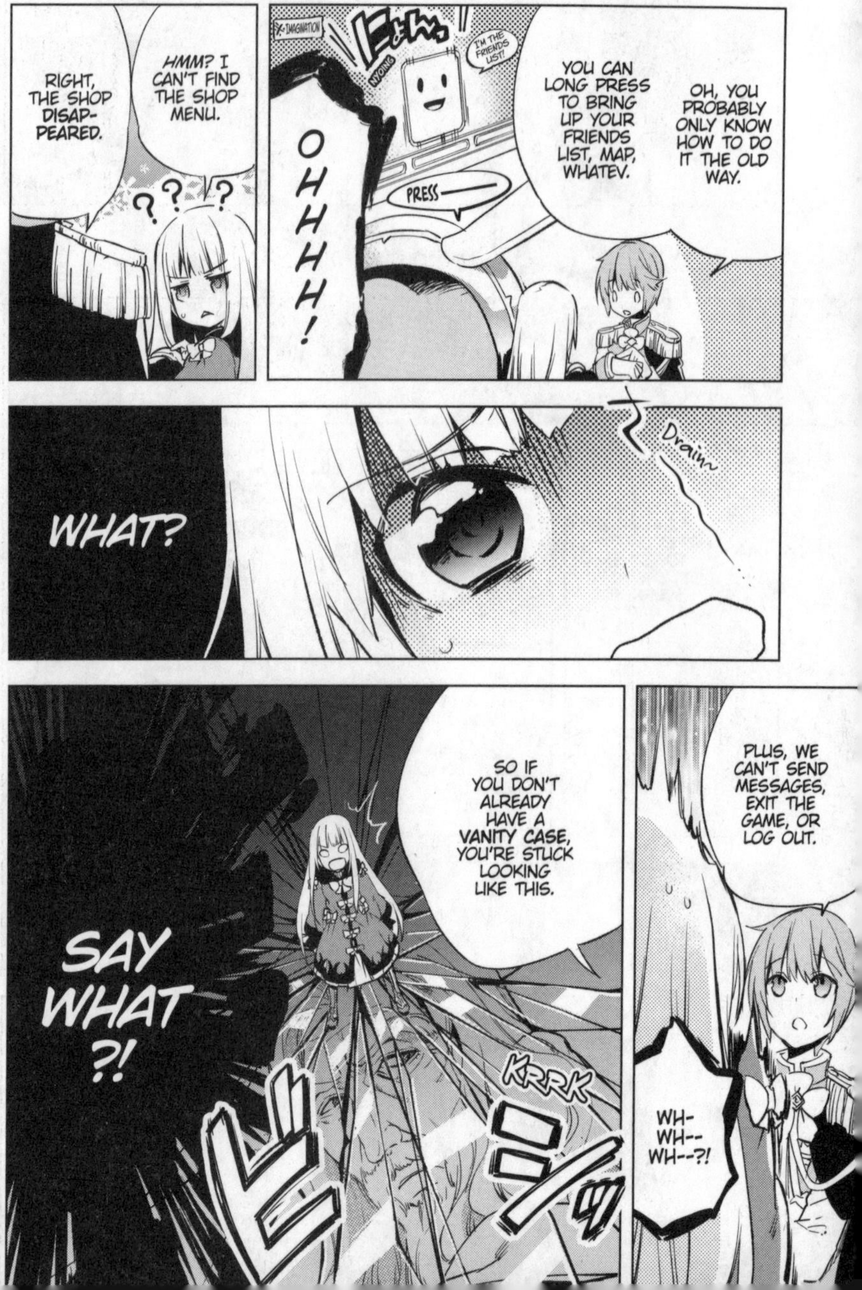
OH, YOU PROBABLY ONLY KNOW HOW TO DO IT THE OLD WAY.
YOU CAN LONG PRESS TO BRING UP YOUR FRIENDS LIST, MAP, WHATEV.
※=IMAGINATION
I'M THE FRIENDS LIST!
NYOING
PRESS—
OHHHHH!
HMM? I CAN'T FIND THE SHOP MENU.
RIGHT, THE SHOP DISAP-PEARED.
Drain~
WHAT?
PLUS, WE CAN'T SEND MESSAGES, EXIT THE GAME, OR LOG OUT.
WH-WH--WH--?!
SO IF YOU DON'T ALREADY HAVE A VANITY CASE, YOU'RE STUCK LOOKING LIKE THIS.
KRRK
SAY WHAT ?!

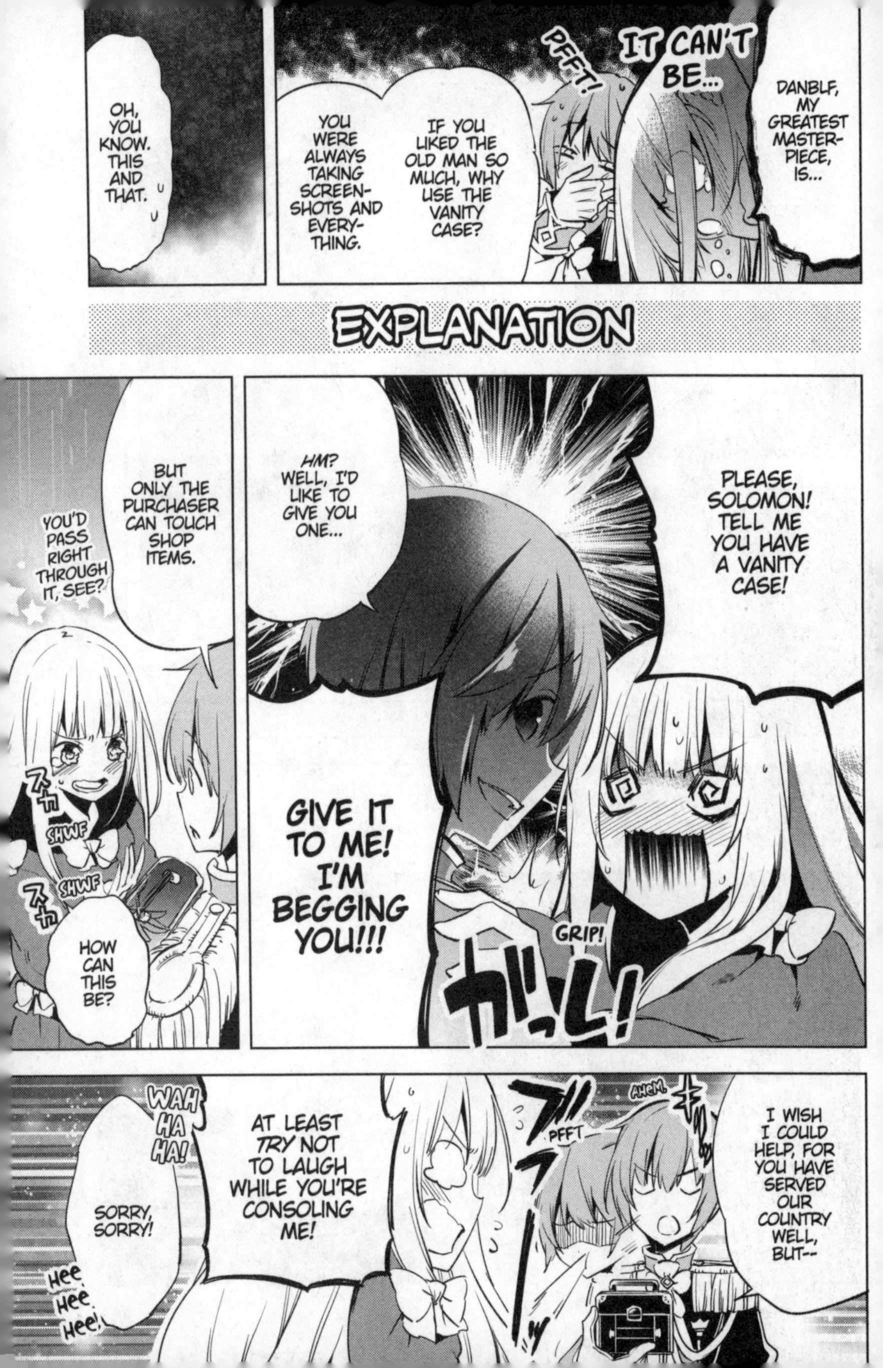
DANBLF, MY GREATEST MASTERPIECE, IS...
IT CAN'T BE...
PFFFT!
IF YOU LIKED THE OLD MAN SO MUCH, WHY USE THE VANITY CASE?
YOU WERE ALWAYS TAKING SCREENSHOTS AND EVERYTHING.
OH, YOU KNOW. THIS AND THAT.
EXPLANATION
PLEASE, SOLOMON! TELL ME YOU HAVE A VANITY CASE!
HM? WELL, I'D LIKE TO GIVE YOU ONE...
GIVE IT TO ME! I'M BEGGING YOU!!!
GRIP!
BUT ONLY THE PURCHASER CAN TOUCH SHOP ITEMS.
YOU'D PASS RIGHT THROUGH IT, SEE?
スカ
SHWF
スカ
SHWF
HOW CAN THIS BE?
I WISH I COULD HELP, FOR YOU HAVE SERVED OUR COUNTRY WELL, BUT--
AHEM.
PFFT
AT LEAST TRY NOT TO LAUGH WHILE YOU'RE CONSOLING ME!
WAH HA HA!
SORRY, SORRY!
HEE HEE HEE!

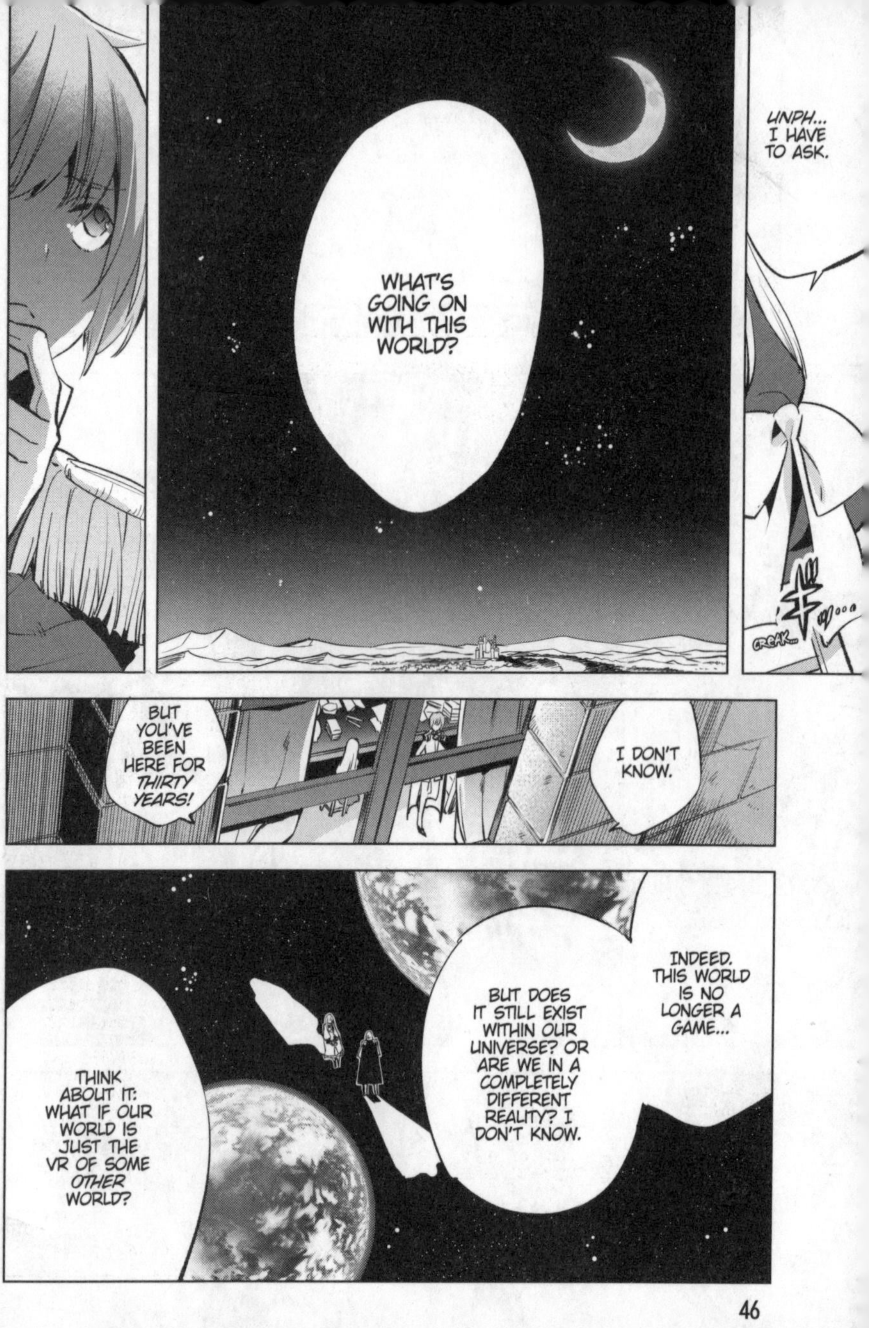
UNPH... I HAVE TO ASK.
CREAK...
WHAT'S GOING ON WITH THIS WORLD?
I DON'T KNOW.
BUT YOU'VE BEEN HERE FOR *THIRTY YEARS!*
INDEED. THIS WORLD IS NO LONGER A GAME...
BUT DOES IT STILL EXIST WITHIN OUR UNIVERSE? OR ARE WE IN A COMPLETELY DIFFERENT REALITY? I DON'T KNOW.
THINK ABOUT IT: WHAT IF OUR WORLD IS JUST THE VR OF SOME *OTHER* WORLD?

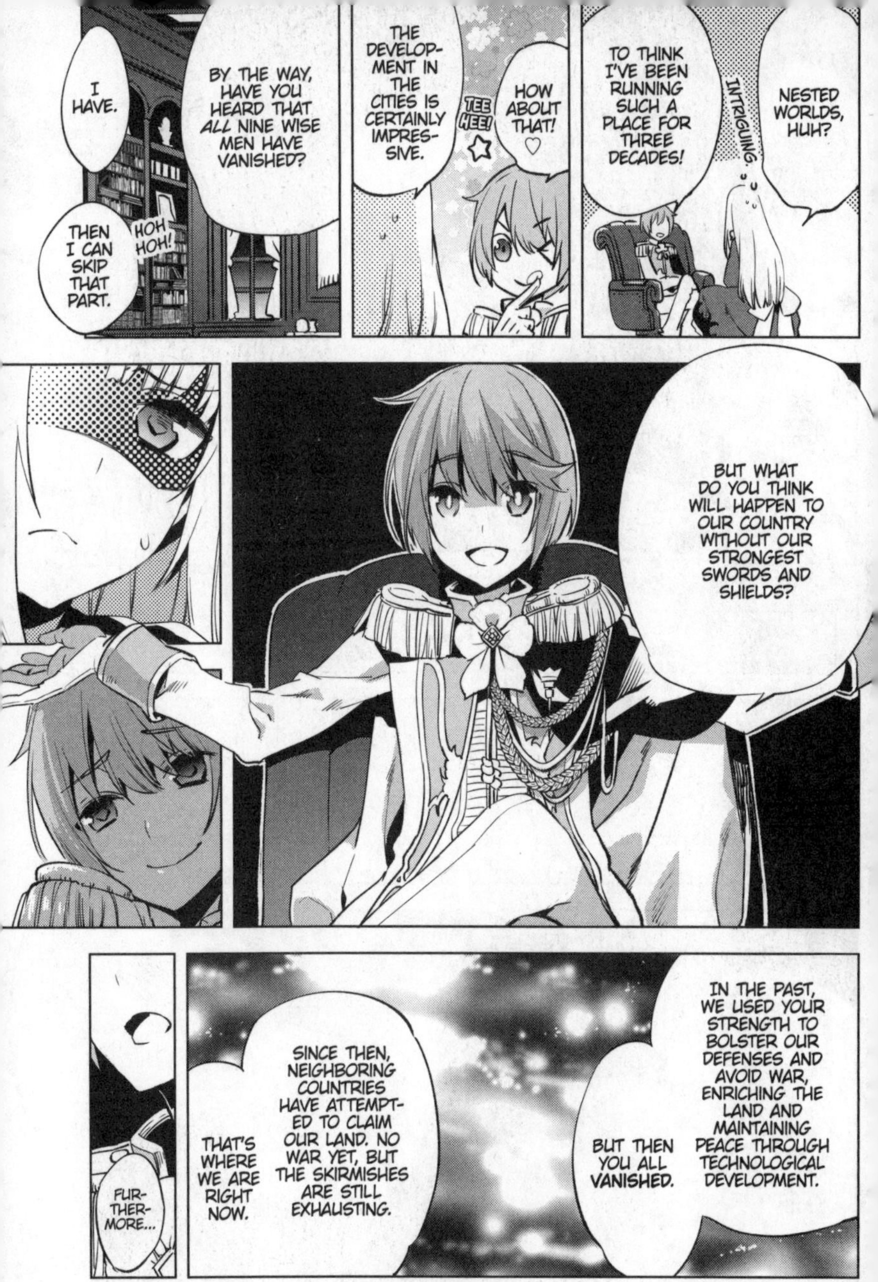
NESTED WORLDS, HUH?
INTRIGUING.
TO THINK I'VE BEEN RUNNING SUCH A PLACE FOR THREE DECADES!
HOW ABOUT THAT! ♡
TEE HEE!
THE DEVELOPMENT IN THE CITIES IS CERTAINLY IMPRESSIVE.
BY THE WAY, HAVE YOU HEARD THAT *ALL* NINE WISE MEN HAVE VANISHED?
I HAVE.
HOH HOH!
THEN I CAN SKIP THAT PART.
BUT WHAT DO YOU THINK WILL HAPPEN TO OUR COUNTRY WITHOUT OUR STRONGEST SWORDS AND SHIELDS?
IN THE PAST, WE USED YOUR STRENGTH TO BOLSTER OUR DEFENSES AND AVOID WAR, ENRICHING THE LAND AND MAINTAINING PEACE THROUGH TECHNOLOGICAL DEVELOPMENT.
BUT THEN YOU ALL **VANISHED.**
SINCE THEN, NEIGHBORING COUNTRIES HAVE ATTEMPTED TO CLAIM OUR LAND. NO WAR YET, BUT THE SKIRMISHES ARE STILL EXHAUSTING.
THAT'S WHERE WE ARE RIGHT NOW.
FURTHERMORE...

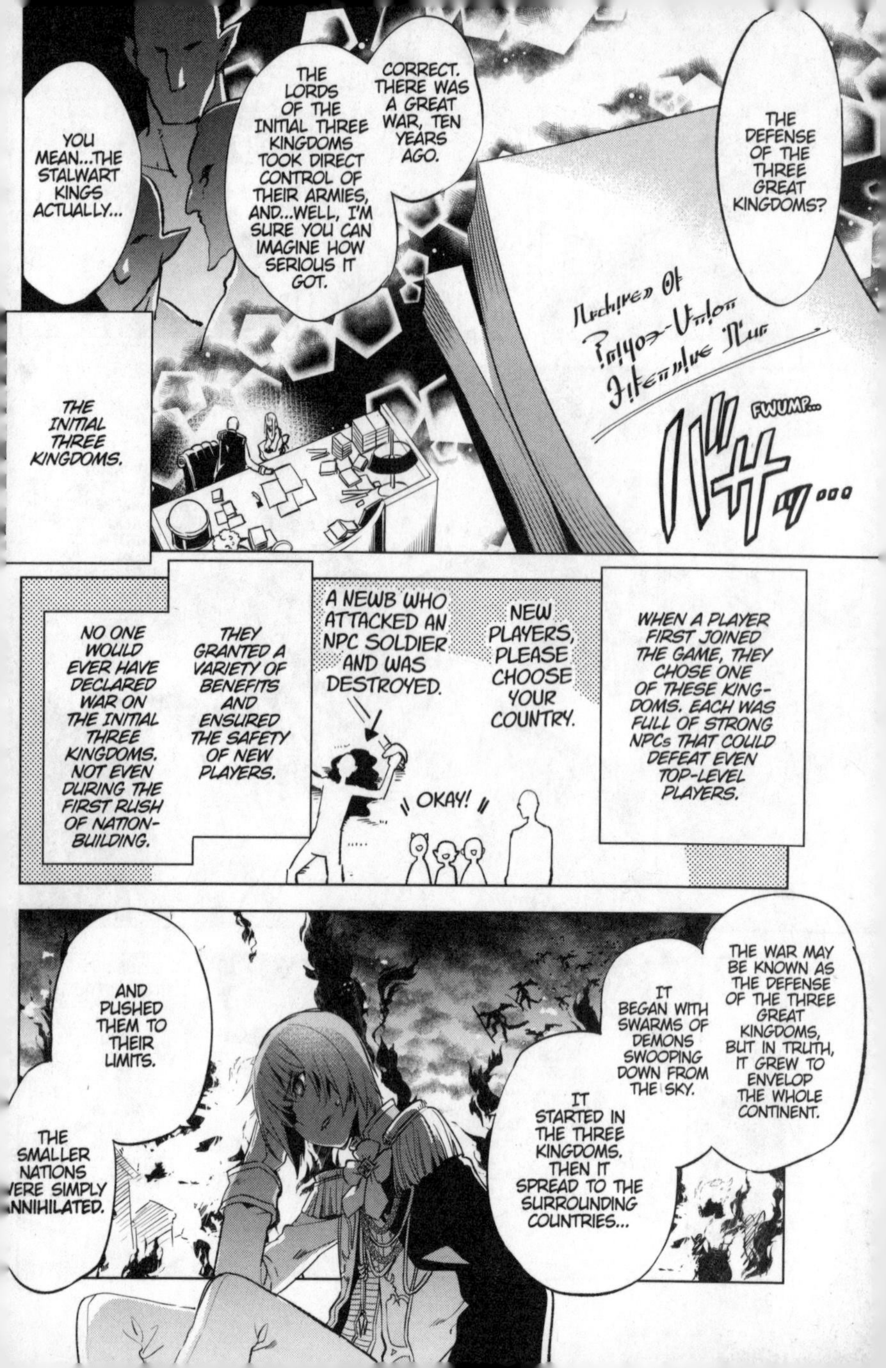

THE DEFENSE OF THE THREE GREAT KINGDOMS?
CORRECT. THERE WAS A GREAT WAR, TEN YEARS AGO.
THE LORDS OF THE INITIAL THREE KINGDOMS TOOK DIRECT CONTROL OF THEIR ARMIES, AND...WELL, I'M SURE YOU CAN IMAGINE HOW SERIOUS IT GOT.
YOU MEAN...THE STALWART KINGS ACTUALLY...
FWUMP...
バサッ...
THE INITIAL THREE KINGDOMS.
WHEN A PLAYER FIRST JOINED THE GAME, THEY CHOSE ONE OF THESE KING-DOMS. EACH WAS FULL OF STRONG NPCs THAT COULD DEFEAT EVEN TOP-LEVEL PLAYERS.
NEW PLAYERS, PLEASE CHOOSE YOUR COUNTRY.
OKAY!
A NEWB WHO ATTACKED AN NPC SOLDIER AND WAS DESTROYED.
THEY GRANTED A VARIETY OF BENEFITS AND ENSURED THE SAFETY OF NEW PLAYERS.
NO ONE WOULD EVER HAVE DECLARED WAR ON THE INITIAL THREE KINGDOMS. NOT EVEN DURING THE FIRST RUSH OF NATION-BUILDING.
THE WAR MAY BE KNOWN AS THE DEFENSE OF THE THREE GREAT KINGDOMS, BUT IN TRUTH, IT GREW TO ENVELOP THE WHOLE CONTINENT.
IT BEGAN WITH SWARMS OF DEMONS SWOOPING DOWN FROM THE SKY.
IT STARTED IN THE THREE KINGDOMS. THEN IT SPREAD TO THE SURROUNDING COUNTRIES...
AND PUSHED THEM TO THEIR LIMITS.
THE SMALLER NATIONS ERE SIMPLY NNIHILATED.

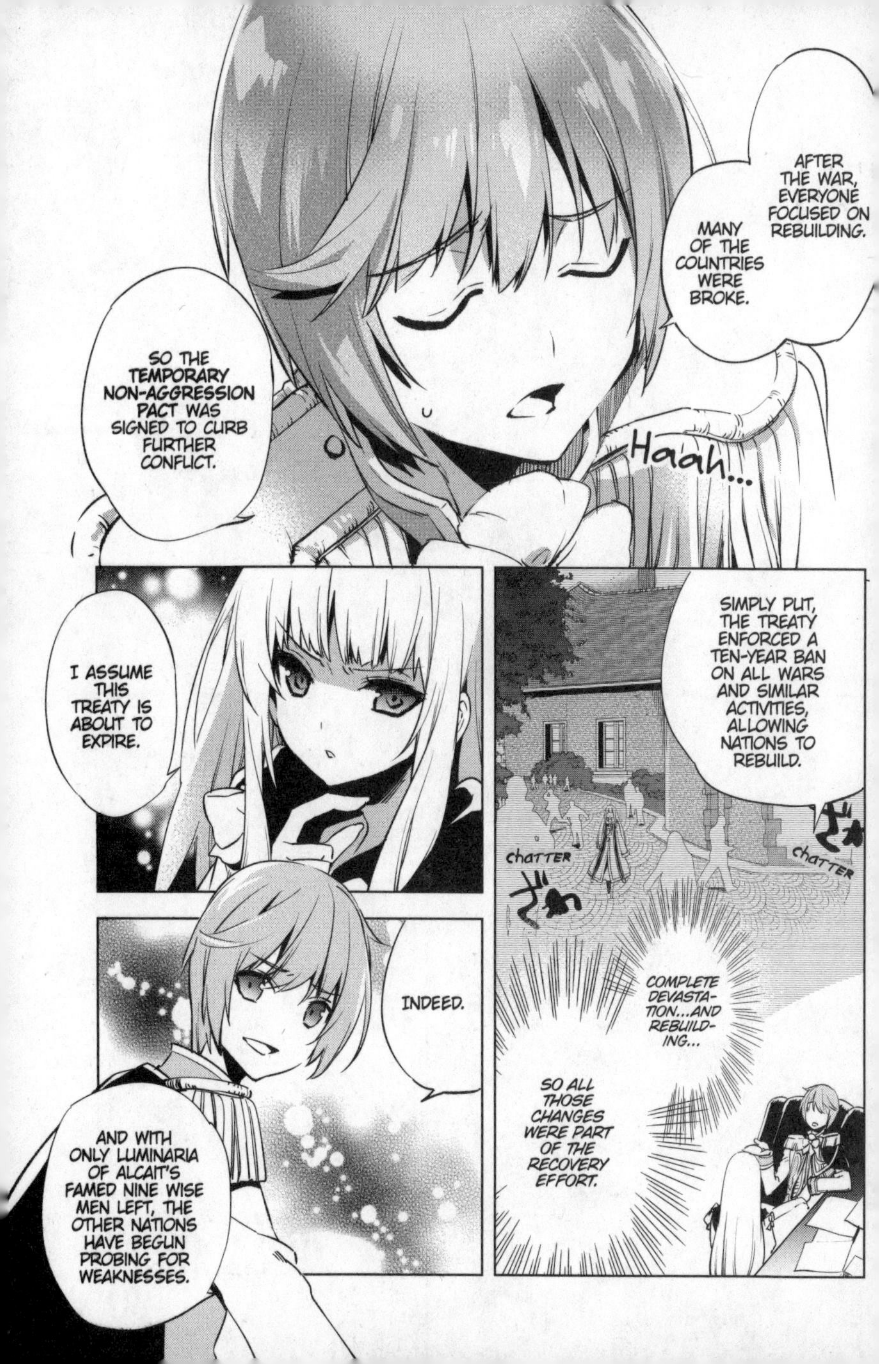
AFTER THE WAR, EVERYONE FOCUSED ON REBUILDING.
MANY OF THE COUNTRIES WERE BROKE.
SO THE TEMPORARY NON-AGGRESSION PACT WAS SIGNED TO CURB FURTHER CONFLICT.
Haah...
SIMPLY PUT, THE TREATY ENFORCED A TEN-YEAR BAN ON ALL WARS AND SIMILAR ACTIVITIES, ALLOWING NATIONS TO REBUILD.
ざわ
chatter
ざわ
chatter
COMPLETE DEVASTATION...AND REBUILDING...
SO ALL THOSE CHANGES WERE PART OF THE RECOVERY EFFORT.
I ASSUME THIS TREATY IS ABOUT TO EXPIRE.
INDEED.
AND WITH ONLY LUMINARIA OF ALCAIT'S FAMED NINE WISE MEN LEFT, THE OTHER NATIONS HAVE BEGUN PROBING FOR WEAKNESSES.

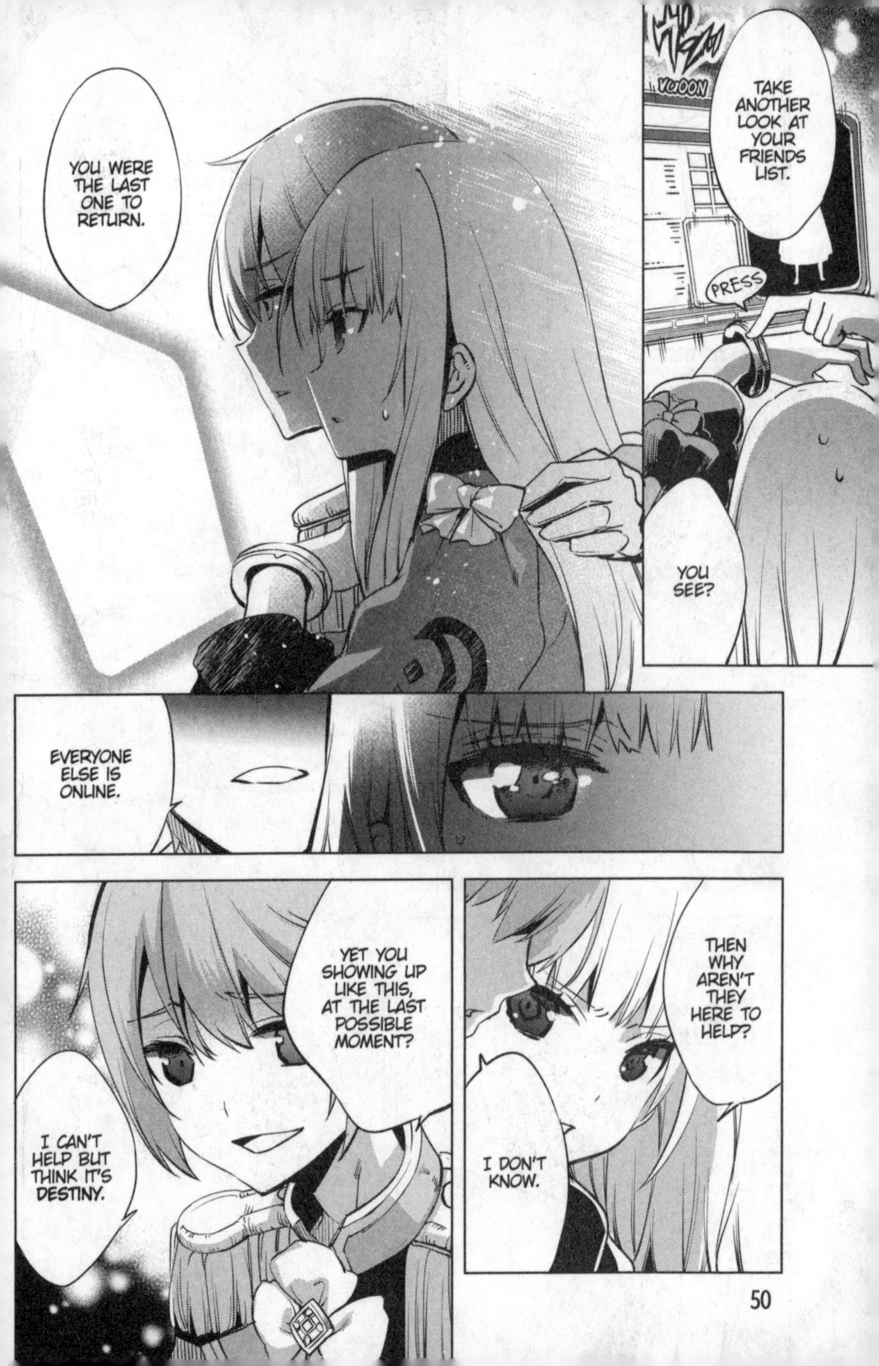
VUOON
TAKE ANOTHER LOOK AT YOUR FRIENDS LIST.
PRESS
YOU SEE?
YOU WERE THE LAST ONE TO RETURN.
EVERYONE ELSE IS ONLINE.
THEN WHY AREN'T THEY HERE TO HELP?
I DON'T KNOW.
YET YOU SHOWING UP LIKE THIS, AT THE LAST POSSIBLE MOMENT?
I CAN'T HELP BUT THINK IT'S DESTINY.

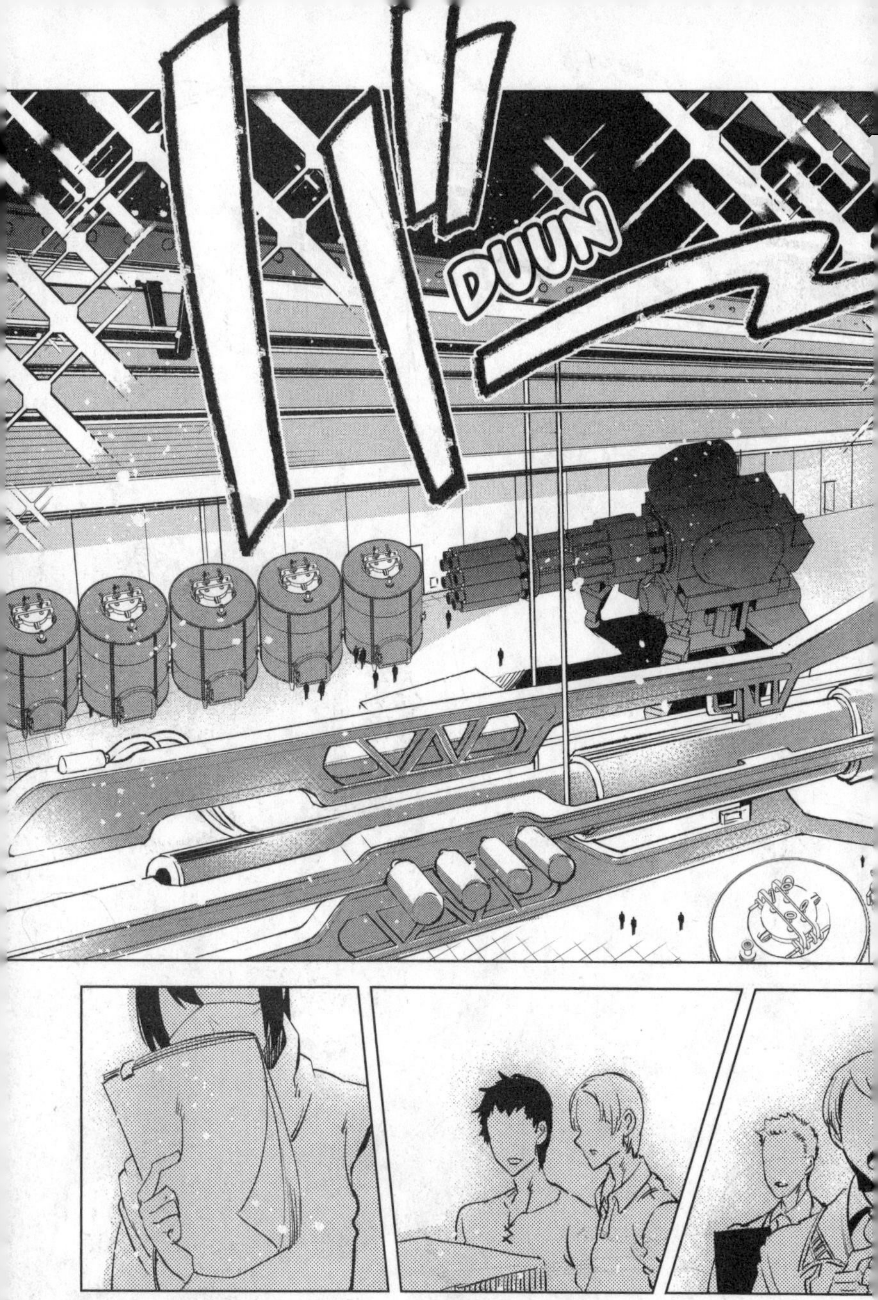
DUUN

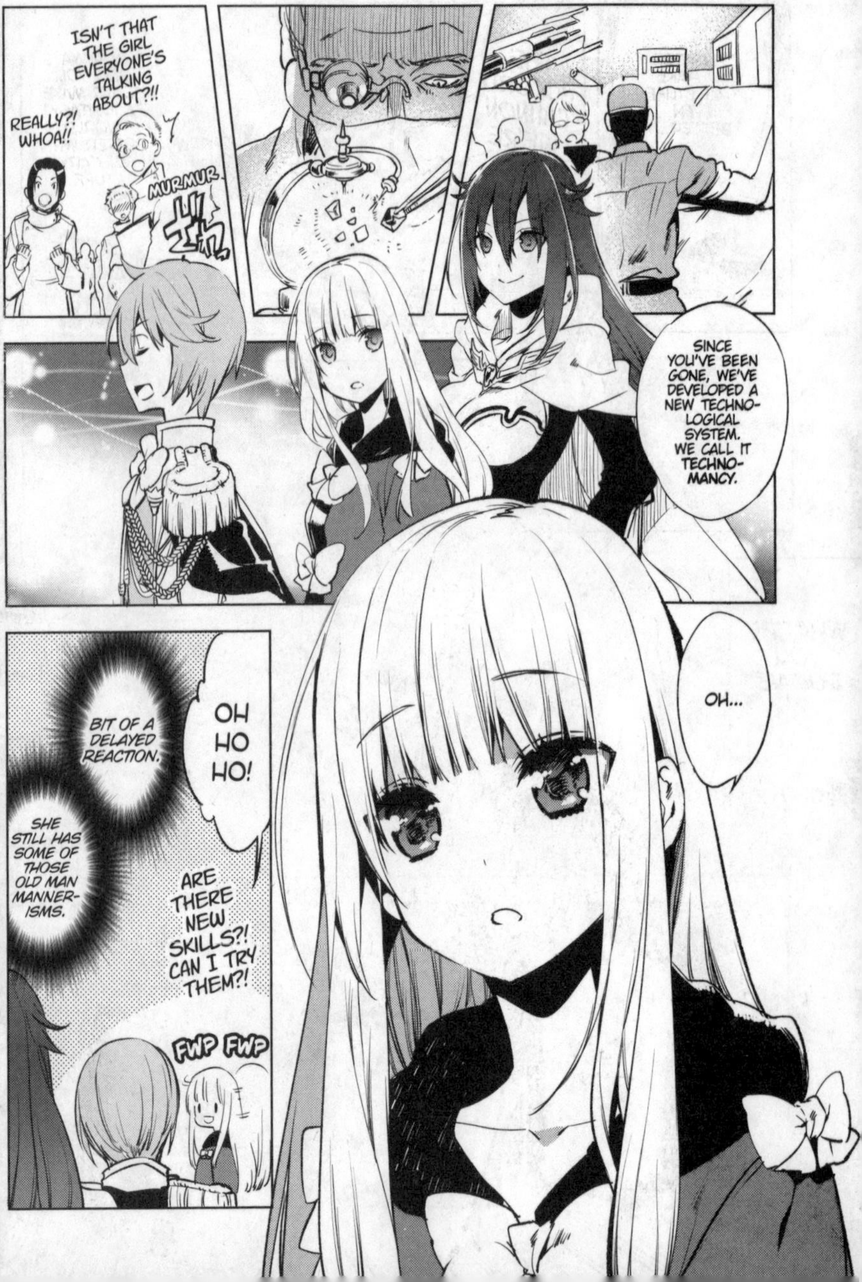
ISN'T THAT THE GIRL EVERYONE'S TALKING ABOUT?!!
REALLY?! WHOA!!
MURMUR
SINCE YOU'VE BEEN GONE, WE'VE DEVELOPED A NEW TECHNO-LOGICAL SYSTEM. WE CALL IT TECHNO-MANCY.
OH...
OH HO HO!
ARE THERE NEW SKILLS?! CAN I TRY THEM?!
BIT OF A DELAYED REACTION.
SHE STILL HAS SOME OF THOSE OLD MAN MANNER-ISMS.
FWP FWP

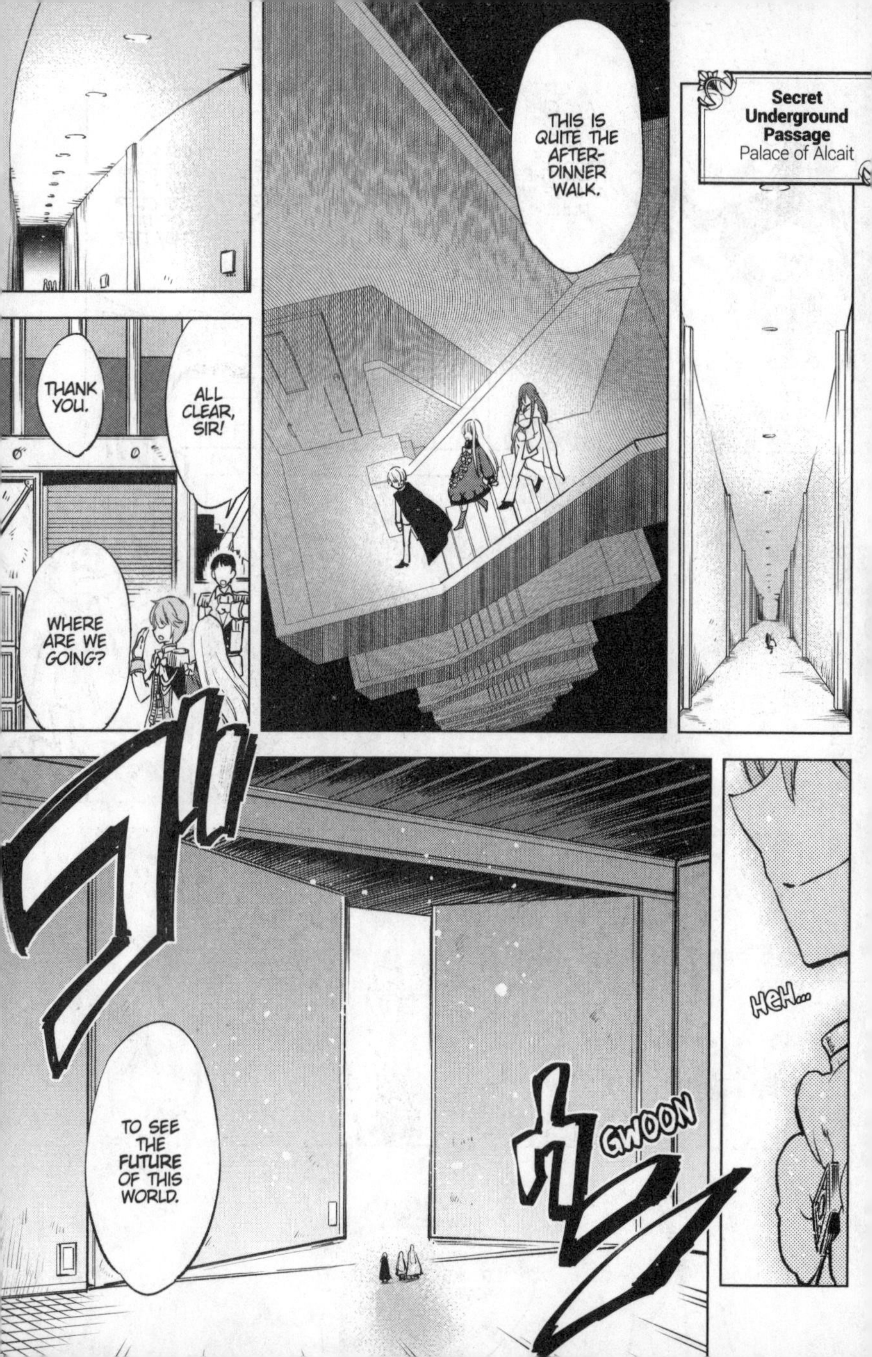
Secret Underground Passage
Palace of Alcait
THIS IS QUITE THE AFTER-DINNER WALK.
ALL CLEAR, SIR!
THANK YOU.
WHERE ARE WE GOING?
HEH...
GWOON
TO SEE THE FUTURE OF THIS WORLD.

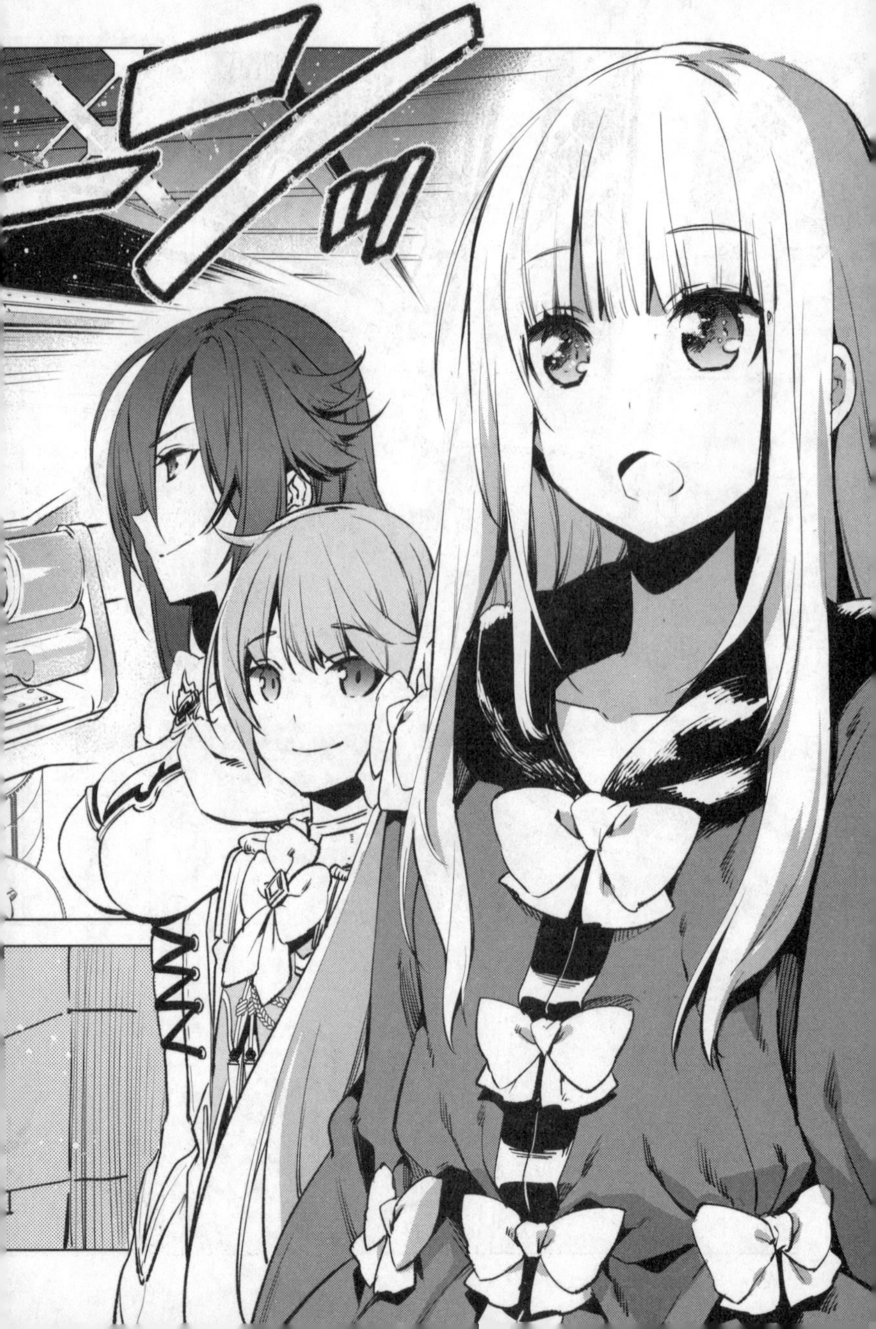

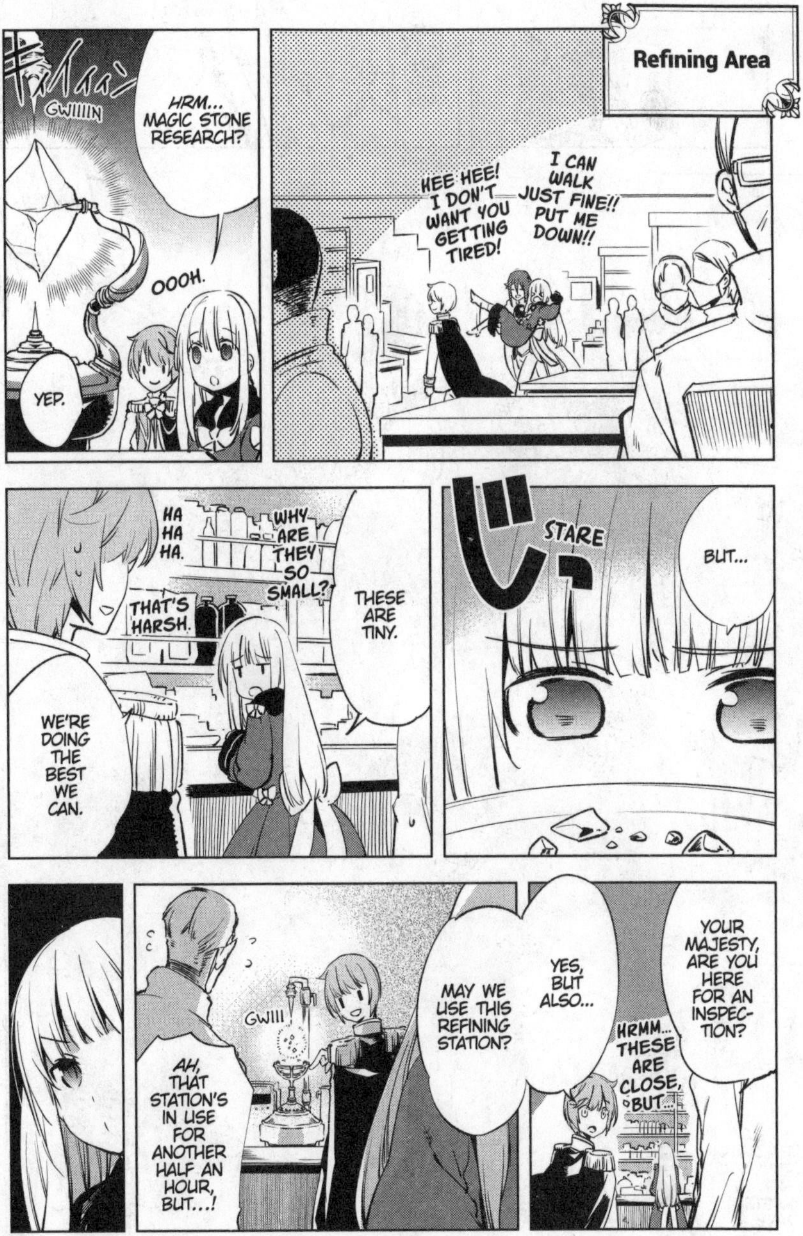
Refining Area
I CAN WALK JUST FINE!! PUT ME DOWN!!
HEE HEE! I DON'T WANT YOU GETTING TIRED!
GWIIIIN
HRM... MAGIC STONE RESEARCH?
OOOH.
YEP.
STARE
BUT...
THESE ARE TINY.
WHY ARE THEY SO SMALL?
HA HA HA.
THAT'S HARSH.
WE'RE DOING THE BEST WE CAN.
YOUR MAJESTY, ARE YOU HERE FOR AN INSPEC-TION?
HRMM... THESE ARE CLOSE, BUT...
YES, BUT ALSO...
MAY WE USE THIS REFINING STATION?
GWIII
AH, THAT STATION'S IN USE FOR ANOTHER HALF AN HOUR, BUT...!

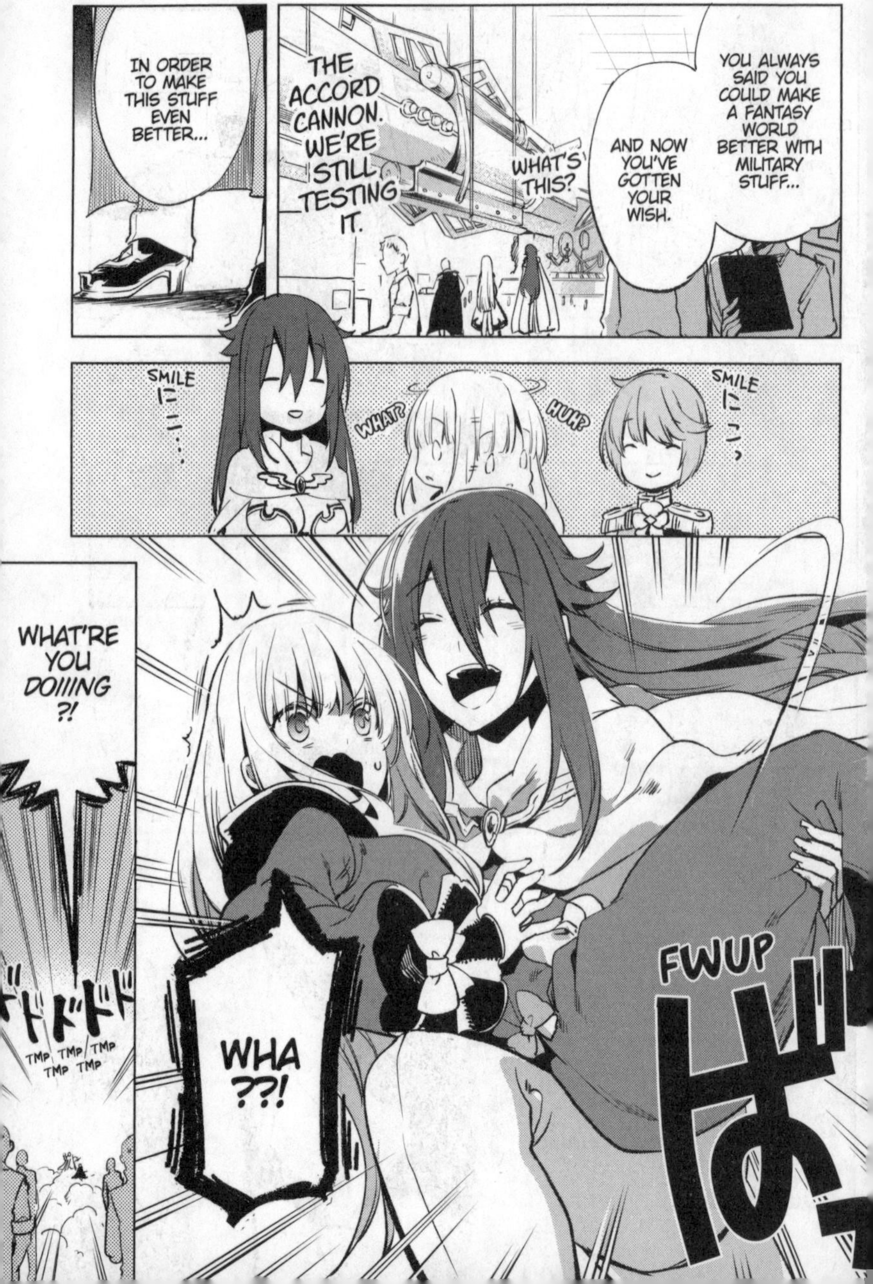
YOU ALWAYS SAID YOU COULD MAKE A FANTASY WORLD BETTER WITH MILITARY STUFF...
AND NOW YOU'VE GOTTEN YOUR WISH.
WHAT'S THIS?
THE ACCORD CANNON. WE'RE STILL TESTING IT.
IN ORDER TO MAKE THIS STUFF EVEN BETTER...
SMILE
HUH?
WHAT?
SMILE
FWUP
WHA ??!
WHAT'RE YOU DOIIING ?!
TMP TMP TMP TMP TMP

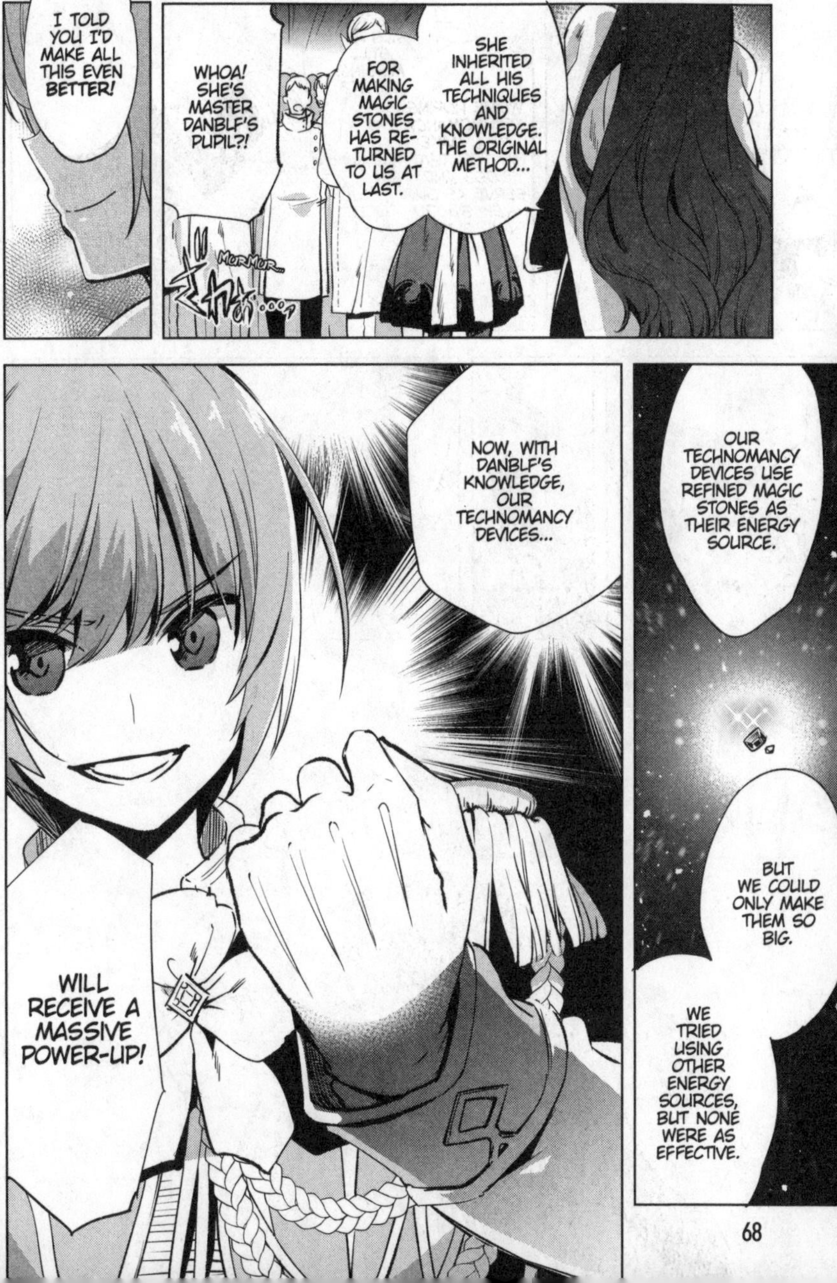
SHE INHERITED ALL HIS TECHNIQUES AND KNOWLEDGE. THE ORIGINAL METHOD...
FOR MAKING MAGIC STONES HAS RE-TURNED TO US AT LAST.
WHOA! SHE'S MASTER DANBLF'S PUPIL?!
MURMUR...
I TOLD YOU I'D MAKE ALL THIS EVEN BETTER!
OUR TECHNOMANCY DEVICES USE REFINED MAGIC STONES AS THEIR ENERGY SOURCE.
BUT WE COULD ONLY MAKE THEM SO BIG.
WE TRIED USING OTHER ENERGY SOURCES, BUT NONE WERE AS EFFECTIVE.
NOW, WITH DANBLF'S KNOWLEDGE, OUR TECHNOMANCY DEVICES...
WILL RECEIVE A MASSIVE POWER-UP!

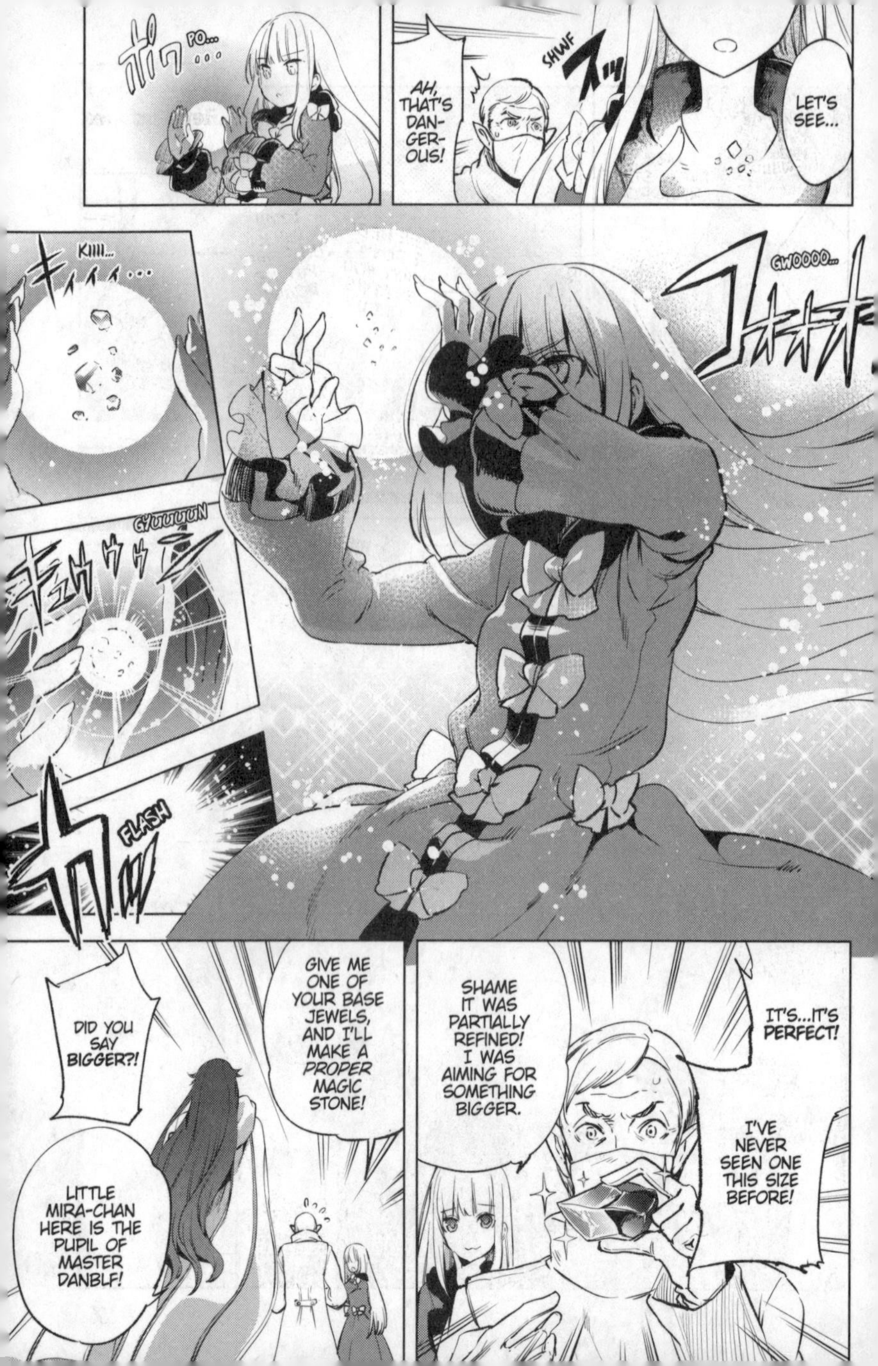
LET'S SEE...
SHWF
AH, THAT'S DAN-GER-OUS!
PO...
GWOOOO...
KIIII...
GYUUUUN
FLASH
IT'S...IT'S PERFECT!
I'VE NEVER SEEN ONE THIS SIZE BEFORE!
SHAME IT WAS PARTIALLY REFINED! I WAS AIMING FOR SOMETHING BIGGER.
GIVE ME ONE OF YOUR BASE JEWELS, AND I'LL MAKE A *PROPER* MAGIC STONE!
DID YOU SAY BIGGER?!
LITTLE MIRA-CHAN HERE IS THE PUPIL OF MASTER DANBLF!

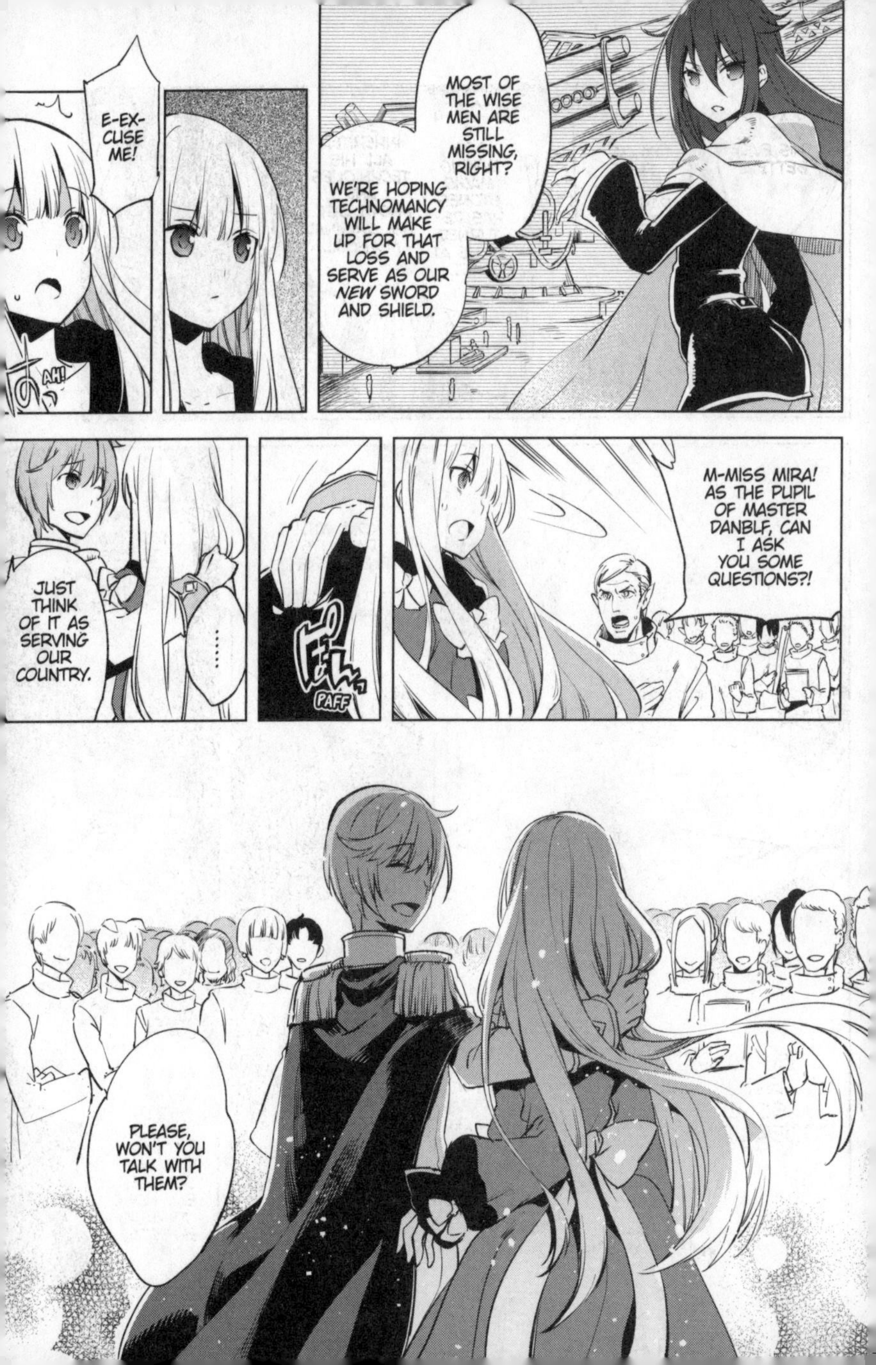
MOST OF THE WISE MEN ARE STILL MISSING, RIGHT?
WE'RE HOPING TECHNOMANCY WILL MAKE UP FOR THAT LOSS AND SERVE AS OUR *NEW* SWORD AND SHIELD.
E-EX-CUSE ME!
AH!
M-MISS MIRA! AS THE PUPIL OF MASTER DANBLF, CAN I ASK YOU SOME QUESTIONS?!
PAFF
JUST THINK OF IT AS SERVING OUR COUNTRY.
......
PLEASE, WON'T YOU TALK WITH THEM?

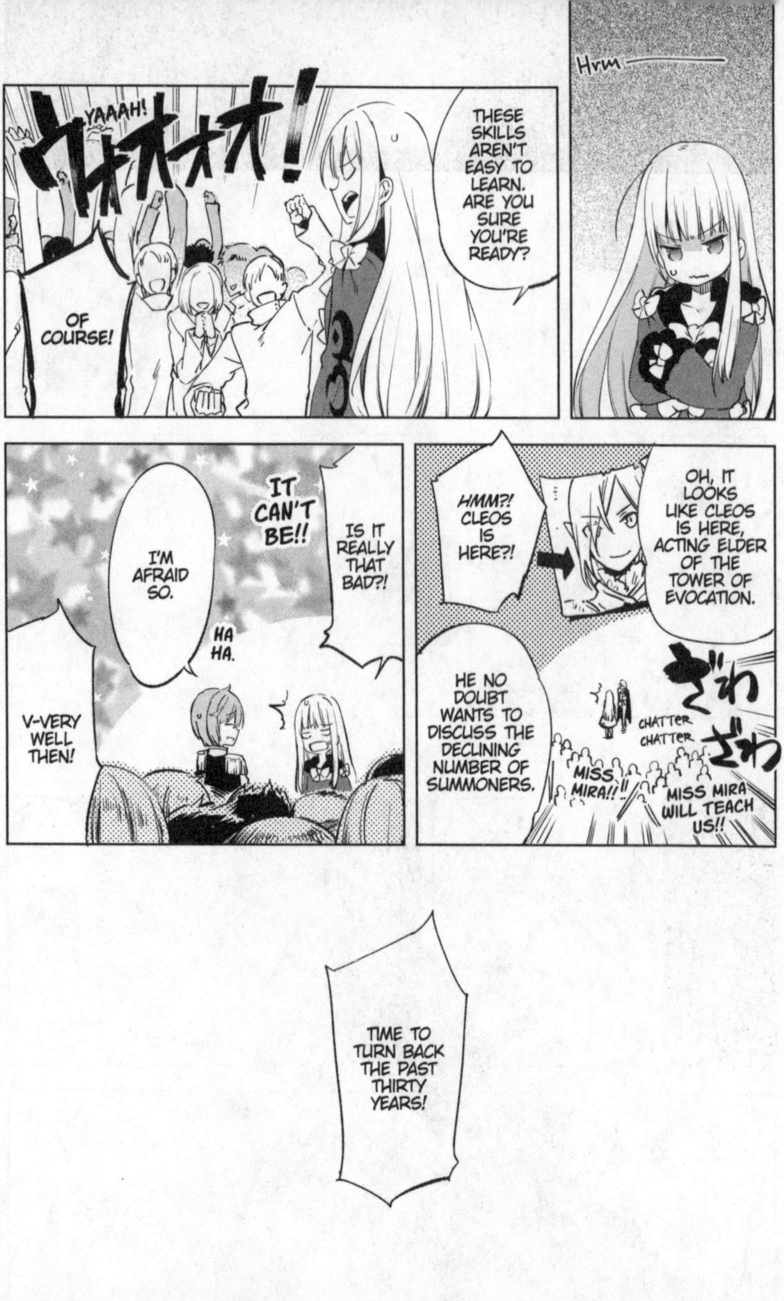
Hrm
THESE SKILLS AREN'T EASY TO LEARN. ARE YOU SURE YOU'RE READY?
YAAAH!
ウォオオオ!
OF COURSE!
OH, IT LOOKS LIKE CLEOS IS HERE, ACTING ELDER OF THE TOWER OF EVOCATION.
HMM?! CLEOS IS HERE?!
ざわ
CHATTER
ざわ
CHATTER
HE NO DOUBT WANTS TO DISCUSS THE DECLINING NUMBER OF SUMMONERS.
MISS MIRA WILL TEACH US!!
MISS MIRA!!
IS IT REALLY THAT BAD?!
IT CAN'T BE!!
I'M AFRAID SO.
HA HA.
V-VERY WELL THEN!
TIME TO TURN BACK THE PAST THIRTY YEARS!

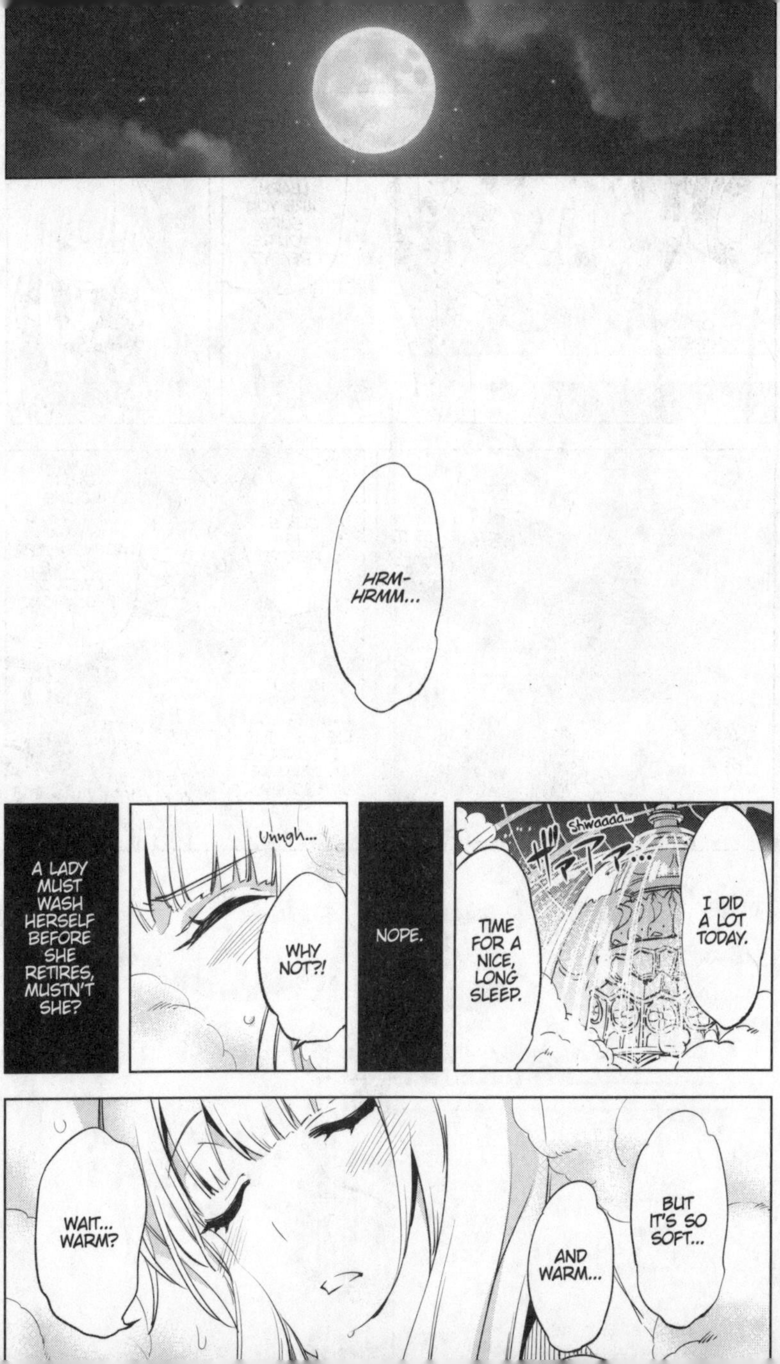
HRM-
HRMM...
I DID A LOT TODAY.
Shwaaaa...
TIME FOR A NICE, LONG SLEEP.
NOPE.
Unngh...
WHY NOT?!
A LADY MUST WASH HERSELF BEFORE SHE RETIRES, MUSTN'T SHE?
BUT IT'S SO SOFT...
AND WARM...
WAIT... WARM?

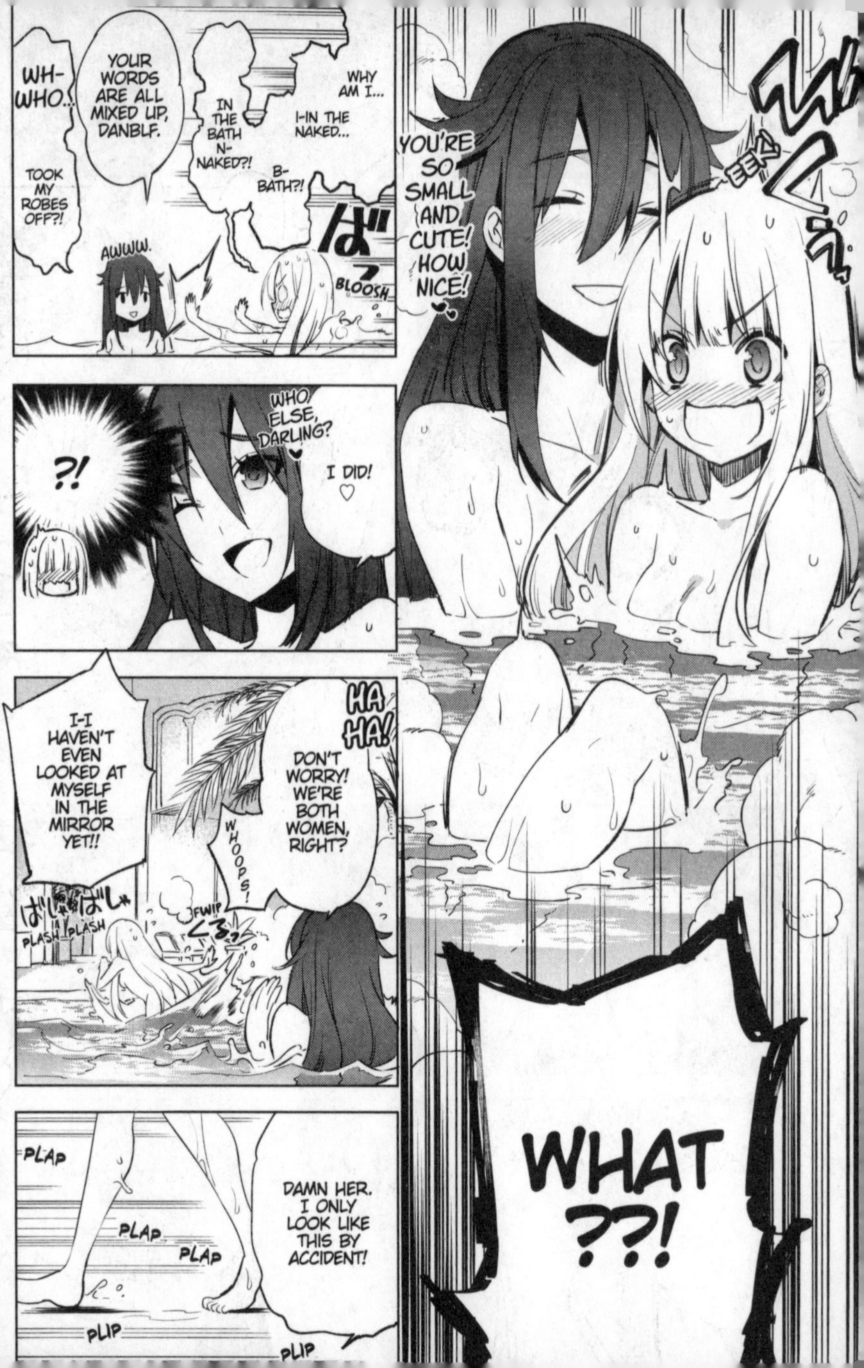
EEK☆
YOU'RE SO SMALL AND CUTE! HOW NICE!
WHAT ??!
WHY AM I... I-IN THE NAKED... B-BATH?!
IN THE BATH N-NAKED?!
YOUR WORDS ARE ALL MIXED UP, DANBLF.
WH-WHO... TOOK MY ROBES OFF?!
BLOOSH
AWWW.
WHO ELSE, DARLING?
I DID! ♡
?!
HA HA!
DON'T WORRY! WE'RE BOTH WOMEN, RIGHT?
I-I HAVEN'T EVEN LOOKED AT MYSELF IN THE MIRROR YET!!
WHOOPS!
FWIP
PLASH PLASH
DAMN HER. I ONLY LOOK LIKE THIS BY ACCIDENT!
PLAP
PLAP
PLAP
PLIP
PLIP

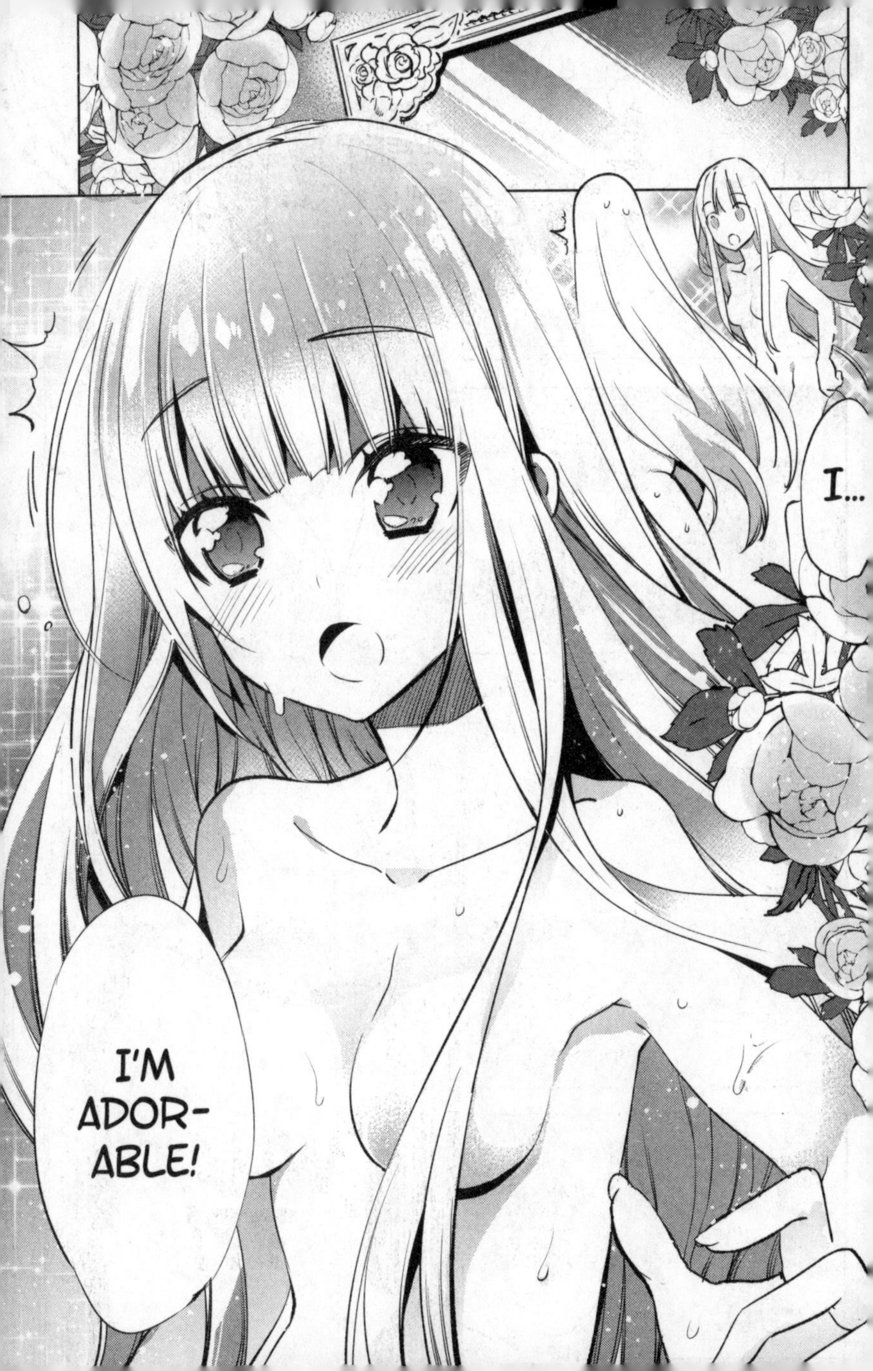
I...
I'M ADORABLE!

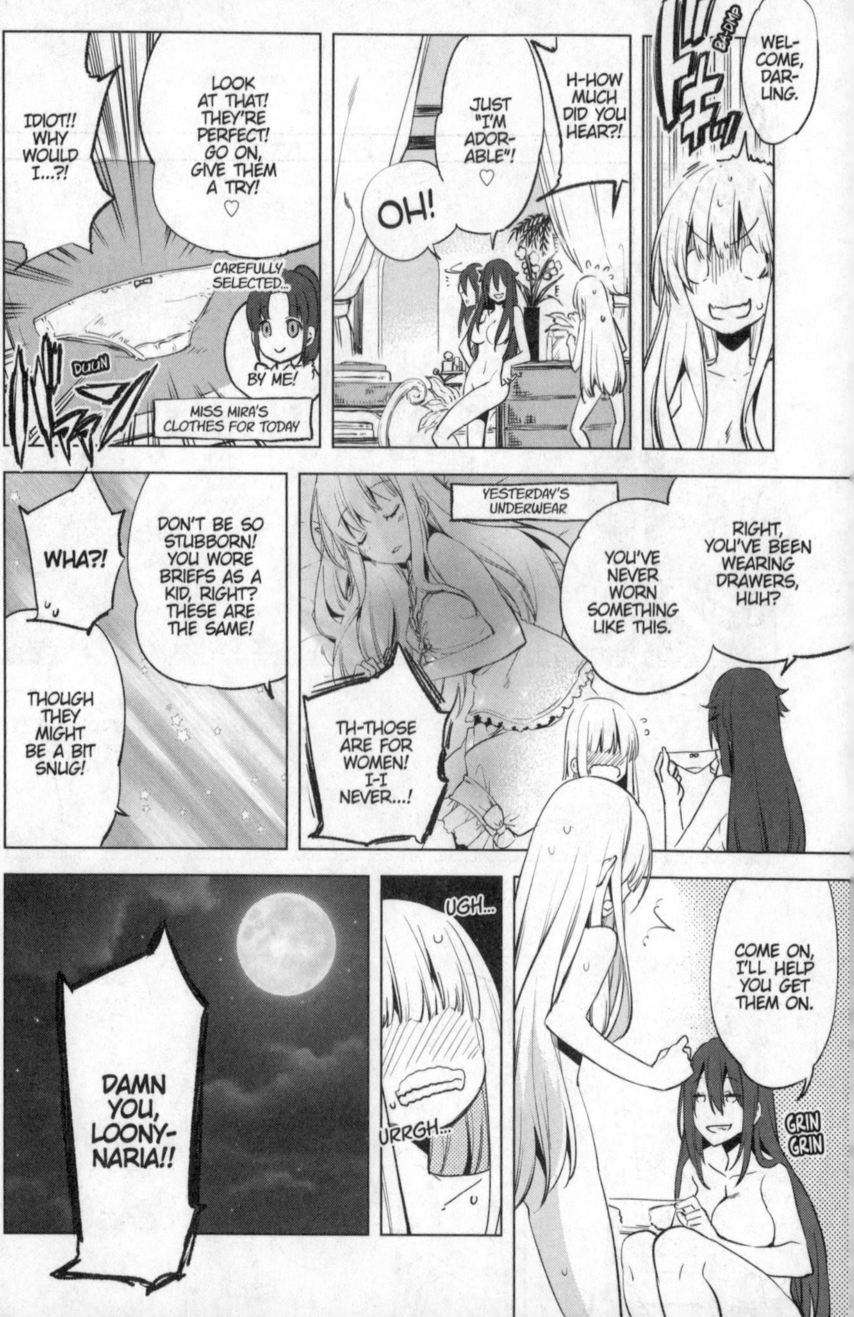
WEL-COME, DAR-LING.
BA-DMP
H-HOW MUCH DID YOU HEAR?!
JUST "I'M ADOR-ABLE"! ♡
OH!
LOOK AT THAT! THEY'RE PERFECT! GO ON, GIVE THEM A TRY! ♡
IDIOT!! WHY WOULD I...?!
CAREFULLY SELECTED...
BY ME!
DUUN
MISS MIRA'S CLOTHES FOR TODAY
RIGHT, YOU'VE BEEN WEARING DRAWERS, HUH?
YOU'VE NEVER WORN SOMETHING LIKE THIS.
YESTERDAY'S UNDERWEAR
TH-THOSE ARE FOR WOMEN! I-I NEVER...!
DON'T BE SO STUBBORN! YOU WORE BRIEFS AS A KID, RIGHT? THESE ARE THE SAME!
WHA?!
THOUGH THEY MIGHT BE A BIT SNUG!
COME ON, I'LL HELP YOU GET THEM ON.
GRIN GRIN
UGH...
URRGH...
DAMN YOU, LOONY-NARIA!!

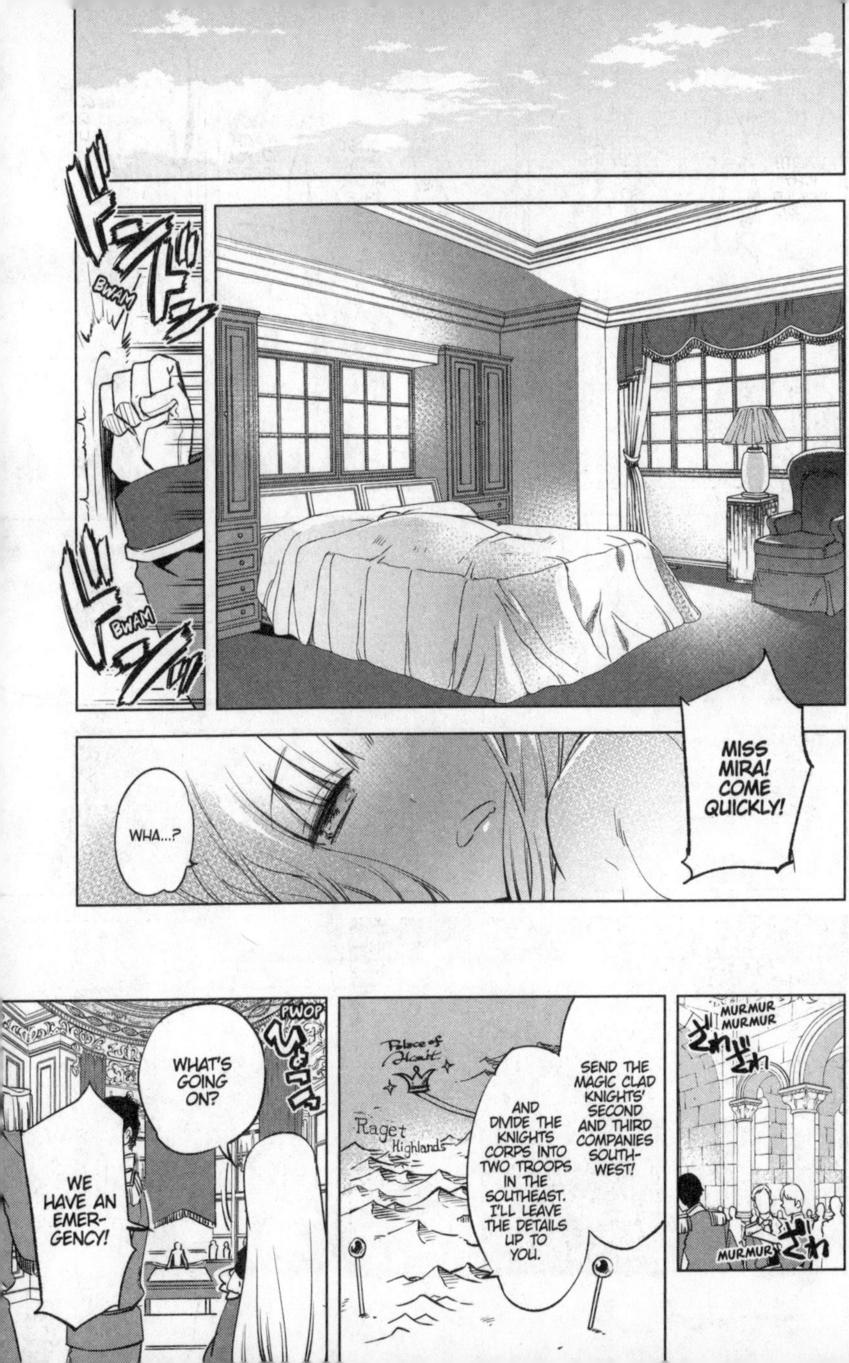
BWAM
BWAM
MISS MIRA! COME QUICKLY!
WHA...?
MURMUR MURMUR
MURMUR
SEND THE MAGIC CLAD KNIGHTS' SECOND AND THIRD COMPANIES SOUTH-WEST!
AND DIVIDE THE KNIGHTS CORPS INTO TWO TROOPS IN THE SOUTHEAST. I'LL LEAVE THE DETAILS UP TO YOU.
Raget Highlands
PWOP
WHAT'S GOING ON?
WE HAVE AN EMER-GENCY!

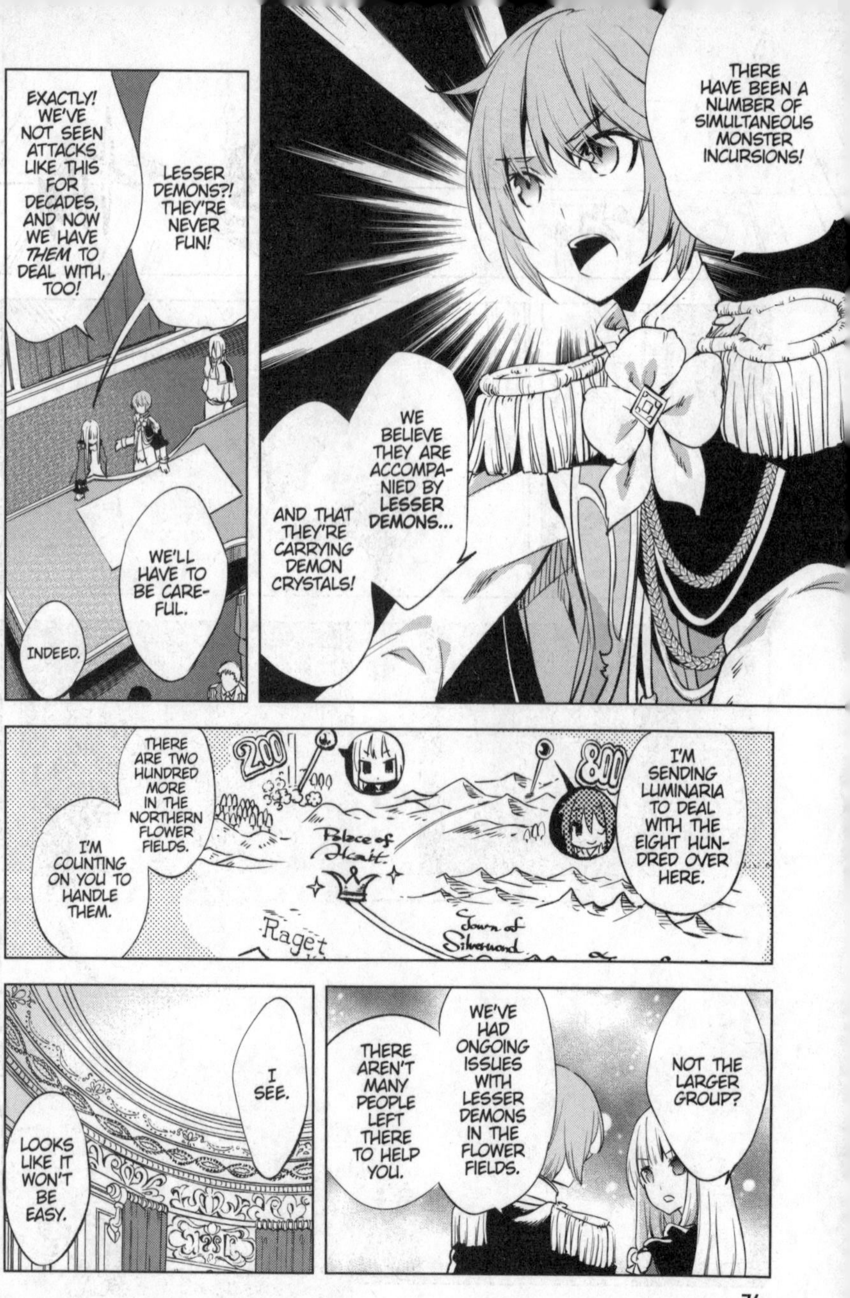
THERE HAVE BEEN A NUMBER OF SIMULTANEOUS MONSTER INCURSIONS!
WE BELIEVE THEY ARE ACCOMPANIED BY LESSER DEMONS...
AND THAT THEY'RE CARRYING DEMON CRYSTALS!
LESSER DEMONS?! THEY'RE NEVER FUN!
EXACTLY! WE'VE NOT SEEN ATTACKS LIKE THIS FOR DECADES, AND NOW WE HAVE *THEM* TO DEAL WITH, TOO!
WE'LL HAVE TO BE CAREFUL.
INDEED.
800
200
Palace of Alcait
Raget
I'M SENDING LUMINARIA TO DEAL WITH THE EIGHT HUNDRED OVER HERE.
THERE ARE TWO HUNDRED MORE IN THE NORTHERN FLOWER FIELDS.
I'M COUNTING ON YOU TO HANDLE THEM.
NOT THE LARGER GROUP?
WE'VE HAD ONGOING ISSUES WITH LESSER DEMONS IN THE FLOWER FIELDS.
THERE AREN'T MANY PEOPLE LEFT THERE TO HELP YOU.
I SEE.
LOOKS LIKE IT WON'T BE EASY.

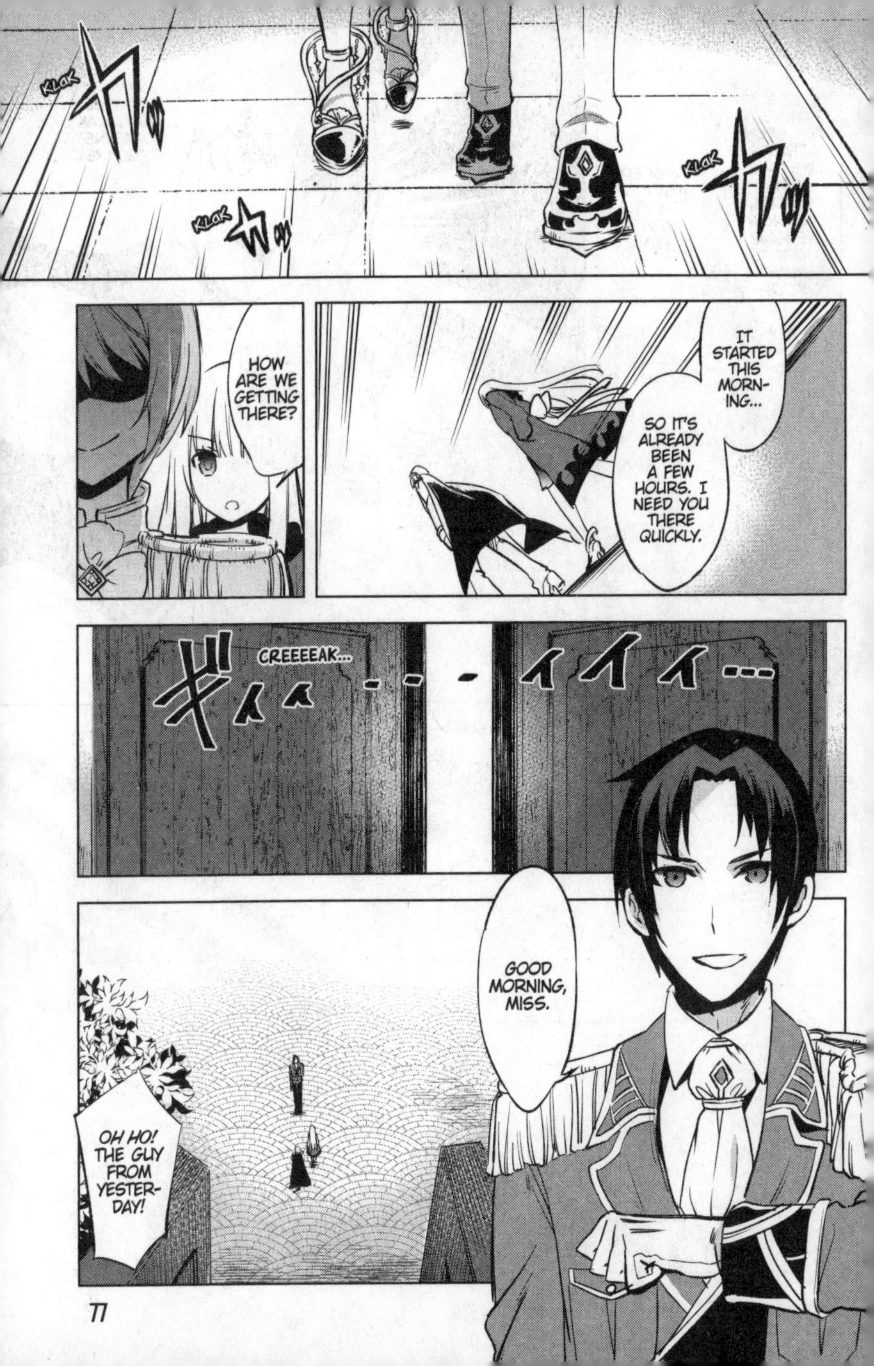
KLAK
KLAK
KLAK
IT STARTED THIS MORNING...
SO IT'S ALREADY BEEN A FEW HOURS. I NEED YOU THERE QUICKLY.
HOW ARE WE GETTING THERE?
CREEEEAK...
GOOD MORNING, MISS.
OH HO! THE GUY FROM YESTERDAY!

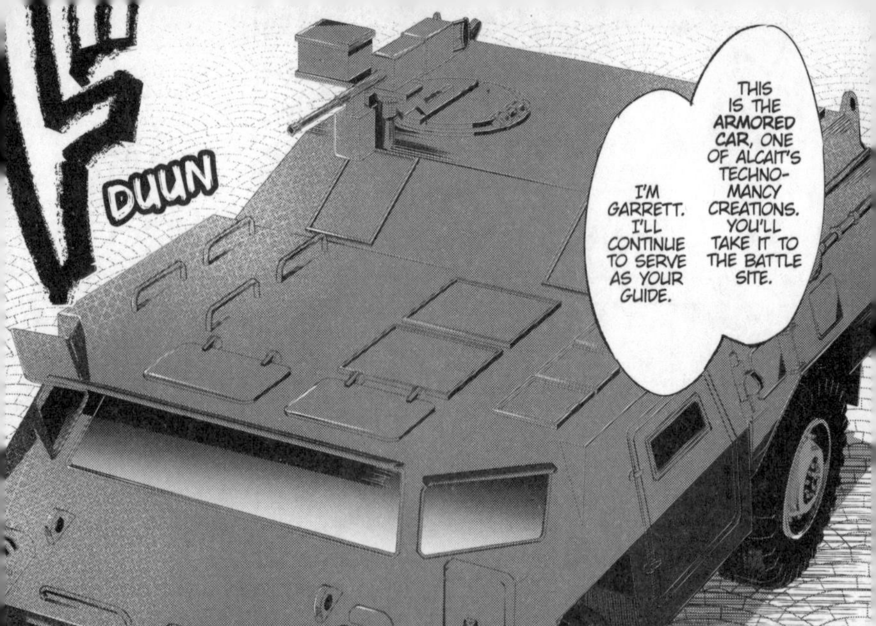
DUUN
THIS IS THE ARMORED CAR, ONE OF ALCAIT'S TECHNO-MANCY CREATIONS. YOU'LL TAKE IT TO THE BATTLE SITE.
I'M GARRETT. I'LL CONTINUE TO SERVE AS YOUR GUIDE.

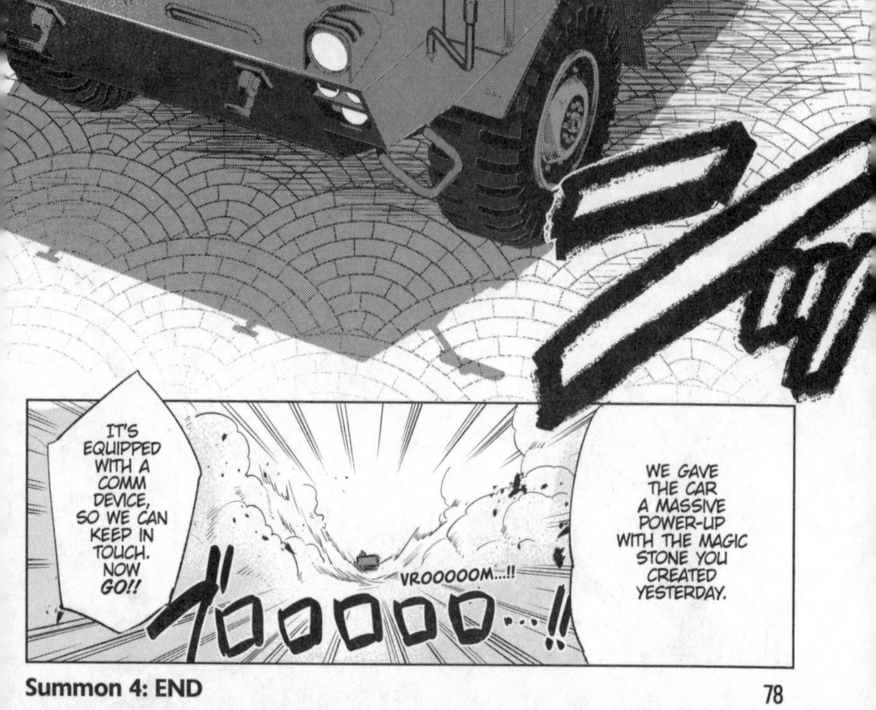
WE GAVE THE CAR A MASSIVE POWER-UP WITH THE MAGIC STONE YOU CREATED YESTERDAY.
VROOOOOM...!!
IT'S EQUIPPED WITH A COMM DEVICE, SO WE CAN KEEP IN TOUCH. NOW *GO!!*

Summon 4: END

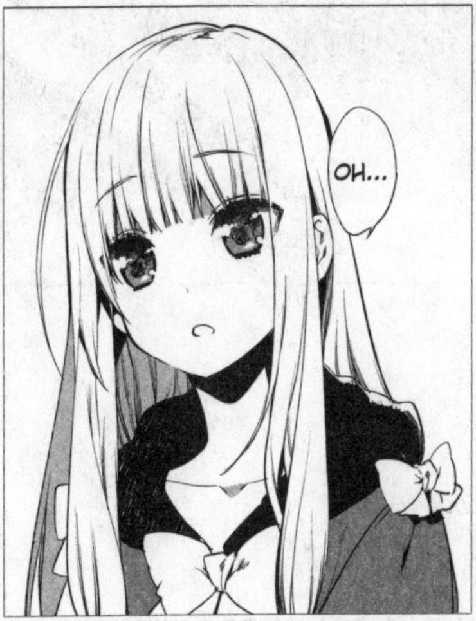
OH...

She
Professed
Herself
Pupil ^{of} the
Wise Man

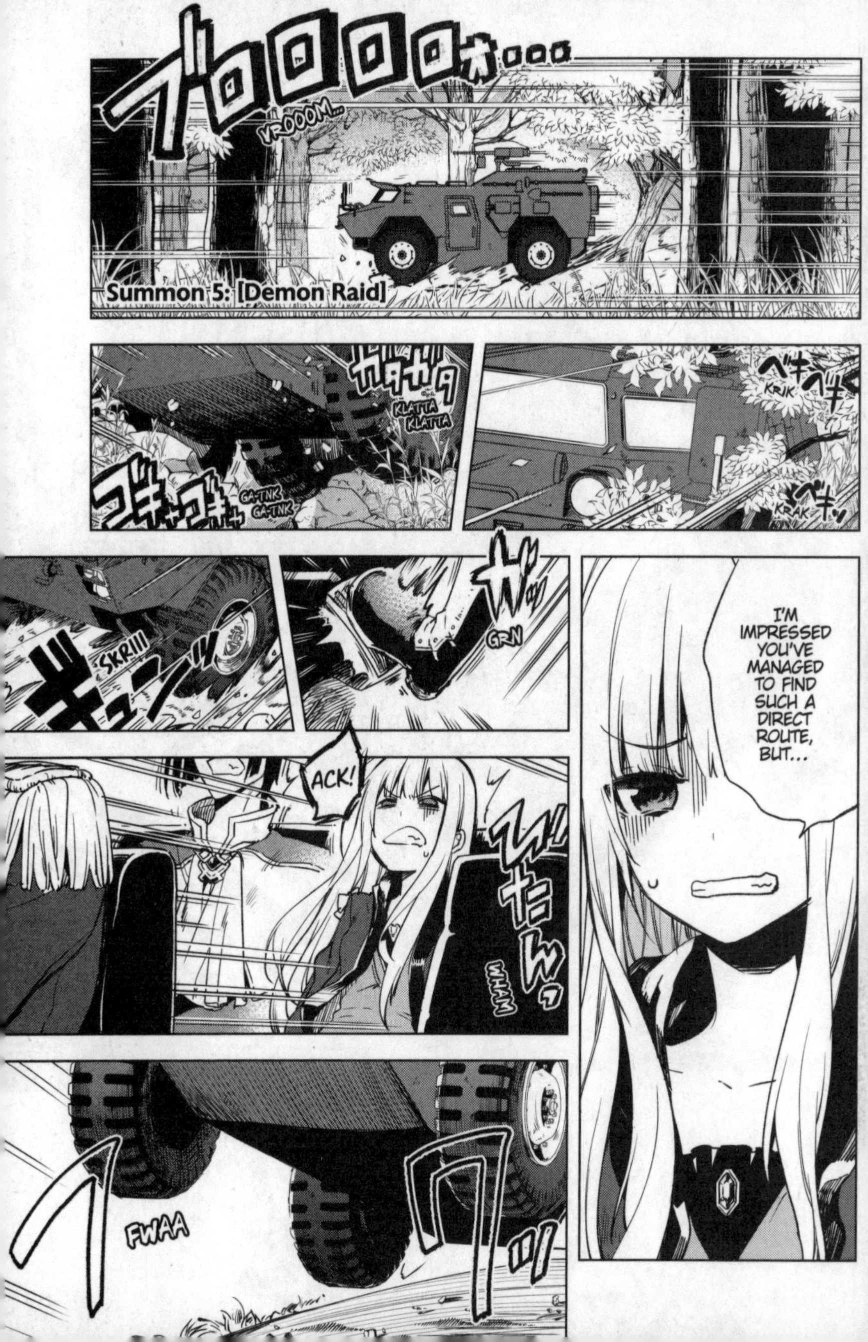
VROOOM...
Summon 5: [Demon Raid]
KRIK
KRAK
KLATTA KLATTA
GA-TNK GA-TNK
I'M IMPRESSED YOU'VE MANAGED TO FIND SUCH A DIRECT ROUTE, BUT...
GRN
SKRIII
ACK!
WHAM
FWAA

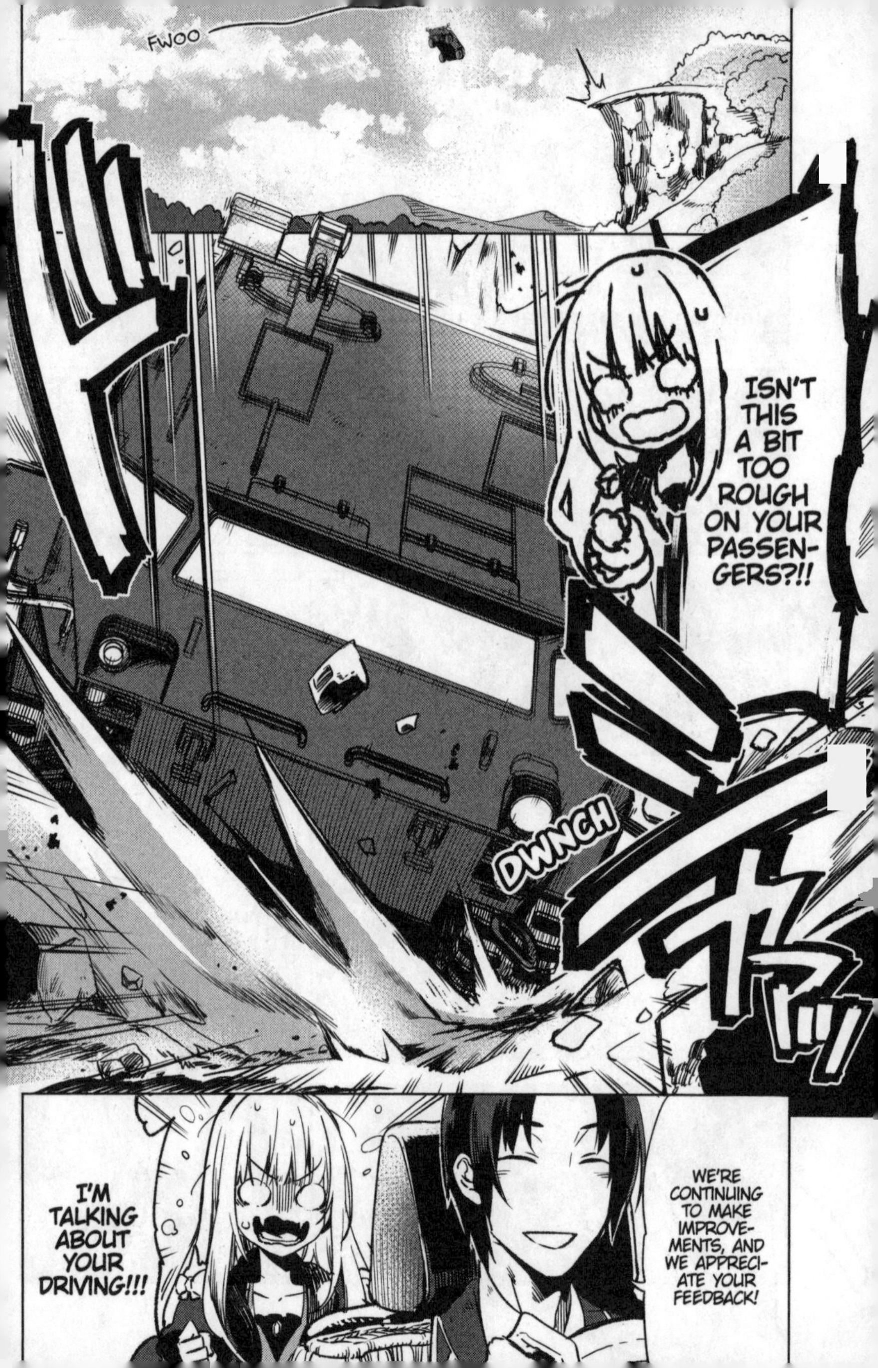
FWOO
ISN'T THIS A BIT TOO ROUGH ON YOUR PASSEN-GERS?!!
DWNCH
WE'RE CONTINUING TO MAKE IMPROVE-MENTS, AND WE APPRECI-ATE YOUR FEEDBACK!
I'M TALKING ABOUT YOUR DRIVING!!!

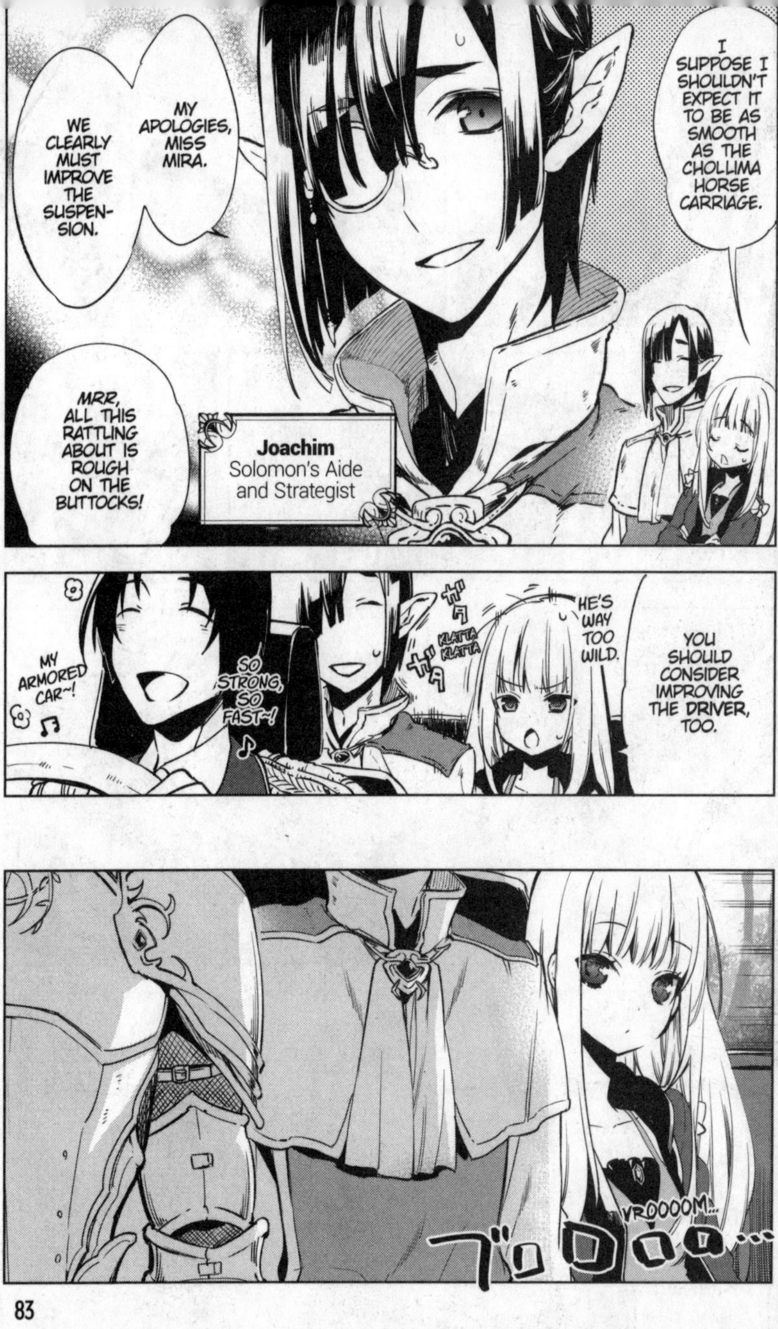
I SUPPOSE I SHOULDN'T EXPECT IT TO BE AS SMOOTH AS THE CHOLLIMA HORSE CARRIAGE.
MY APOLOGIES, MISS MIRA.
WE CLEARLY MUST IMPROVE THE SUSPEN-SION.
Joachim
Solomon's Aide and Strategist
MRR, ALL THIS RATTLING ABOUT IS ROUGH ON THE BUTTOCKS!
YOU SHOULD CONSIDER IMPROVING THE DRIVER, TOO.
HE'S WAY TOO WILD.
ガタ ガタ
KLATTA KLATTA
SO STRONG, SO FAST~!
MY ARMORED CAR~!
VROOOOM...
ブロロロロ…

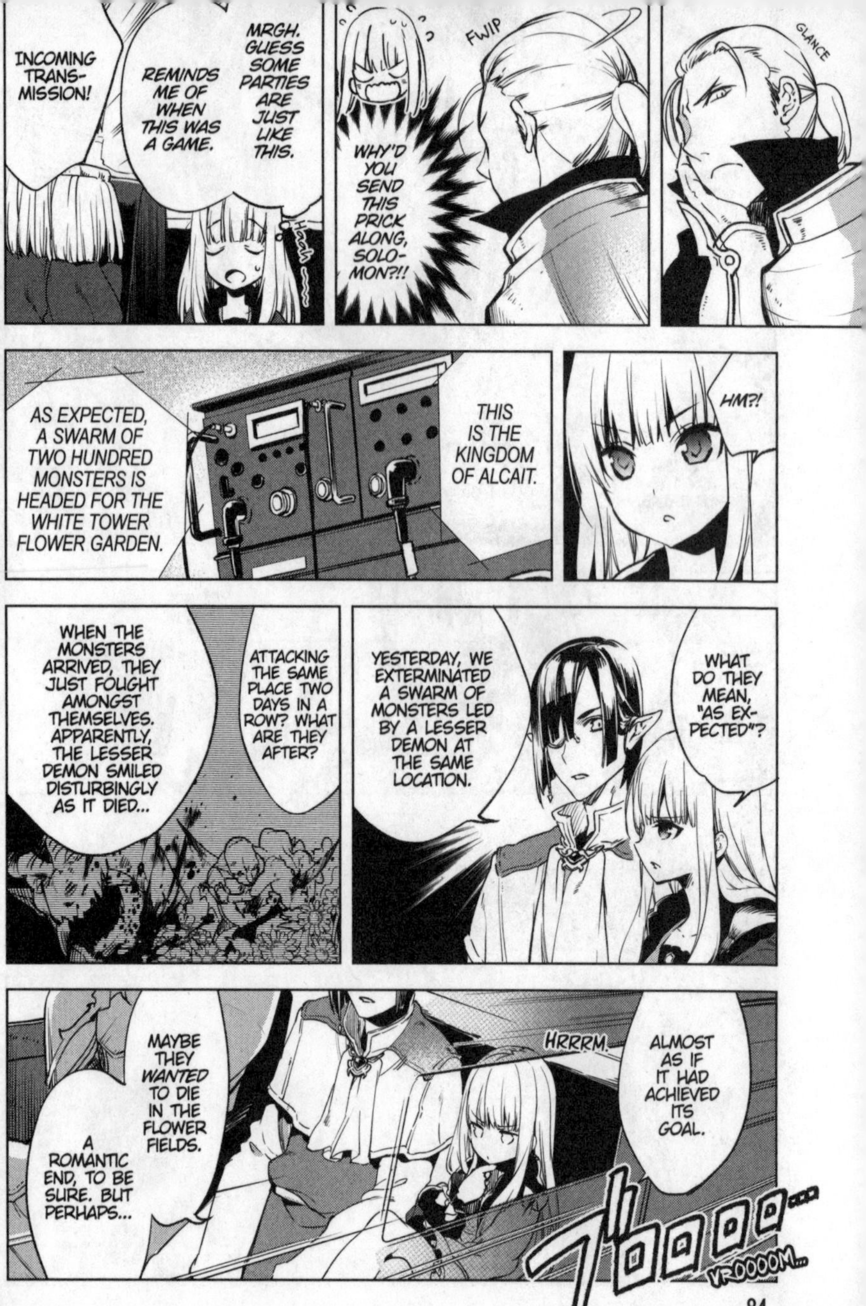
GLANCE
FWIP
WHY'D YOU SEND THIS PRICK ALONG, SOLOMON?!!
MRGH. GUESS SOME PARTIES ARE JUST LIKE THIS.
REMINDS ME OF WHEN THIS WAS A GAME.
Hach~
INCOMING TRANSMISSION!
HM?!
THIS IS THE KINGDOM OF ALCAIT.
AS EXPECTED, A SWARM OF TWO HUNDRED MONSTERS IS HEADED FOR THE WHITE TOWER FLOWER GARDEN.
WHAT DO THEY MEAN, "AS EXPECTED"?
YESTERDAY, WE EXTERMINATED A SWARM OF MONSTERS LED BY A LESSER DEMON AT THE SAME LOCATION.
ATTACKING THE SAME PLACE TWO DAYS IN A ROW? WHAT ARE THEY AFTER?
WHEN THE MONSTERS ARRIVED, THEY JUST FOUGHT AMONGST THEMSELVES. APPARENTLY, THE LESSER DEMON SMILED DISTURBINGLY AS IT DIED...
VROOOOM...
ALMOST AS IF IT HAD ACHIEVED ITS GOAL.
HRRRM.
MAYBE THEY WANTED TO DIE IN THE FLOWER FIELDS.
A ROMANTIC END, TO BE SURE. BUT PERHAPS...

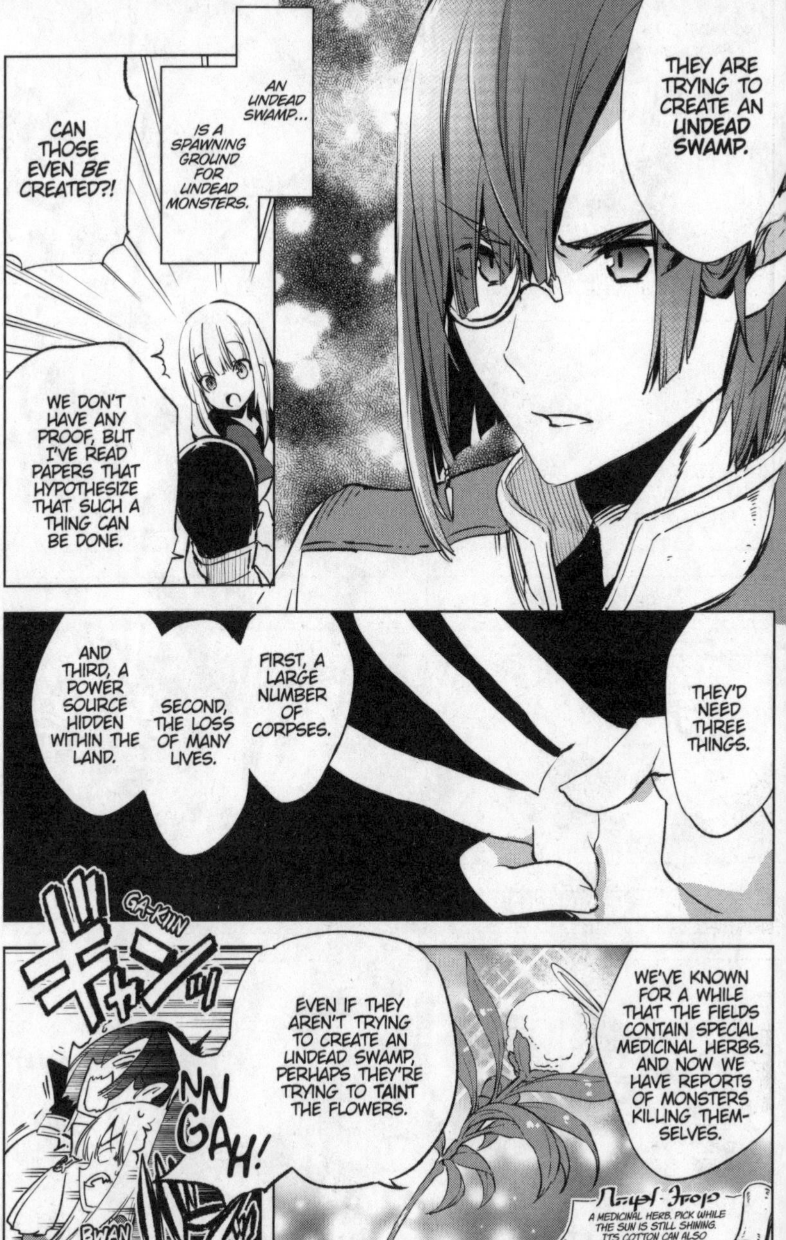
THEY ARE TRYING TO CREATE AN UNDEAD SWAMP.
AN UNDEAD SWAMP... IS A SPAWNING GROUND FOR UNDEAD MONSTERS.
CAN THOSE EVEN *BE* CREATED?!
WE DON'T HAVE ANY PROOF, BUT I'VE READ PAPERS THAT HYPOTHESIZE THAT SUCH A THING CAN BE DONE.
THEY'D NEED THREE THINGS.
FIRST, A LARGE NUMBER OF CORPSES.
SECOND, THE LOSS OF MANY LIVES.
AND THIRD, A POWER SOURCE HIDDEN WITHIN THE LAND.
WE'VE KNOWN FOR A WHILE THAT THE FIELDS CONTAIN SPECIAL MEDICINAL HERBS. AND NOW WE HAVE REPORTS OF MONSTERS KILLING THEMSELVES.
A MEDICINAL HERB. PICK WHILE THE SUN IS STILL SHINING. ITS COTTON CAN ALSO BE USED FOR THREAD.
EVEN IF THEY AREN'T TRYING TO CREATE AN UNDEAD SWAMP, PERHAPS THEY'RE TRYING TO TAINT THE FLOWERS.
GA-KIIN
NN GAH!
BWAN

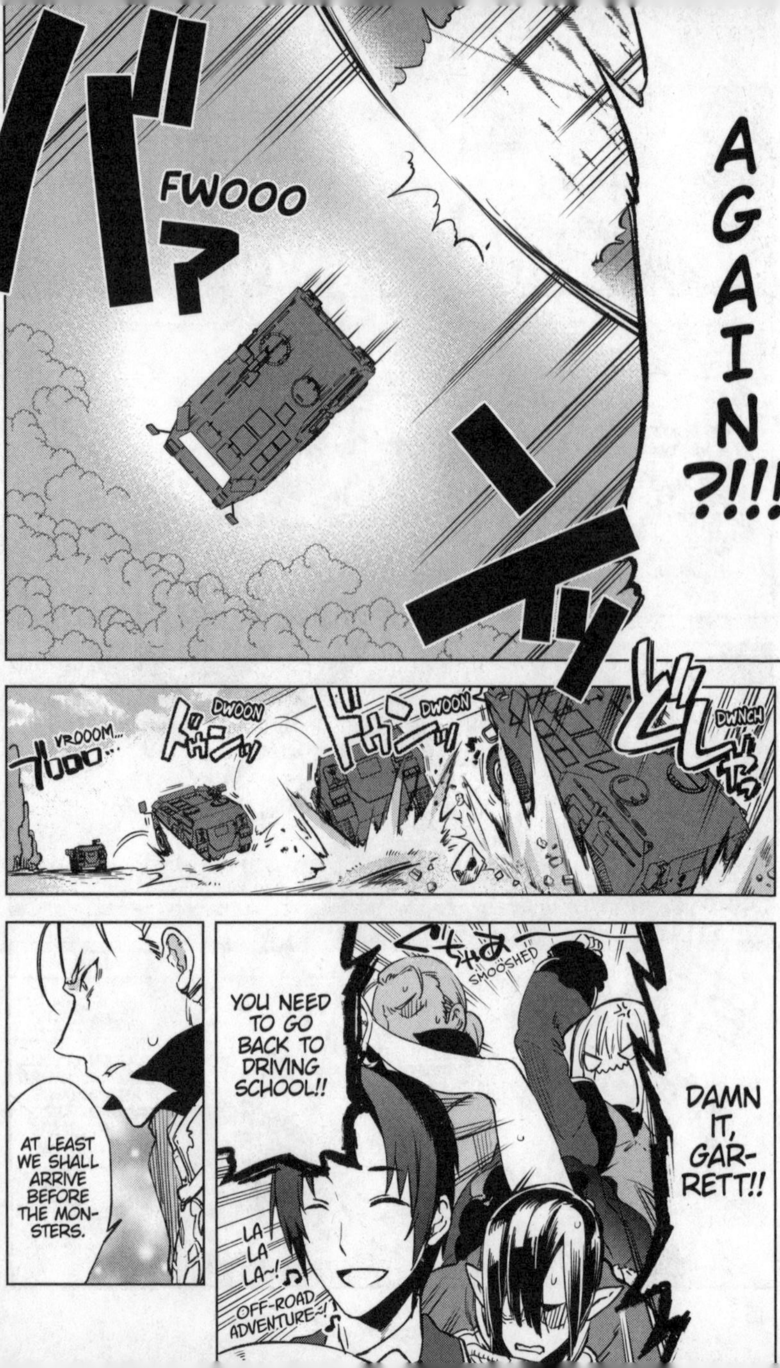
AGAIN?!!!
FWOOO
DWNCH
DWOON
DWOON
VROOOM...
SMOOSHED
DAMN IT, GAR-RETT!!
YOU NEED TO GO BACK TO DRIVING SCHOOL!!
LA LA LA~!
OFF-ROAD ADVENTURE~!
AT LEAST WE SHALL ARRIVE BEFORE THE MON-STERS.

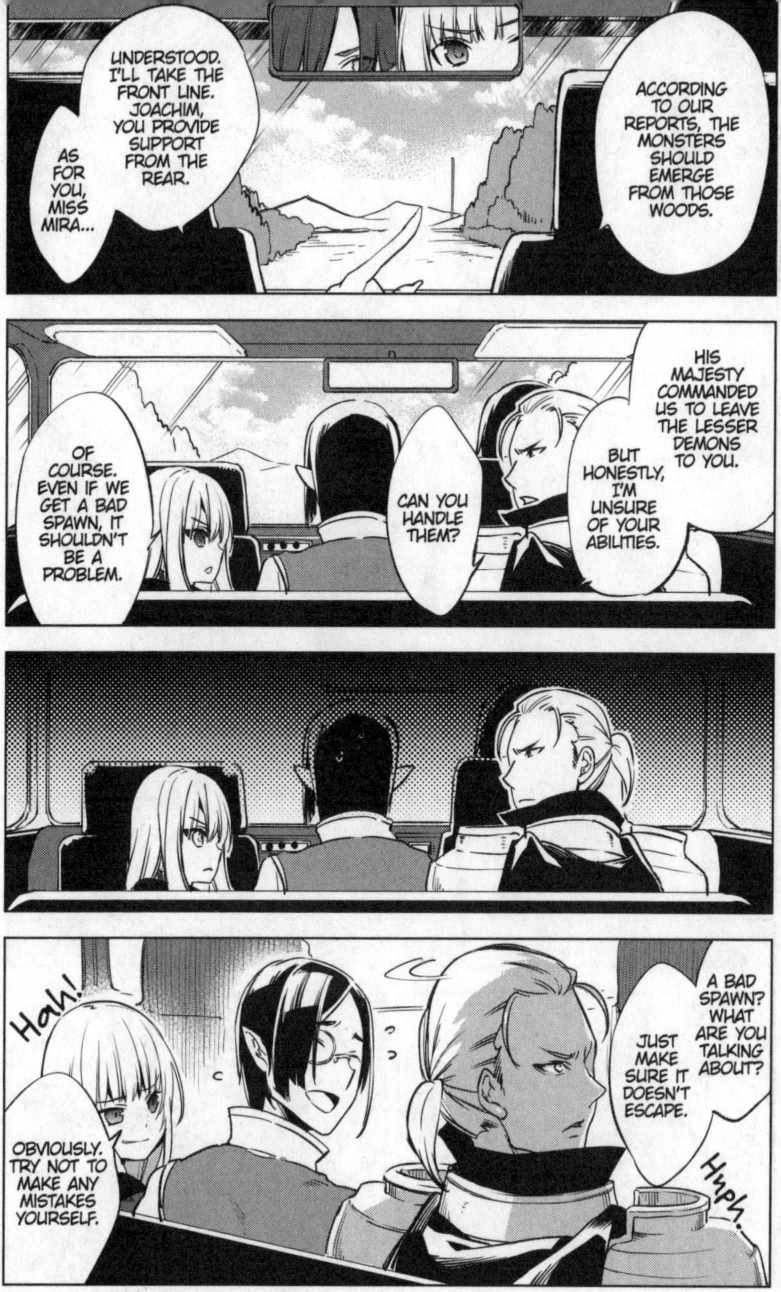
ACCORDING TO OUR REPORTS, THE MONSTERS SHOULD EMERGE FROM THOSE WOODS.
UNDERSTOOD. I'LL TAKE THE FRONT LINE. JOACHIM, YOU PROVIDE SUPPORT FROM THE REAR.
AS FOR YOU, MISS MIRA...
HIS MAJESTY COMMANDED US TO LEAVE THE LESSER DEMONS TO YOU.
BUT HONESTLY, I'M UNSURE OF YOUR ABILITIES.
CAN YOU HANDLE THEM?
OF COURSE. EVEN IF WE GET A BAD SPAWN, IT SHOULDN'T BE A PROBLEM.
A BAD SPAWN? WHAT ARE YOU TALKING ABOUT?
JUST MAKE SURE IT DOESN'T ESCAPE.
Hmph.
OBVIOUSLY. TRY NOT TO MAKE ANY MISTAKES YOURSELF.
Hah!

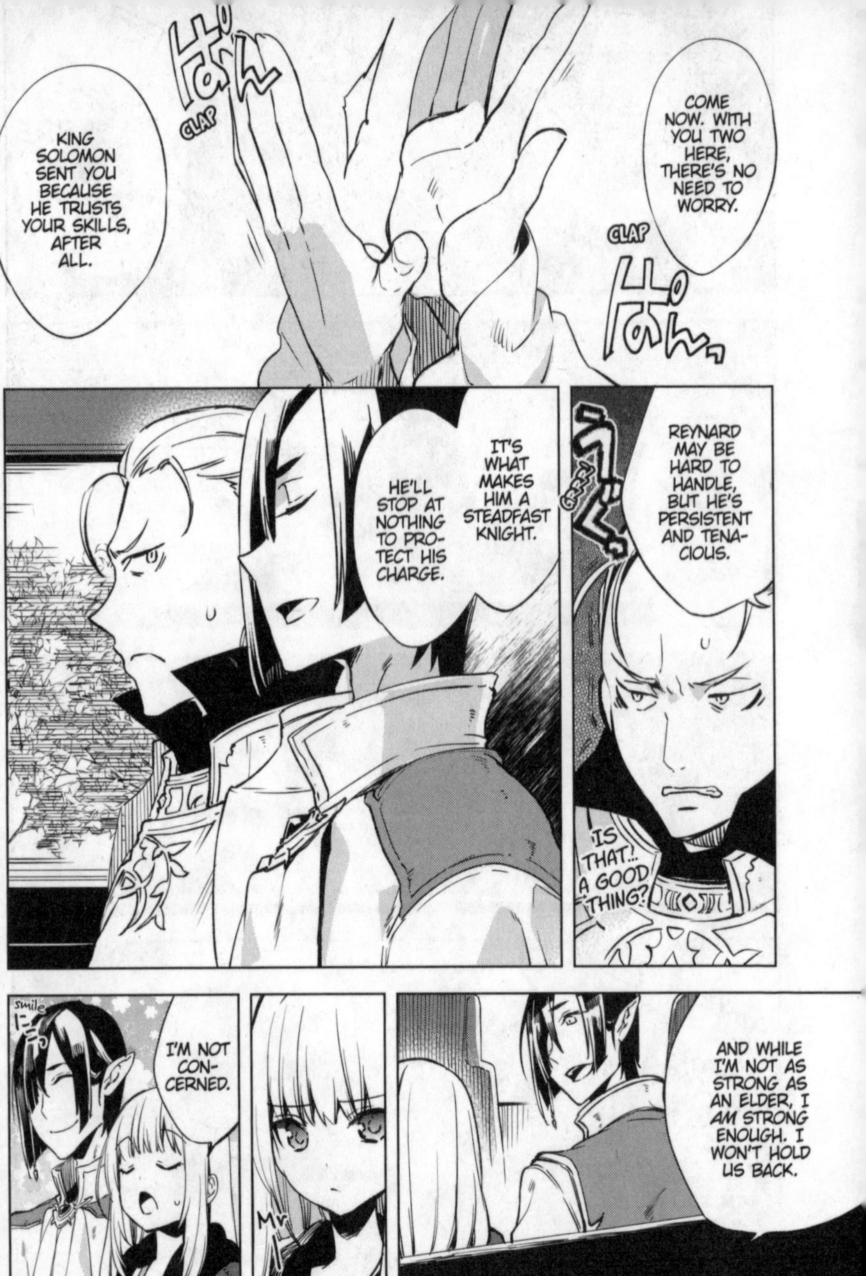
COME NOW. WITH YOU TWO HERE, THERE'S NO NEED TO WORRY.
CLAP
CLAP
KING SOLOMON SENT YOU BECAUSE HE TRUSTS YOUR SKILLS, AFTER ALL.
REYNARD MAY BE HARD TO HANDLE, BUT HE'S PERSISTENT AND TENACIOUS.
IS THAT... A GOOD THING?
IT'S WHAT MAKES HIM A STEADFAST KNIGHT.
HE'LL STOP AT NOTHING TO PROTECT HIS CHARGE.
AND WHILE I'M NOT AS STRONG AS AN ELDER, I AM STRONG ENOUGH. I WON'T HOLD US BACK.
Mr
I'M NOT CONCERNED.
smile

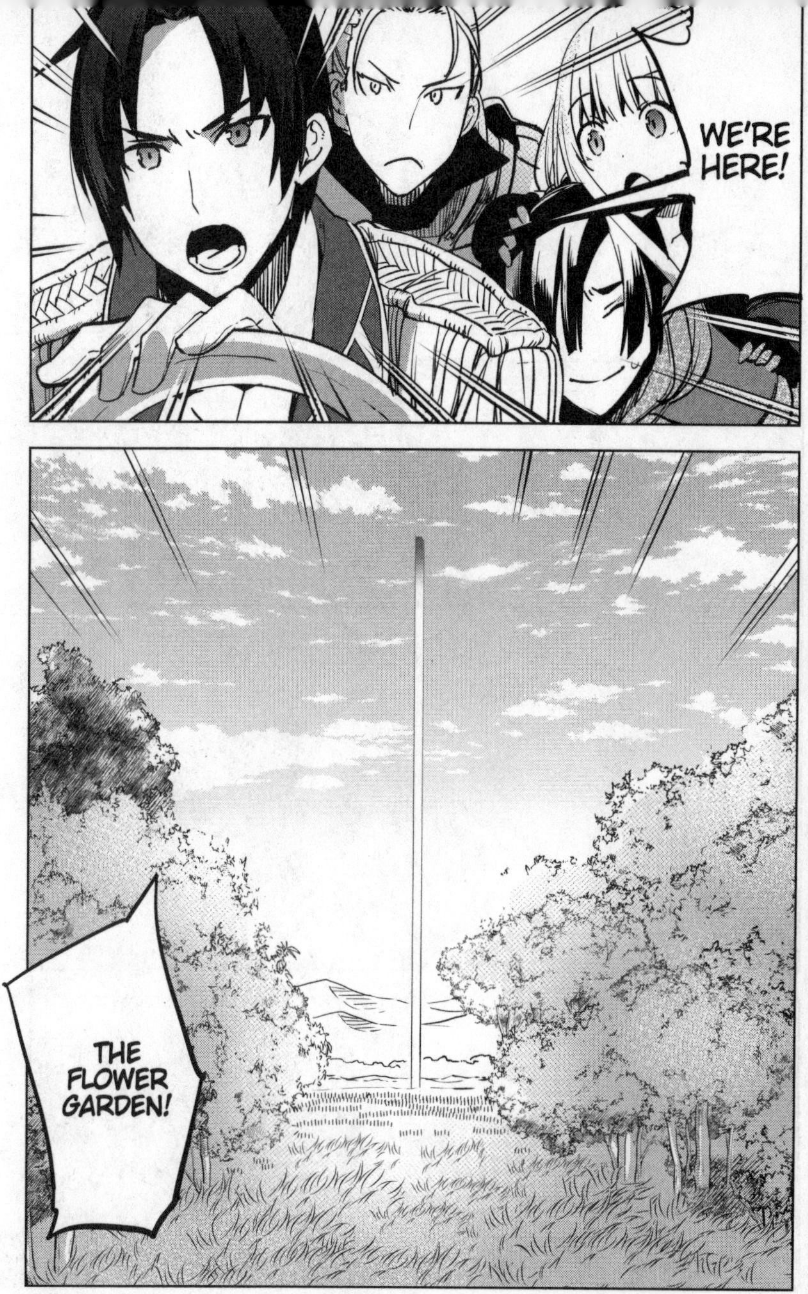
WE'RE HERE!
THE FLOWER GARDEN!

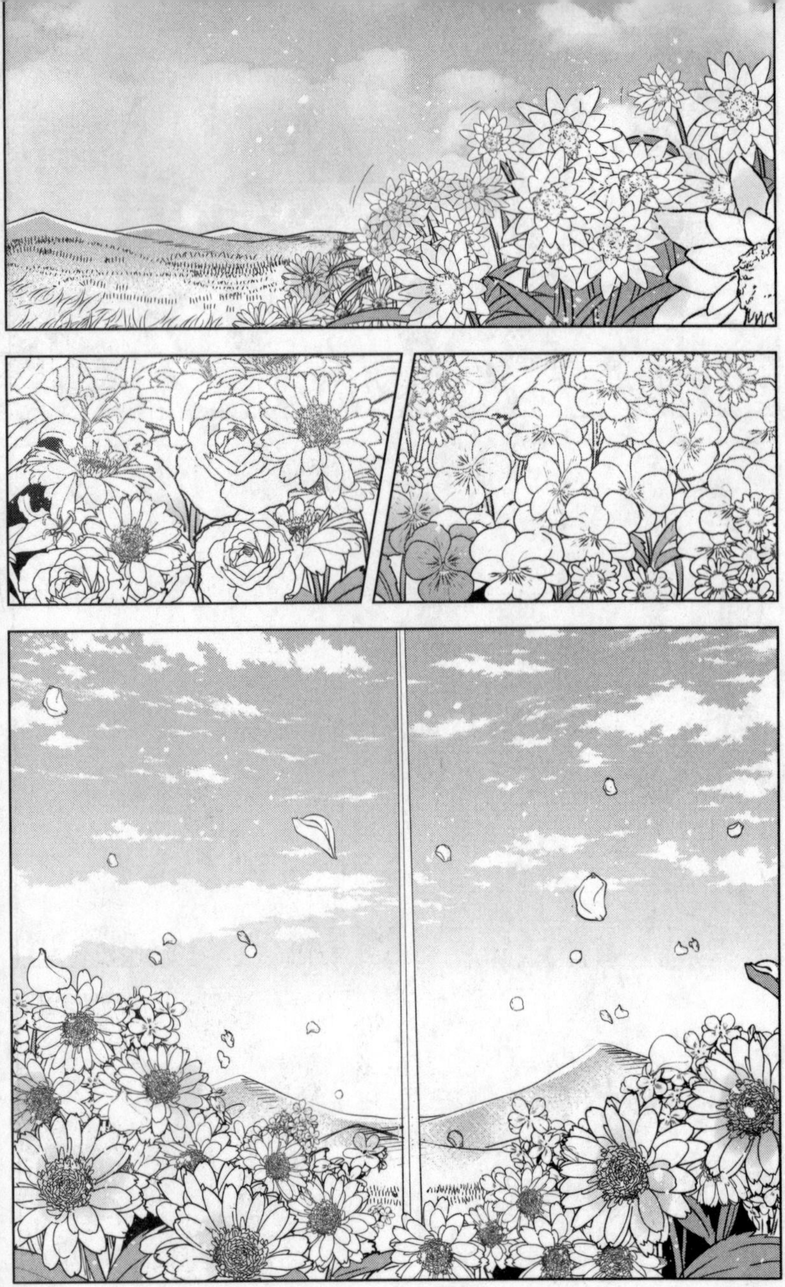

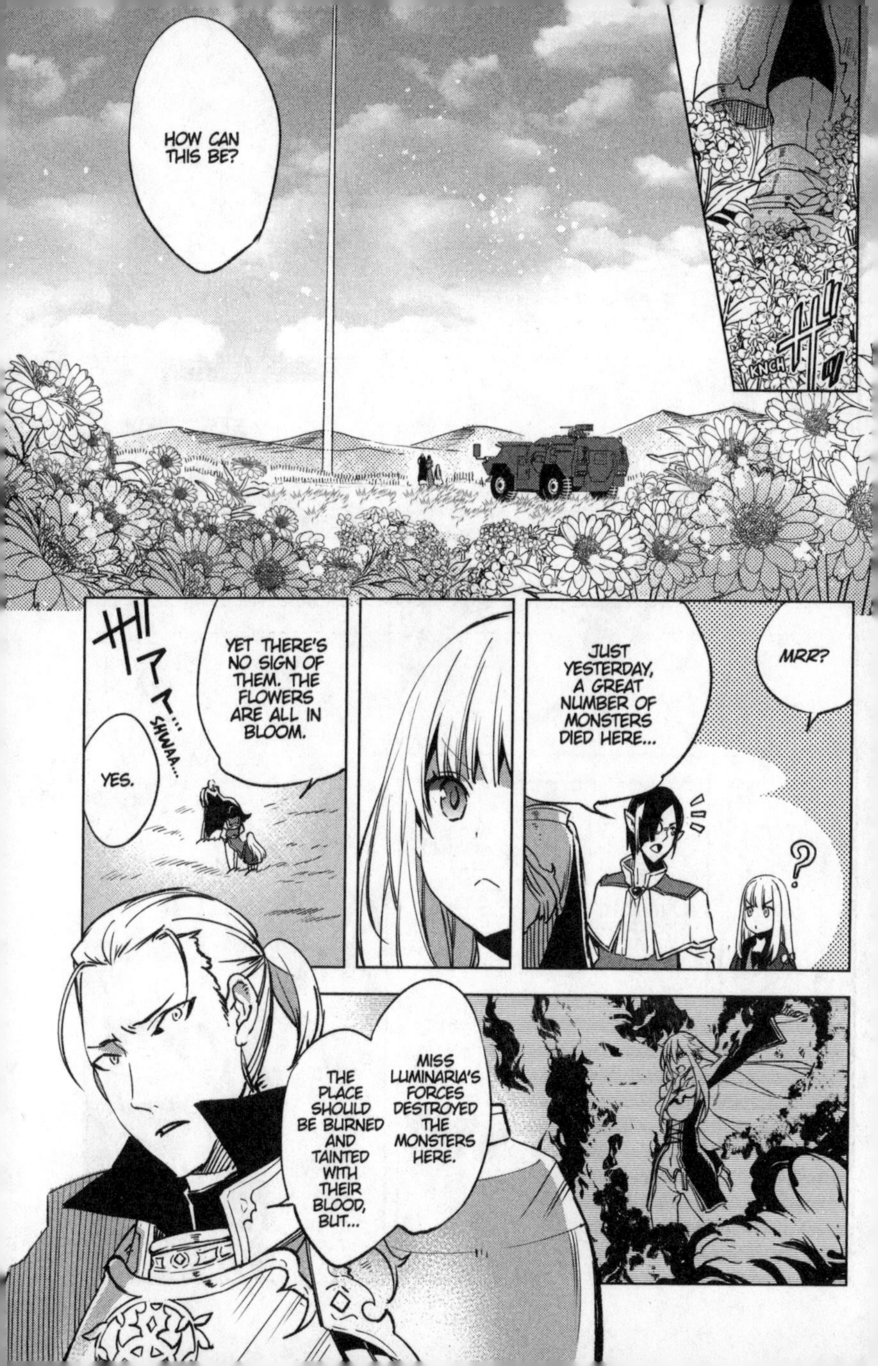
KNCH
HOW CAN THIS BE?
MRR?
JUST YESTERDAY, A GREAT NUMBER OF MONSTERS DIED HERE...
YET THERE'S NO SIGN OF THEM. THE FLOWERS ARE ALL IN BLOOM.
SHWAA...
YES.
MISS LUMINARIA'S FORCES DESTROYED THE MONSTERS HERE.
THE PLACE SHOULD BE BURNED AND TAINTED WITH THEIR BLOOD, BUT...

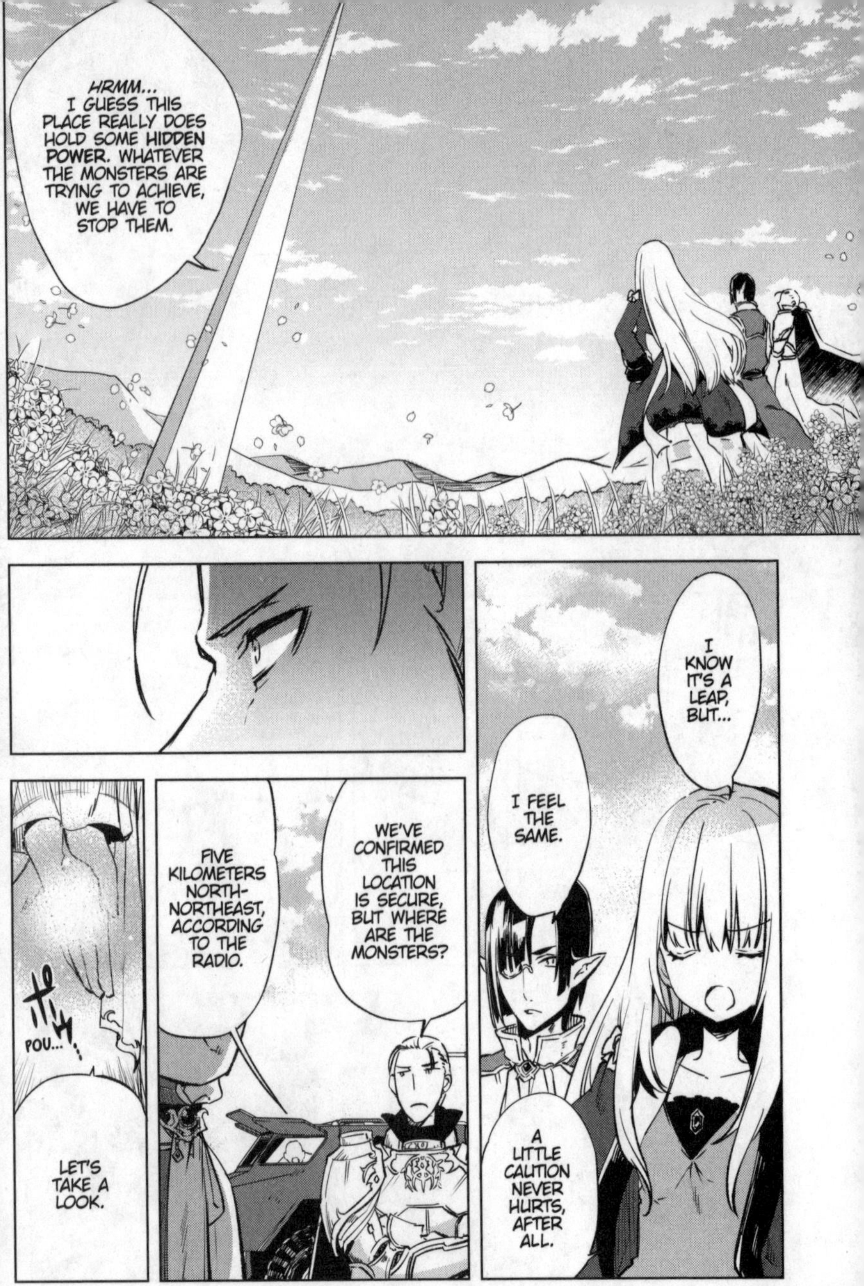
HRMM... I GUESS THIS PLACE REALLY DOES HOLD SOME HIDDEN POWER. WHATEVER THE MONSTERS ARE TRYING TO ACHIEVE, WE HAVE TO STOP THEM.
I KNOW IT'S A LEAP, BUT...
I FEEL THE SAME.
A LITTLE CAUTION NEVER HURTS, AFTER ALL.
WE'VE CONFIRMED THIS LOCATION IS SECURE, BUT WHERE ARE THE MONSTERS?
FIVE KILOMETERS NORTH-NORTHEAST, ACCORDING TO THE RADIO.
POU...
LET'S TAKE A LOOK.

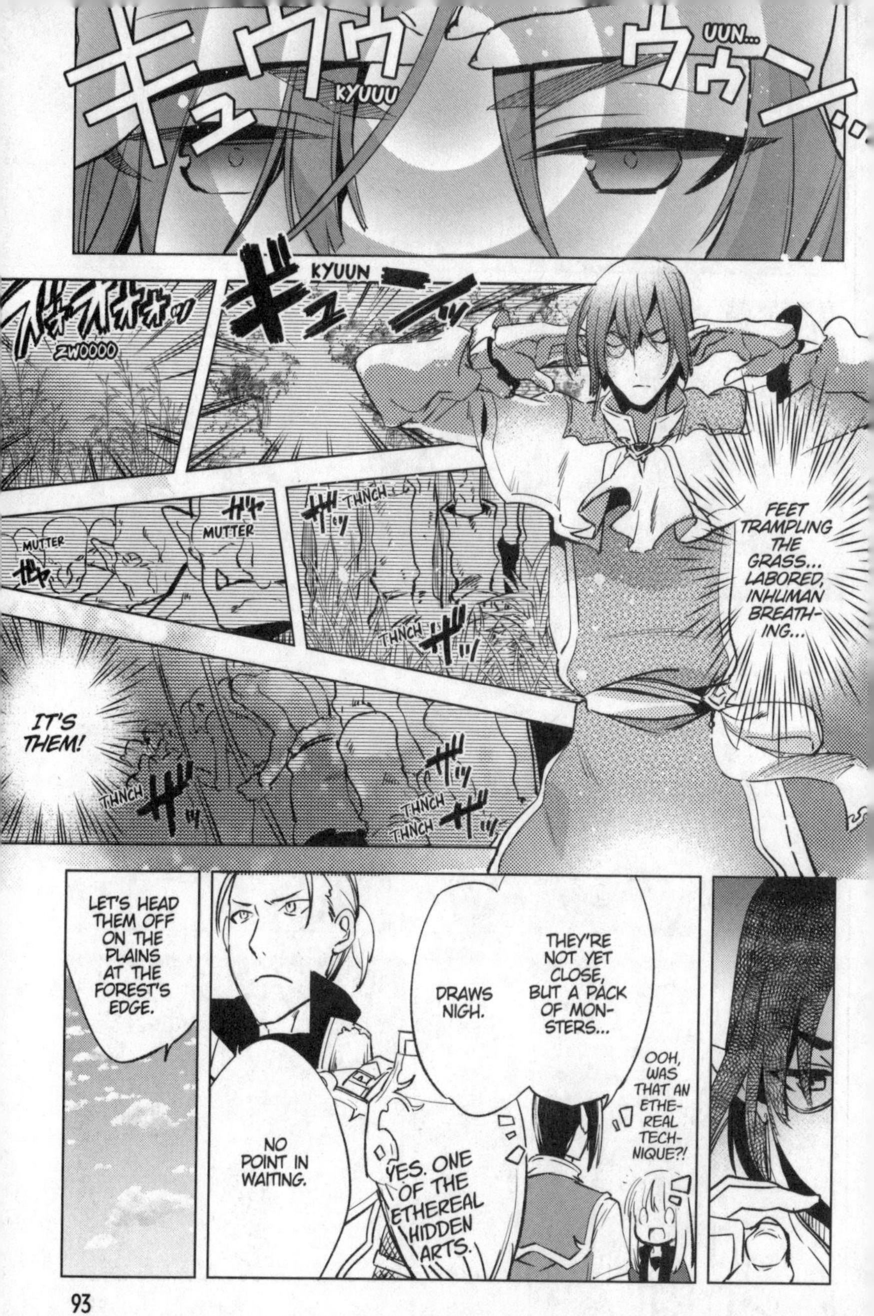
KYUUU
UUN...
KYUUN
ZWOOOO
FEET TRAMPLING THE GRASS... LABORED, INHUMAN BREATHING...
MUTTER
MUTTER
THNCH
THNCH
IT'S THEM!
THNCH
THNCH
THNCH
THEY'RE NOT YET CLOSE, BUT A PACK OF MONSTERS...
DRAWS NIGH.
OOH, WAS THAT AN ETHEREAL TECHNIQUE?!
YES. ONE OF THE ETHEREAL HIDDEN ARTS.
NO POINT IN WAITING.
LET'S HEAD THEM OFF ON THE PLAINS AT THE FOREST'S EDGE.

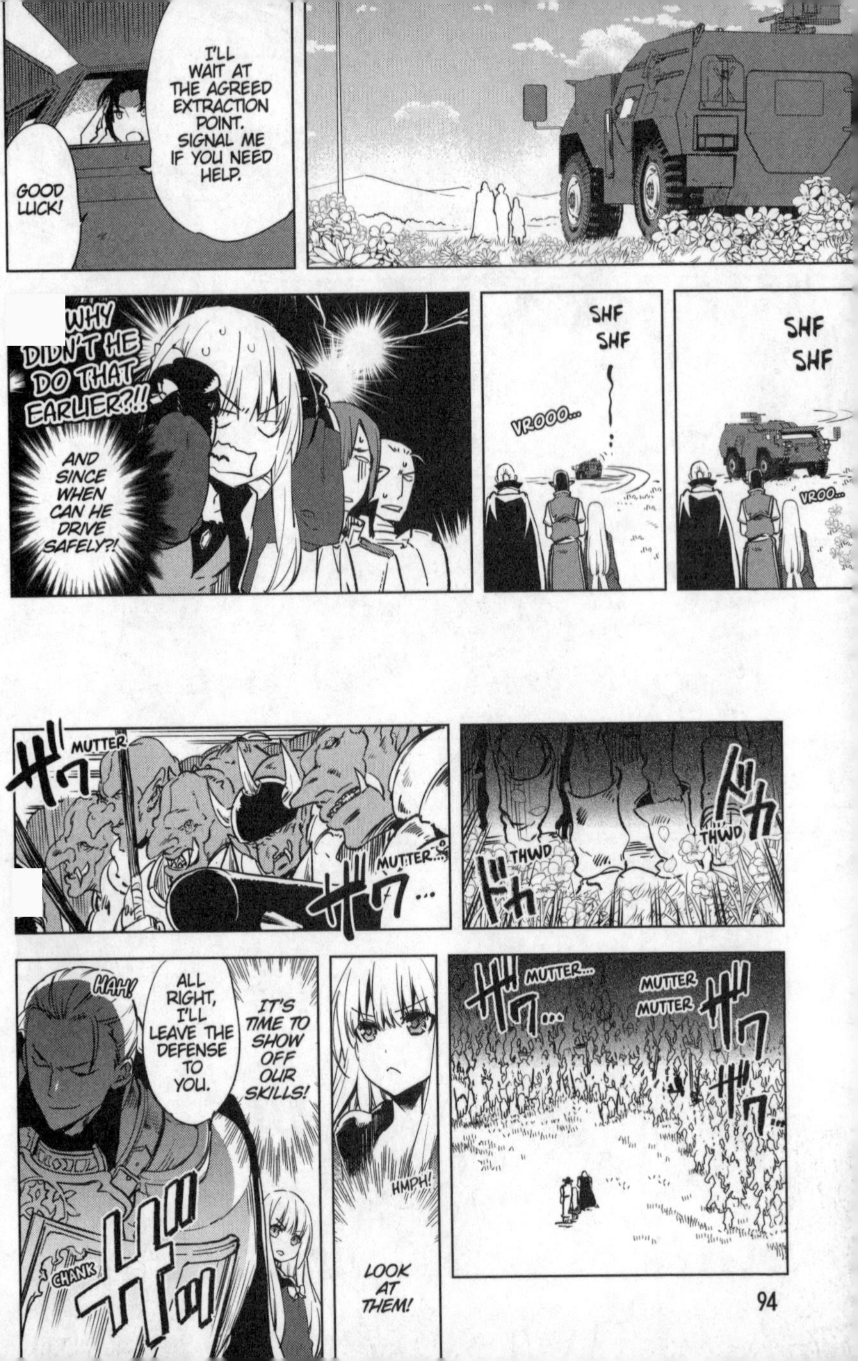
I'LL WAIT AT THE AGREED EXTRACTION POINT. SIGNAL ME IF YOU NEED HELP.
GOOD LUCK!
SHF SHF
VROO...
SHF SHF
VROOO...
WHY DIDN'T HE DO THAT EARLIER?!!
AND SINCE WHEN CAN HE DRIVE SAFELY?!
ドカ
THWD
ドカ
THWD
MUTTER
ザワ
MUTTER...
ザワ...
MUTTER MUTTER
ザワ
MUTTER...
ザワ...
ザワ...
HMPH!
LOOK AT THEM!
IT'S TIME TO SHOW OFF OUR SKILLS!
ALL RIGHT, I'LL LEAVE THE DEFENSE TO YOU.
HAH!
CHANK
ガッ

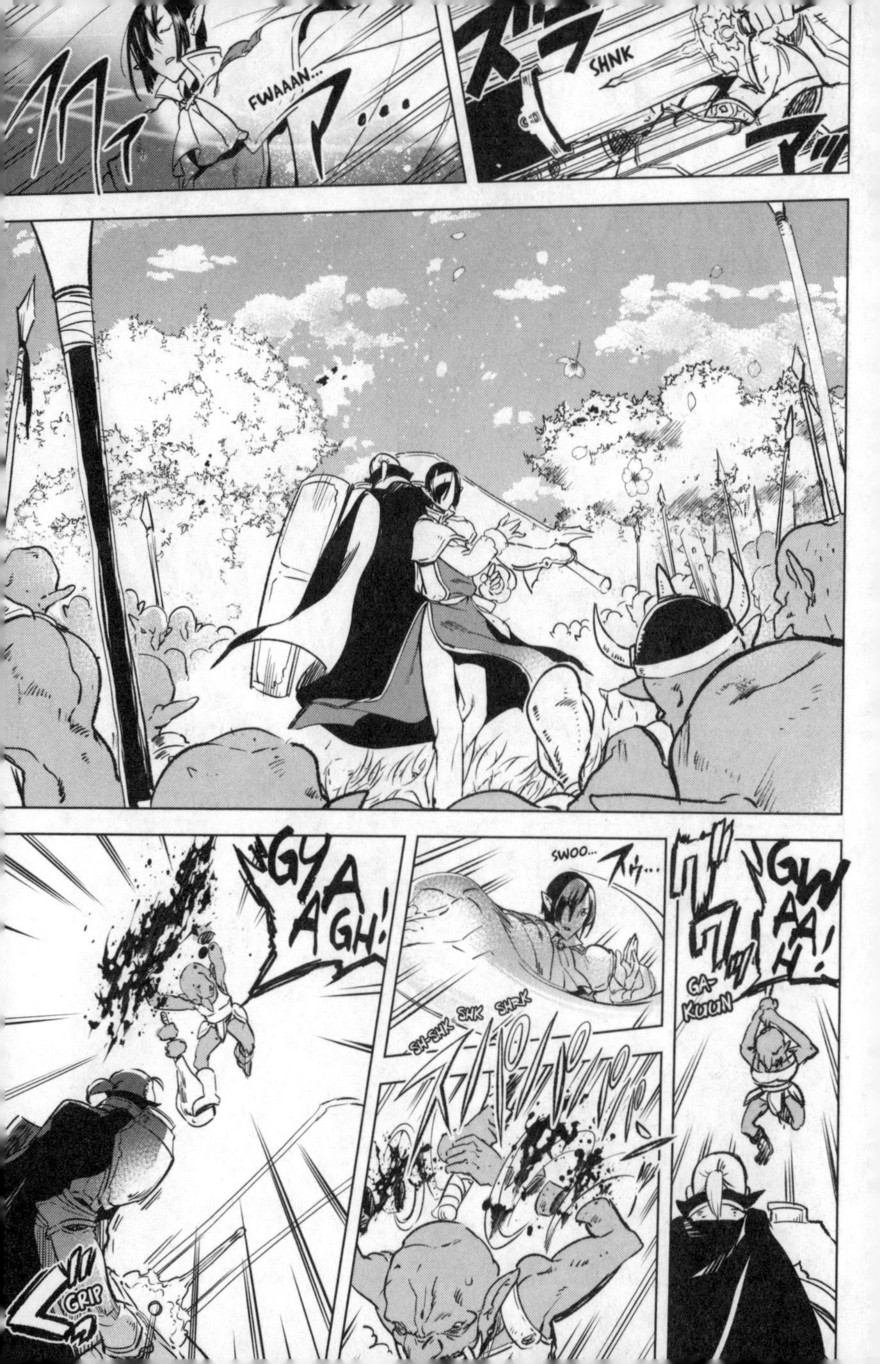
SHNK
FWAAAN...
GWAAAH!
GA-KUUN
SWOO...
SH-SHK SHK SHRK
GYAAGH!
GRIP

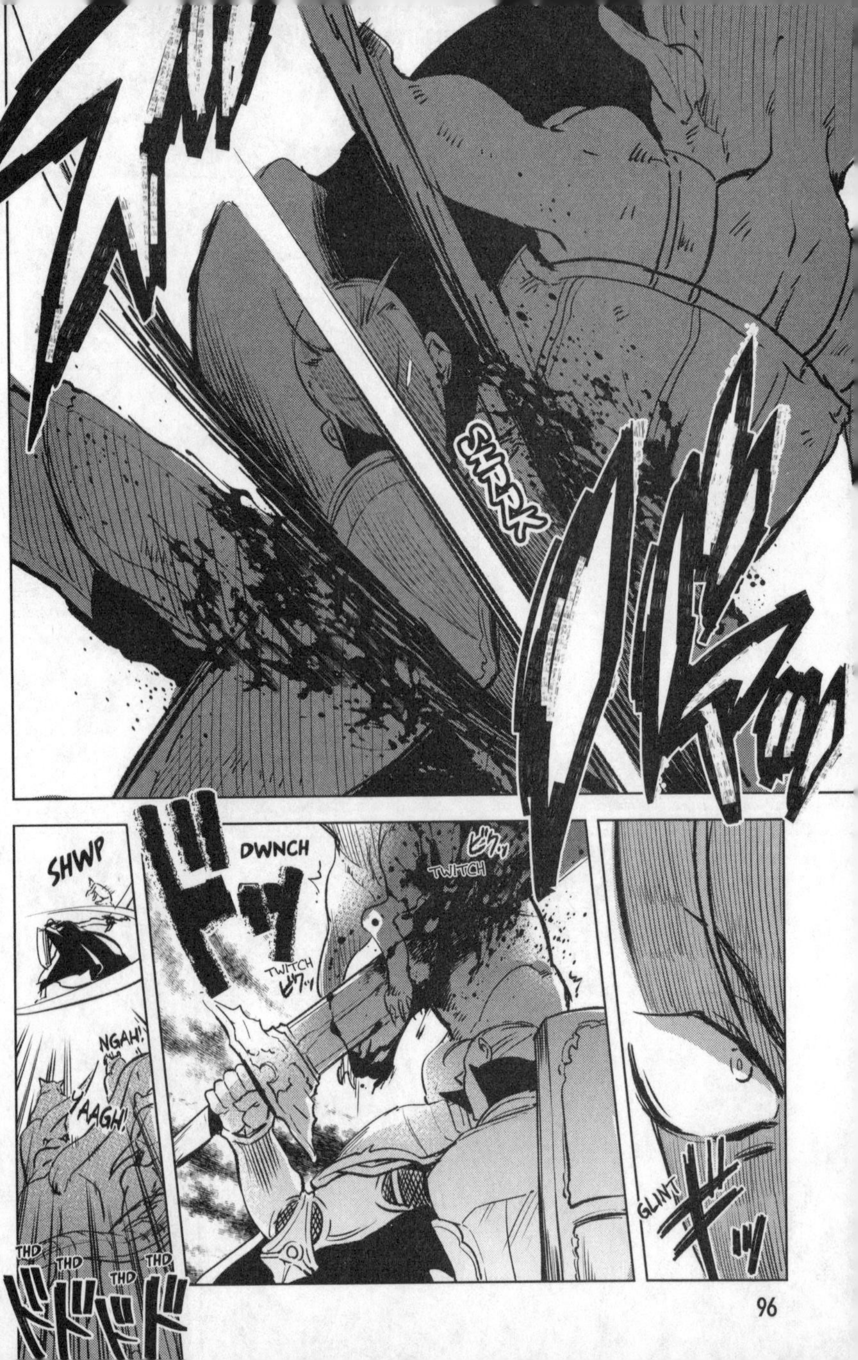
SHRRK
GLINT
DWNCH
TWITCH
TWITCH
SHWP
NGAH!
YAAGH!
THD
THD
THD
THD

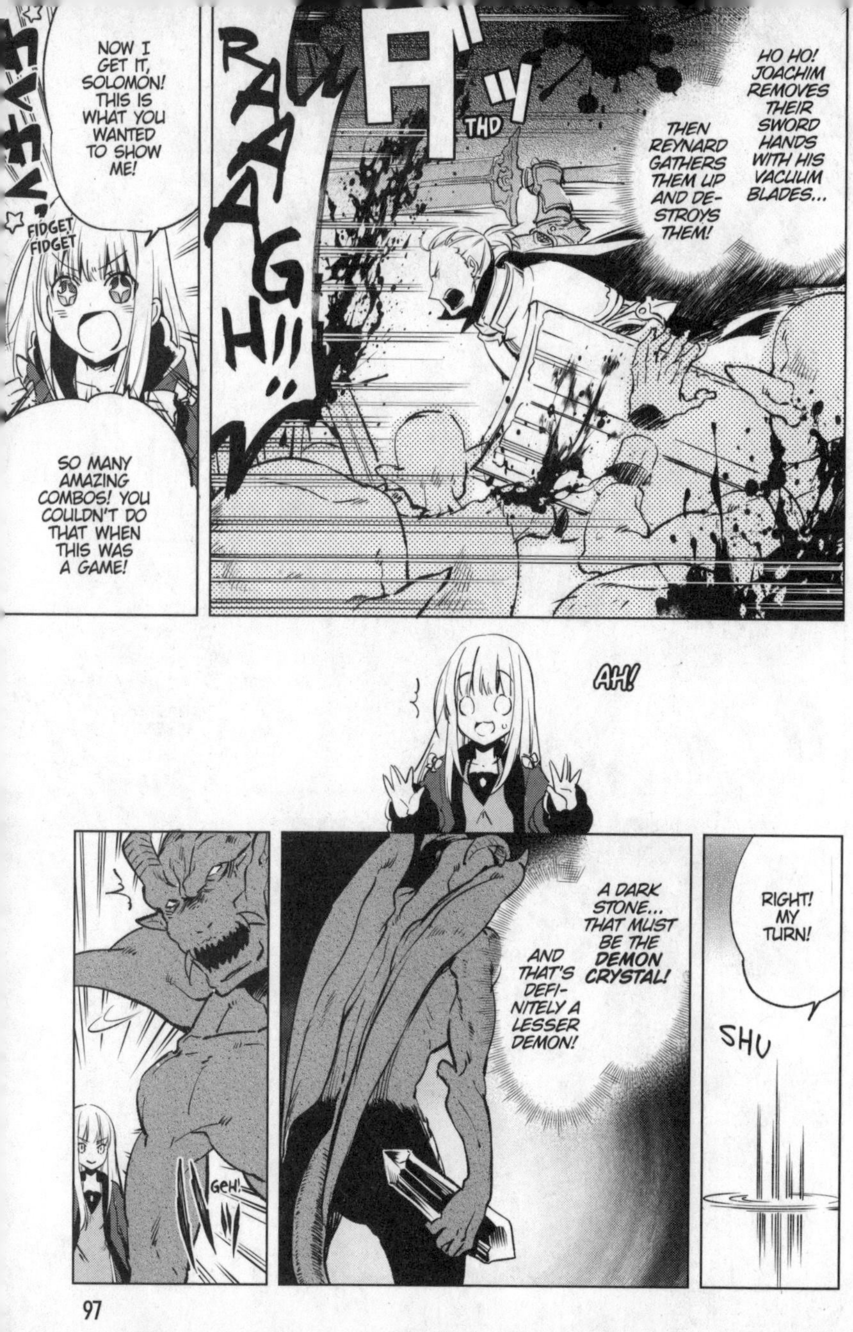
HO HO! JOACHIM REMOVES THEIR SWORD HANDS WITH HIS VACUUM BLADES...
THEN REYNARD GATHERS THEM UP AND DE-STROYS THEM!
THD
RAAAGH!!
NOW I GET IT, SOLOMON! THIS IS WHAT YOU WANTED TO SHOW ME!
FIDGET FIDGET
SO MANY AMAZING COMBOS! YOU COULDN'T DO THAT WHEN THIS WAS A GAME!
AH!
RIGHT! MY TURN!
SHU
A DARK STONE... THAT MUST BE THE DEMON CRYSTAL!
AND THAT'S DEFI-NITELY A LESSER DEMON!
GEH!

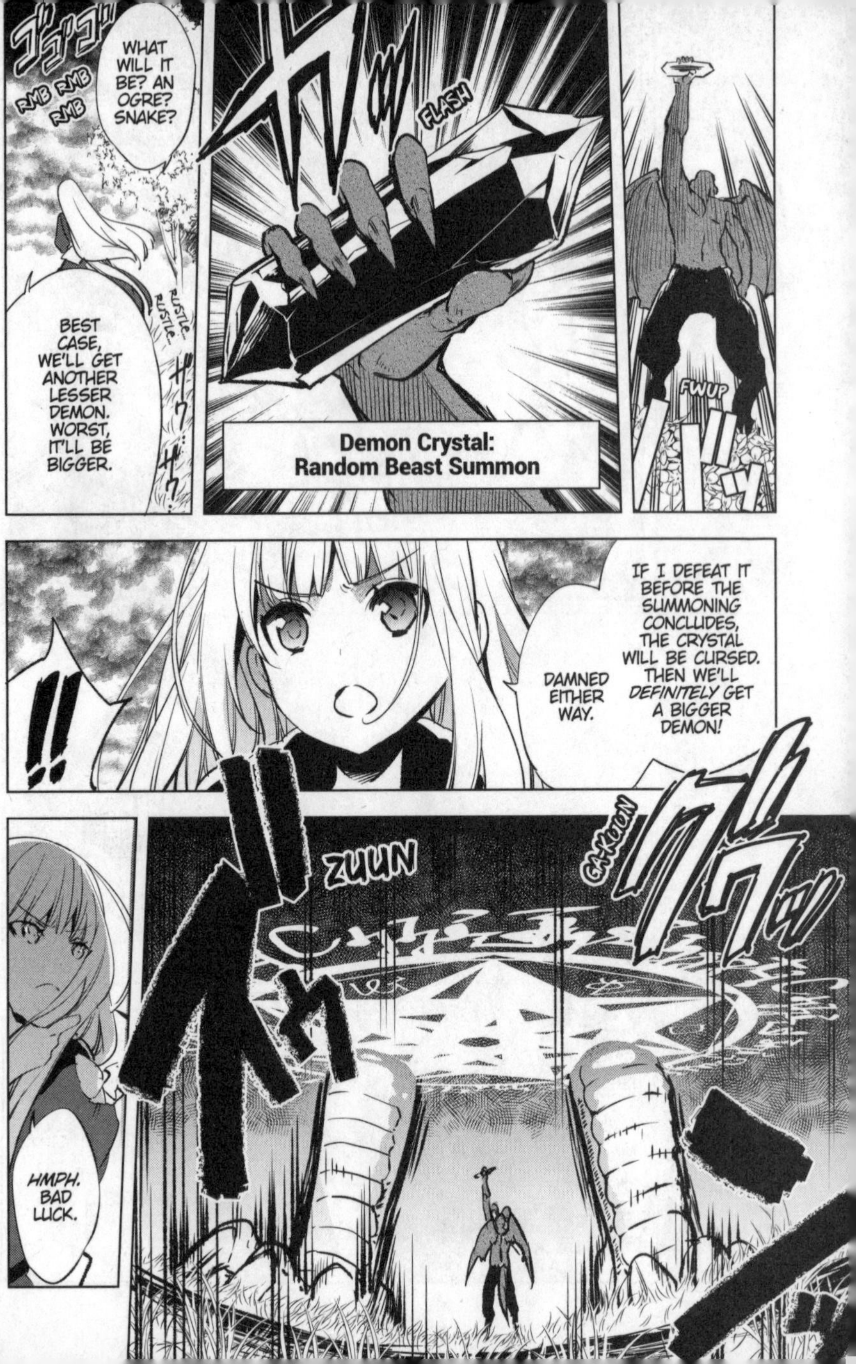
RMB RMB RMB
WHAT WILL IT BE? AN OGRE? SNAKE?
FLASH
BEST CASE, WE'LL GET ANOTHER LESSER DEMON. WORST, IT'LL BE BIGGER.
RUSTLE... RUSTLE...
FWUP
Demon Crystal: Random Beast Summon
!!
IF I DEFEAT IT BEFORE THE SUMMONING CONCLUDES, THE CRYSTAL WILL BE CURSED. THEN WE'LL DEFINITELY GET A BIGGER DEMON!
DAMNED EITHER WAY.
GA-KOOON
ZUUN
HMPH. BAD LUCK.

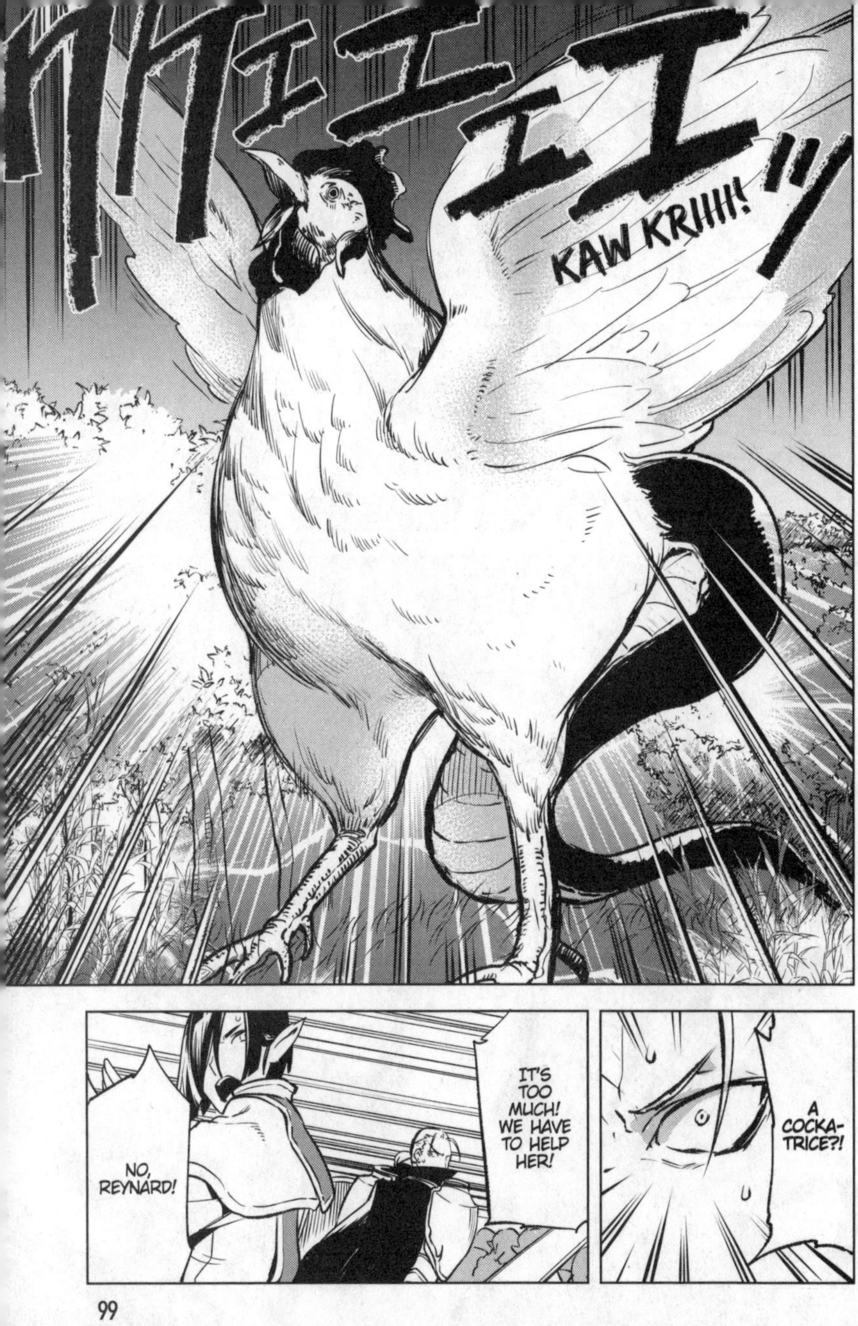
KAW KRIHH!
A COCKA-TRICE?!
IT'S TOO MUCH! WE HAVE TO HELP HER!
NO, REYNARD!

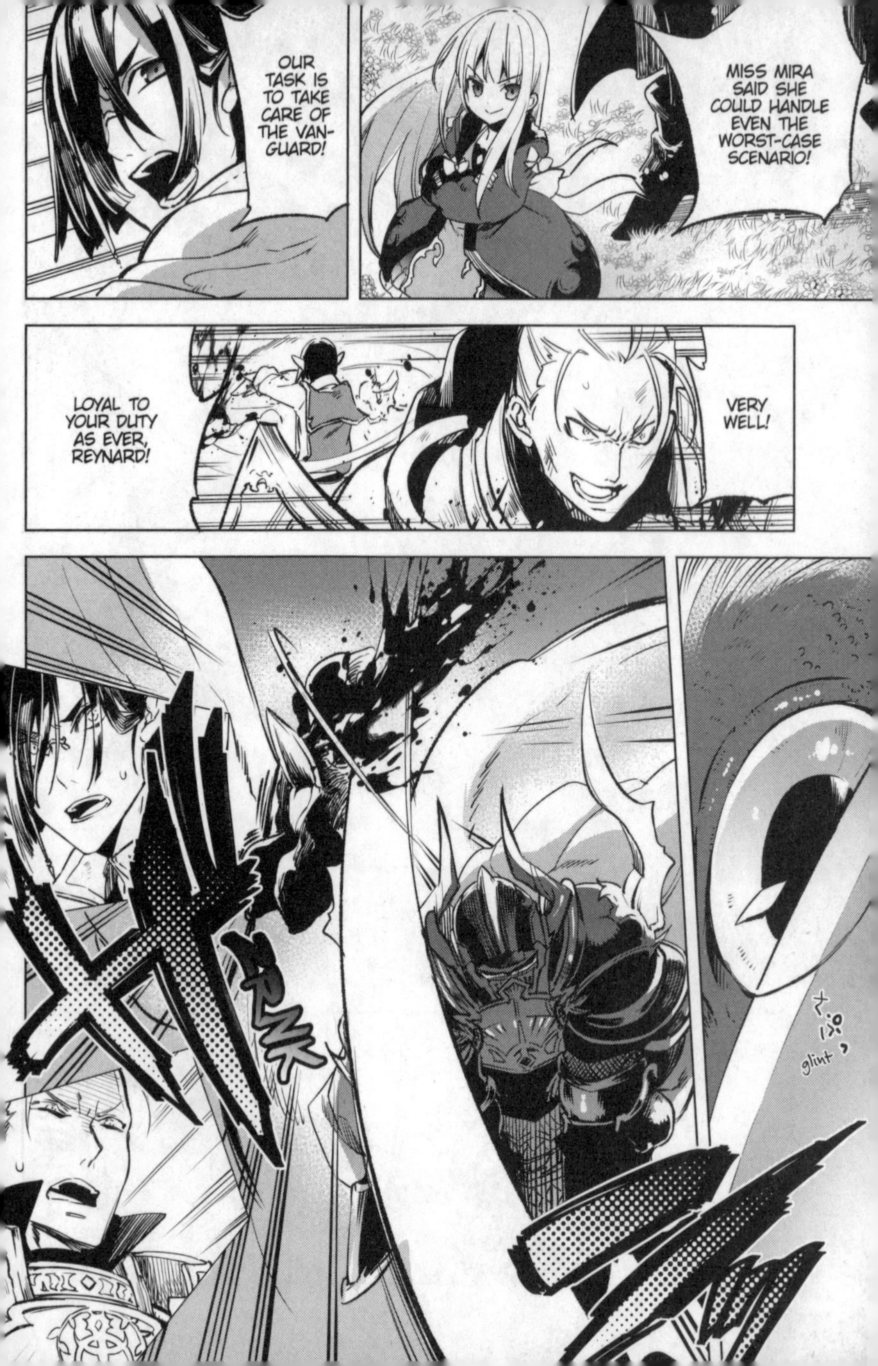
MISS MIRA SAID SHE COULD HANDLE EVEN THE WORST-CASE SCENARIO!
OUR TASK IS TO TAKE CARE OF THE VAN-GUARD!
VERY WELL!
LOYAL TO YOUR DUTY AS EVER, REYNARD!
さぷっ
glint
SRNK

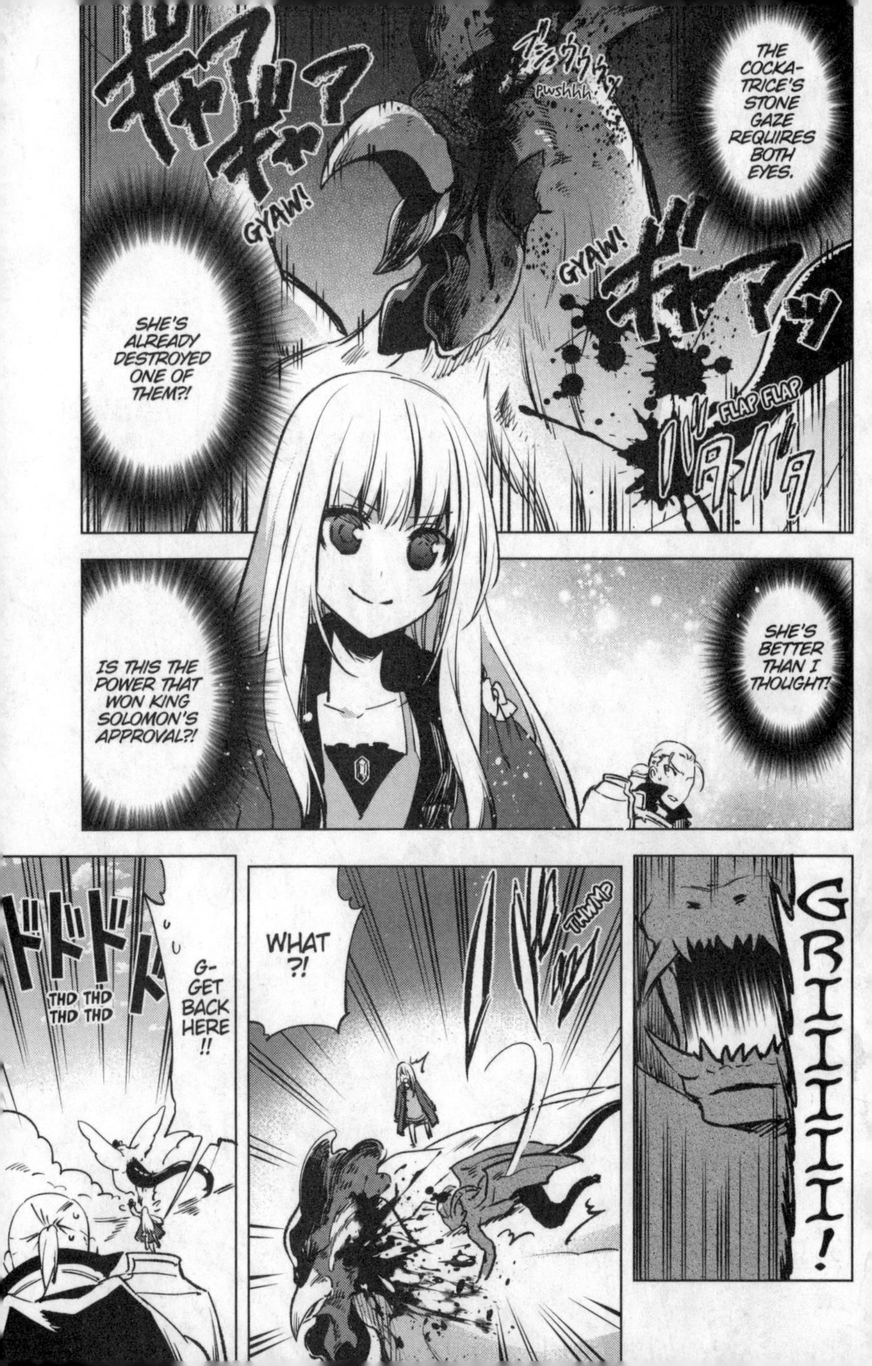
THE COCKA-TRICE'S STONE GAZE REQUIRES BOTH EYES.
pwshhh
GYAW!
GYAW!
FLAP FLAP
SHE'S ALREADY DESTROYED ONE OF THEM?!
SHE'S BETTER THAN I THOUGHT!
IS THIS THE POWER THAT WON KING SOLOMON'S APPROVAL?!
GRIIII!
THWMP
WHAT?!
G-GET BACK HERE!!
THD THD THD THD

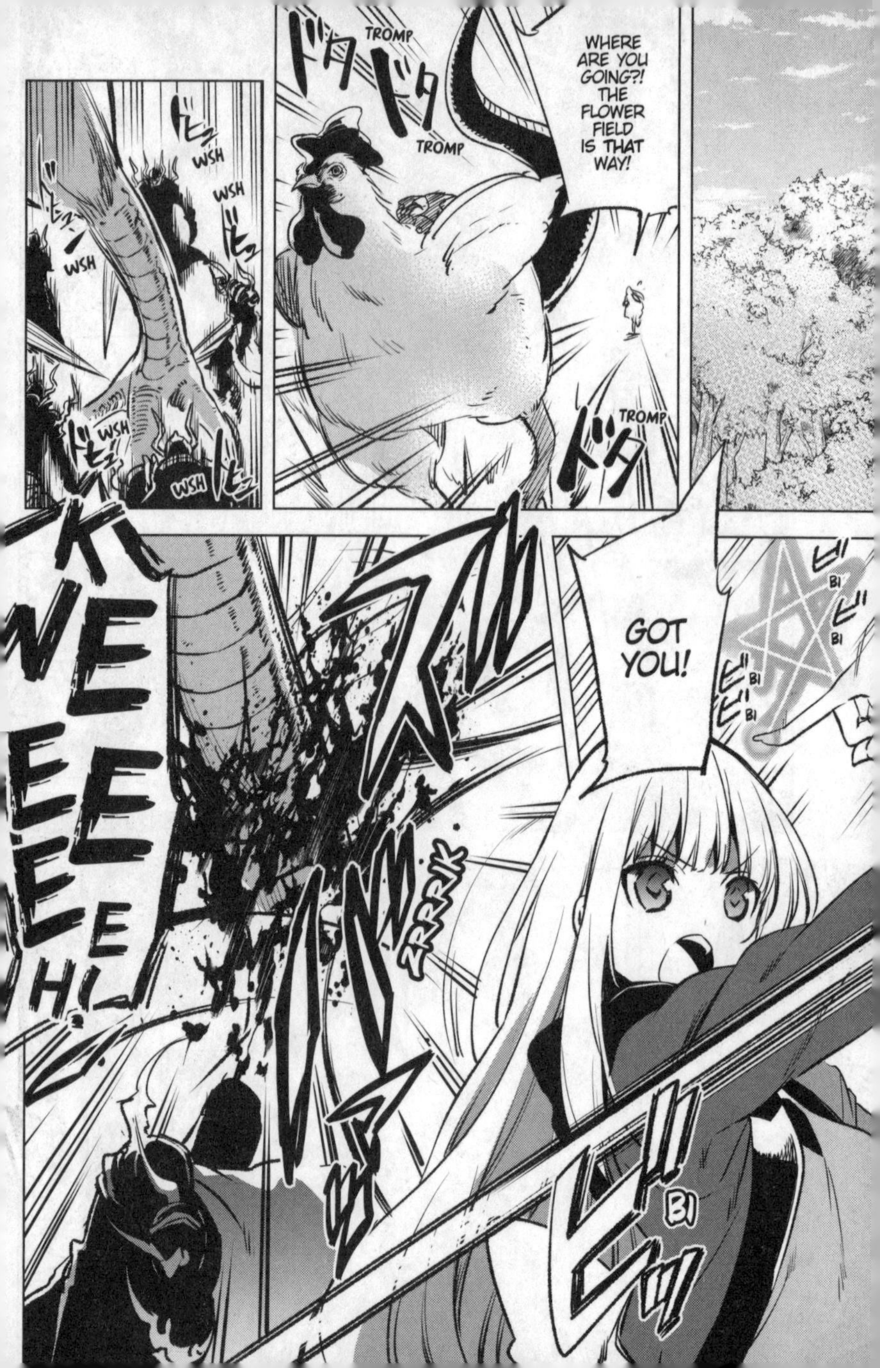
WHERE ARE YOU GOING?! THE FLOWER FIELD IS THAT WAY!
TROMP
TROMP
TROMP
WSH
WSH
WSH
WSH
WSH
GOT YOU!
BI
BI
BI
BI
BI
ZRRRRK
KWEEEEEEEH!

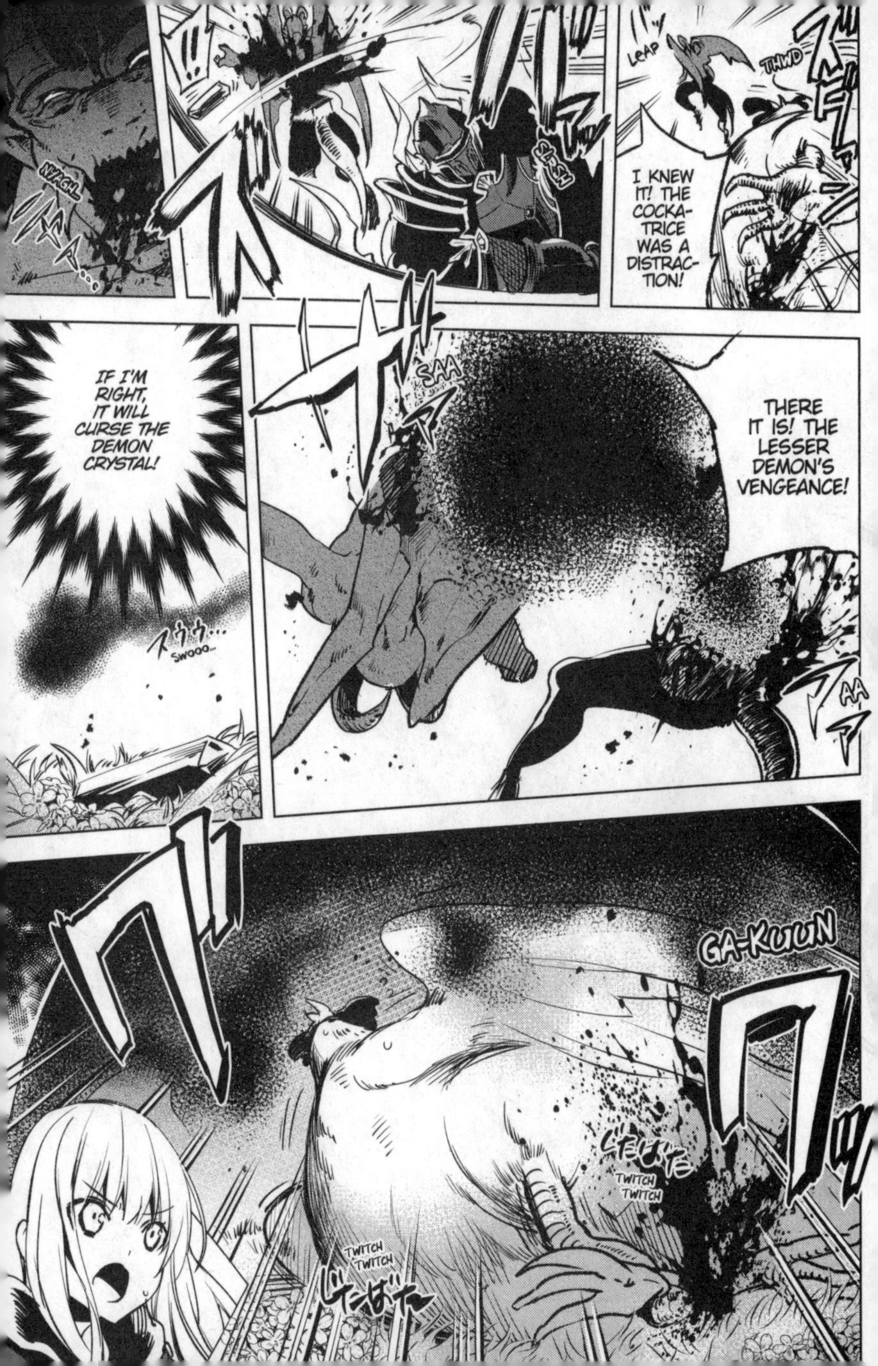
LEAP
THWD
I KNEW IT! THE COCKATRICE WAS A DISTRACTION!
SLASH
NYAGH...
SAA
THERE IT IS! THE LESSER DEMON'S VENGEANCE!
AA
IF I'M RIGHT, IT WILL CURSE THE DEMON CRYSTAL!
SWOOO...
GA-KUUN
TWITCH TWITCH
TWITCH TWITCH

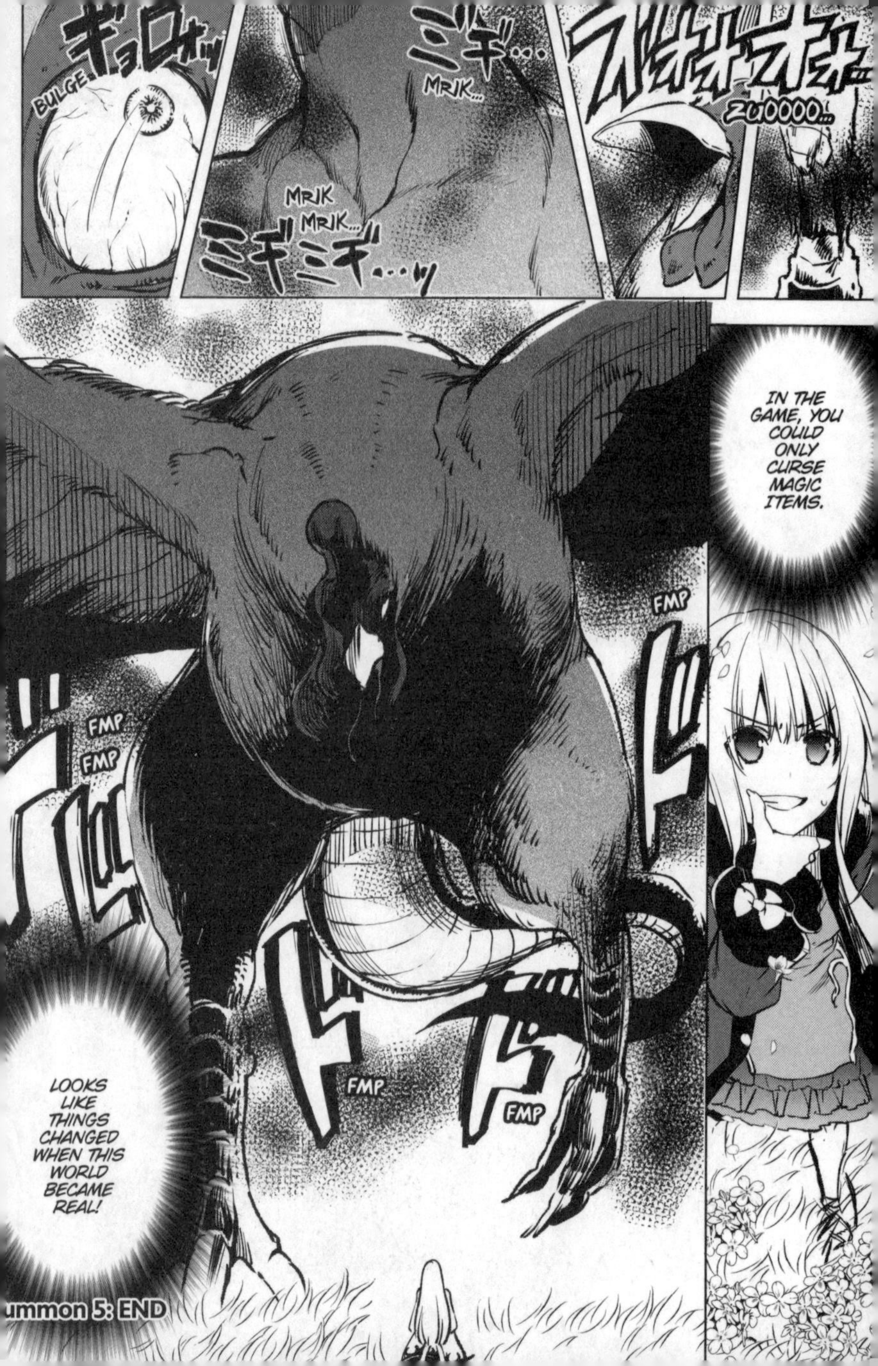
ZUOOOO...
MRIK...
MRIK
MRIK...
BULGE
IN THE GAME, YOU COULD ONLY CURSE MAGIC ITEMS.
FMP
FMP
FMP
FMP
FMP
LOOKS LIKE THINGS CHANGED WHEN THIS WORLD BECAME REAL!
ummon 5: END

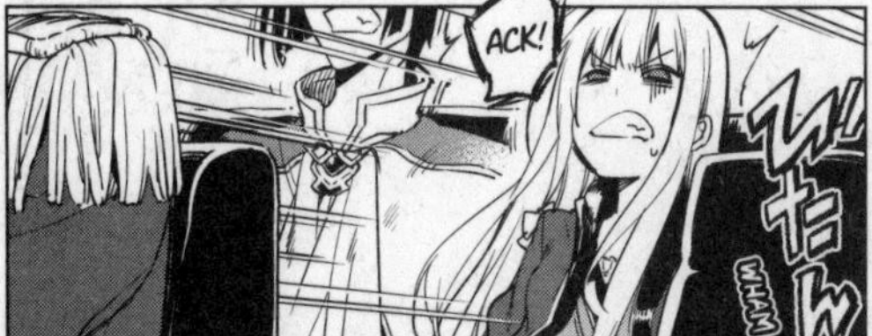
ACK!
WHAM

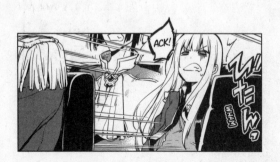

She
Professed
Herself
Pupil of the
Wise Man

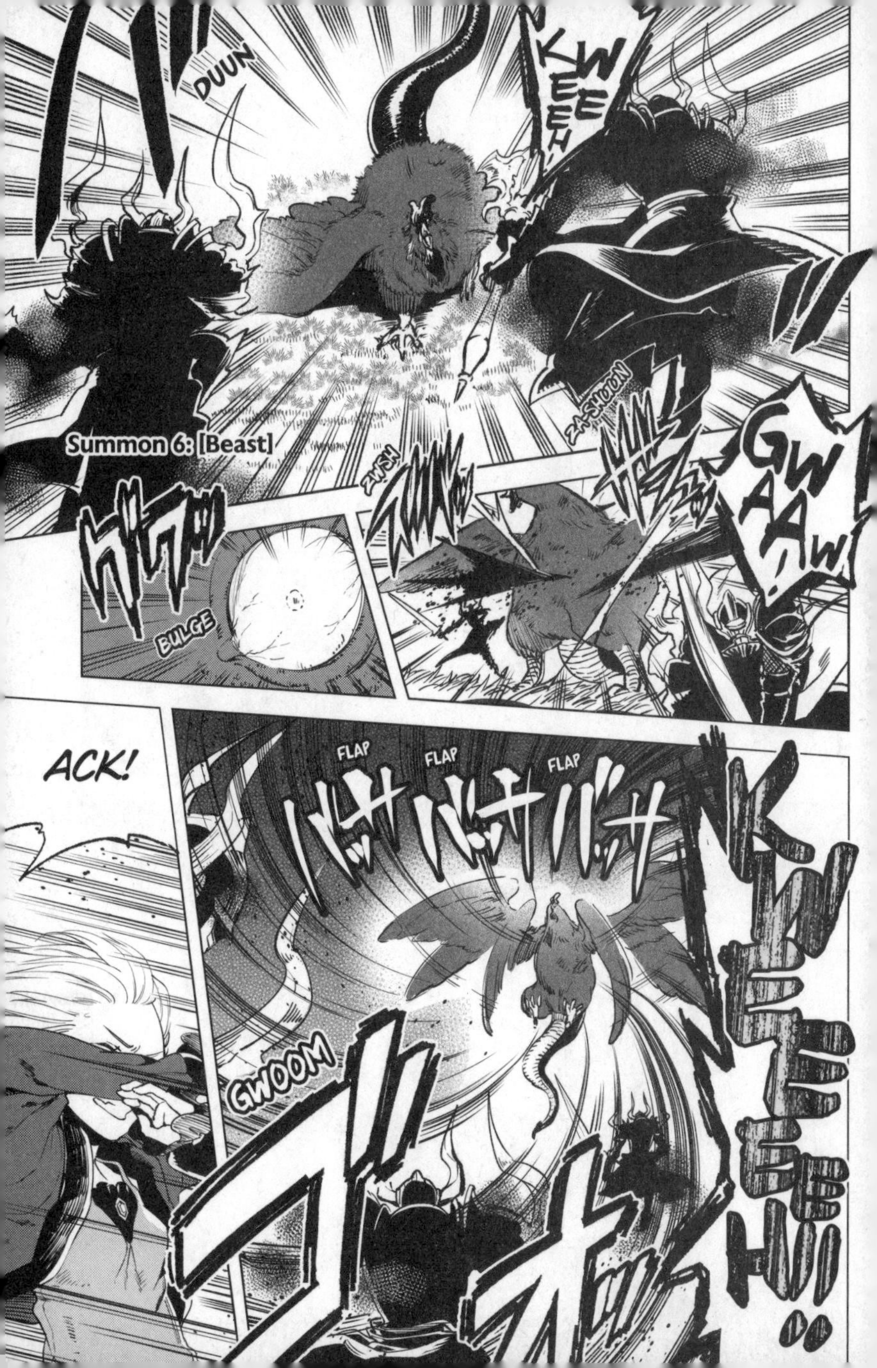
KWEEEH!
DUUN
Summon 6: [Beast]
GWAAAW!
ZA-SHOOON
ZWSH
BULGE
KWEEEEEEH!!
FLAP
FLAP
FLAP
GWOOM
ACK!

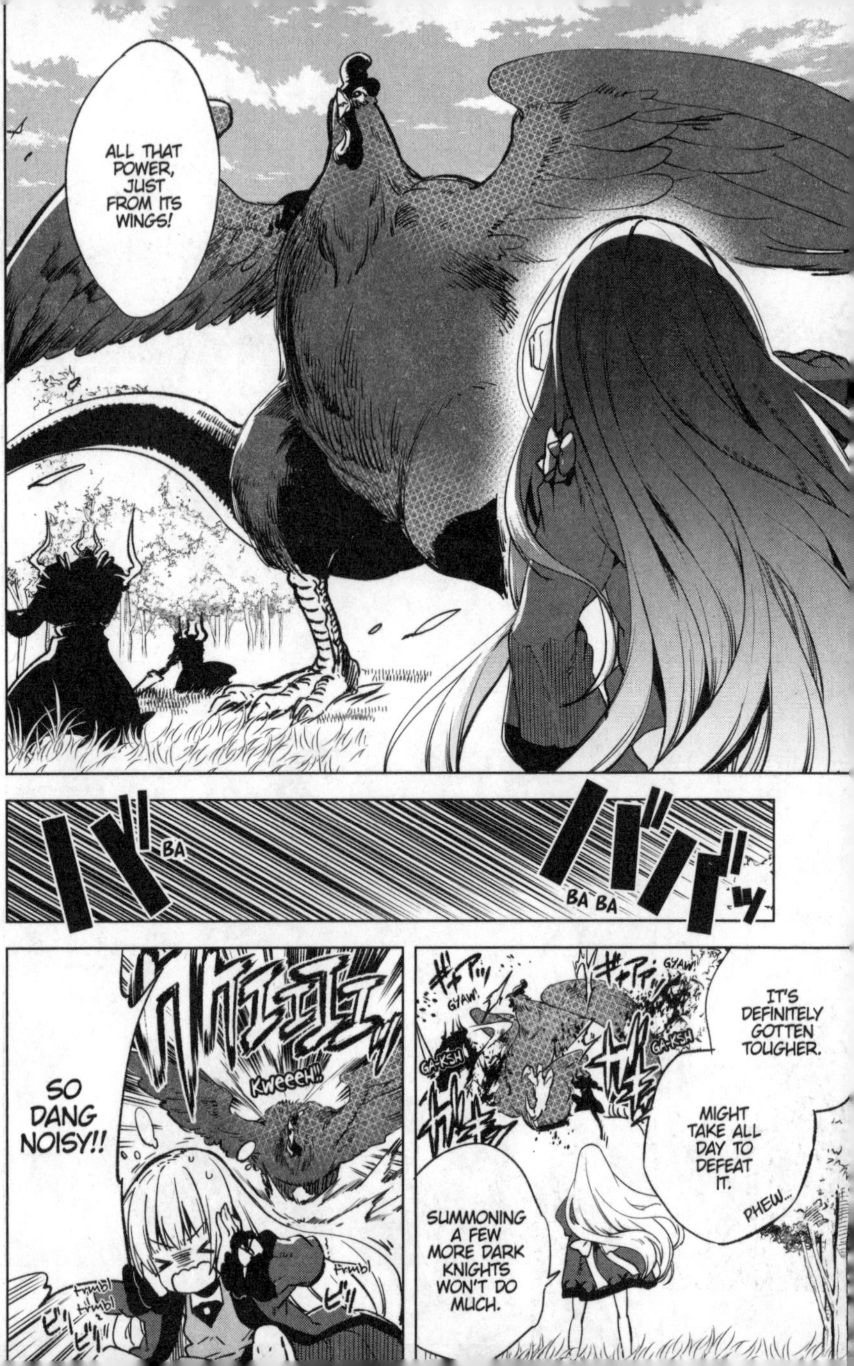
ALL THAT POWER, JUST FROM ITS WINGS!
BA BA
BA
GYAW!
GYAW!
GA-KSH
GA-KSH
IT'S DEFINITELY GOTTEN TOUGHER.
MIGHT TAKE ALL DAY TO DEFEAT IT.
PHEW...
SUMMONING A FEW MORE DARK KNIGHTS WON'T DO MUCH.
KWEEEH!!
SO DANG NOISY!!
trmbl
trmbl
trmbl

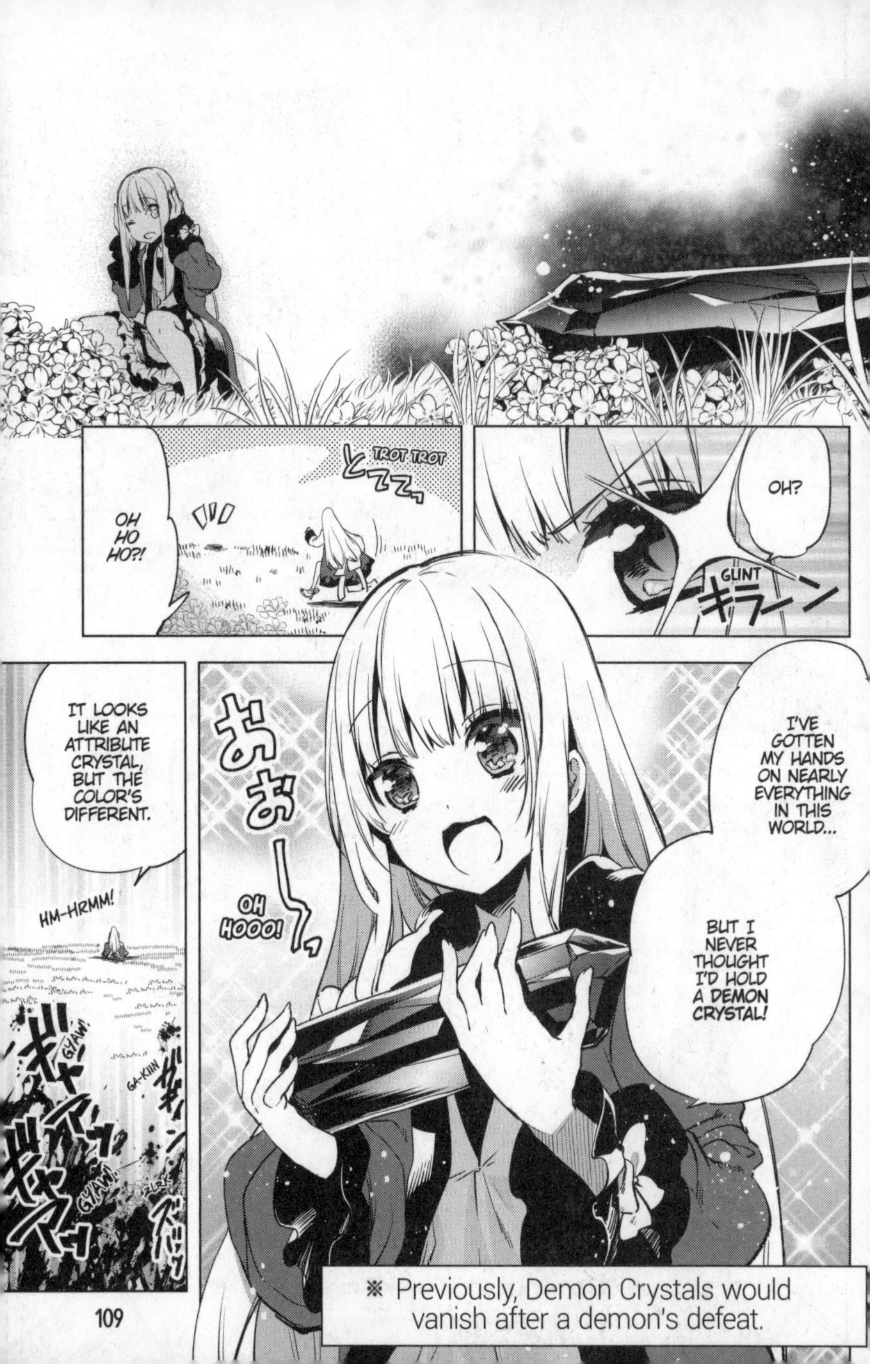
OH?
GLINT
キラーン
TROT TROT
とててっ
OH HO HO?!
I'VE GOTTEN MY HANDS ON NEARLY EVERYTHING IN THIS WORLD...
BUT I NEVER THOUGHT I'D HOLD A DEMON CRYSTAL!
OH HOOO!
IT LOOKS LIKE AN ATTRIBUTE CRYSTAL, BUT THE COLOR'S DIFFERENT.
HM-HRMM!
GYAW!
GA-KIIN
GYAW!
ZURK

※ Previously, Demon Crystals would vanish after a demon's defeat.

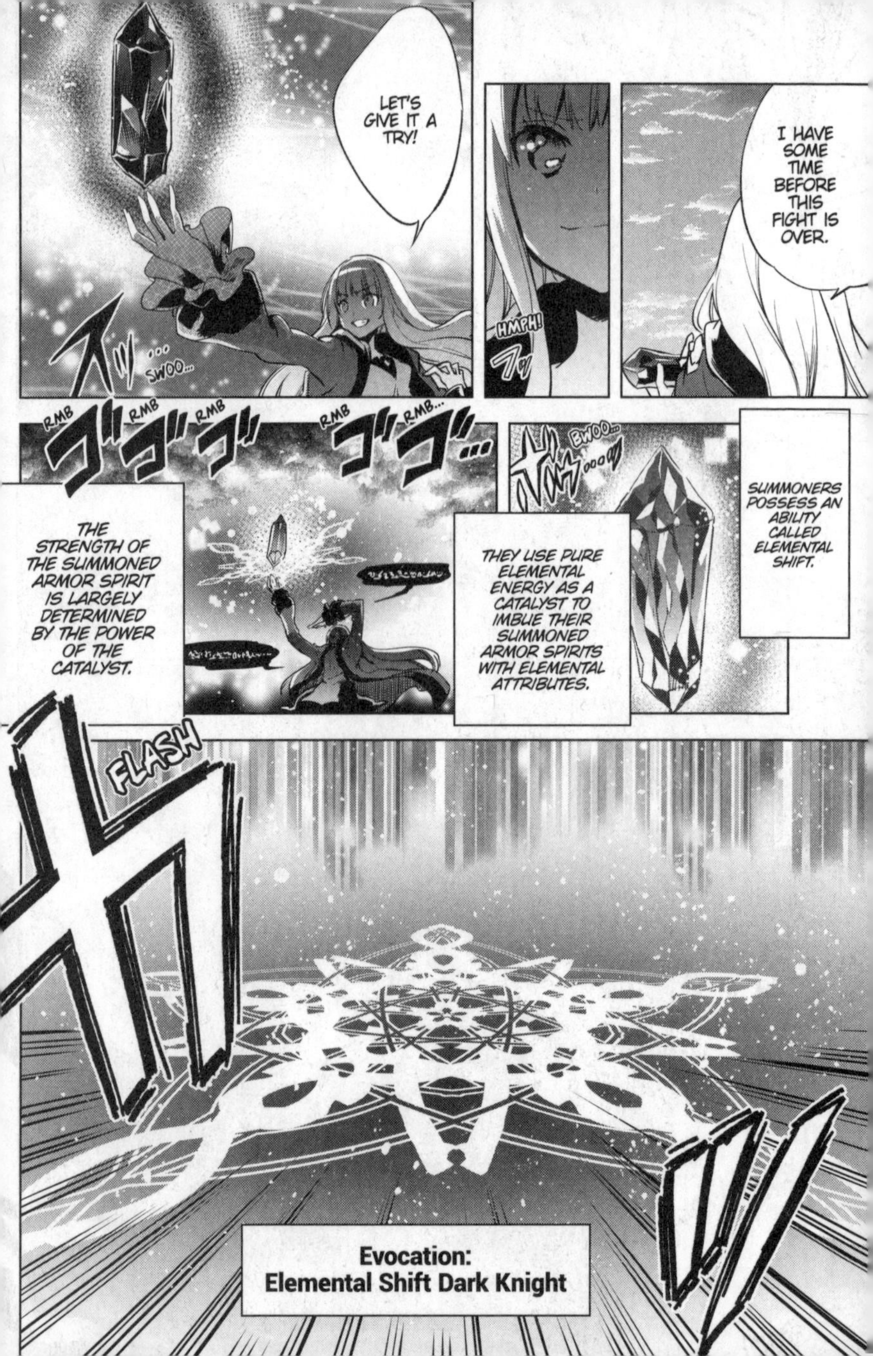
I HAVE SOME TIME BEFORE THIS FIGHT IS OVER.
HMPH!
LET'S GIVE IT A TRY!
SWOO...
BWOO...
SUMMONERS POSSESS AN ABILITY CALLED ELEMENTAL SHIFT.
THEY USE PURE ELEMENTAL ENERGY AS A CATALYST TO IMBUE THEIR SUMMONED ARMOR SPIRITS WITH ELEMENTAL ATTRIBUTES.
RMB RMB RMB
RMB RMB...
THE STRENGTH OF THE SUMMONED ARMOR SPIRIT IS LARGELY DETERMINED BY THE POWER OF THE CATALYST.
FLASH
Evocation:
Elemental Shift Dark Knight

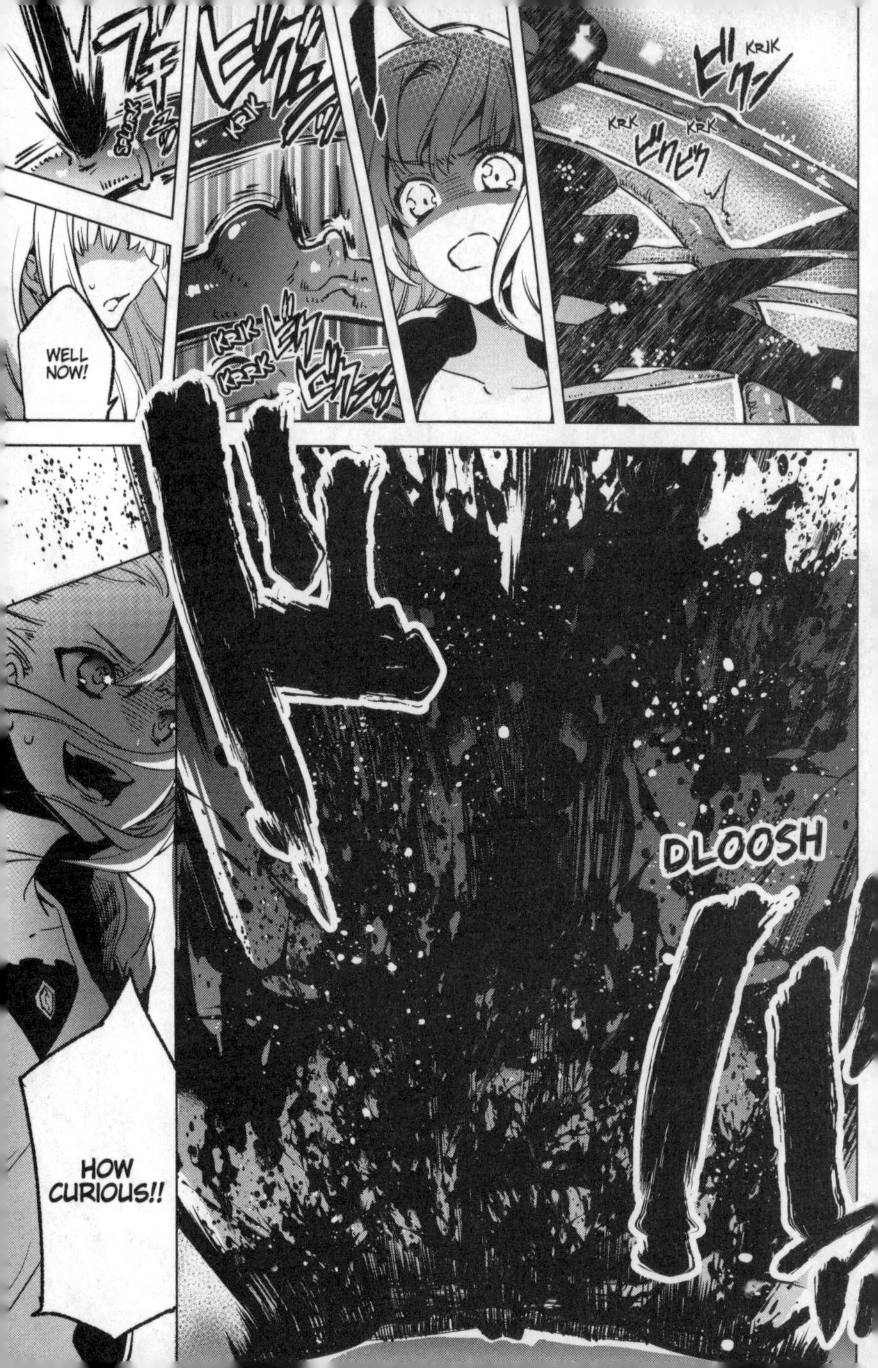
KRIK
KRK
KRK
KRIK
KRIK
KRRK
SPLURK
WELL NOW!
DLOOSH
HOW CURIOUS!!

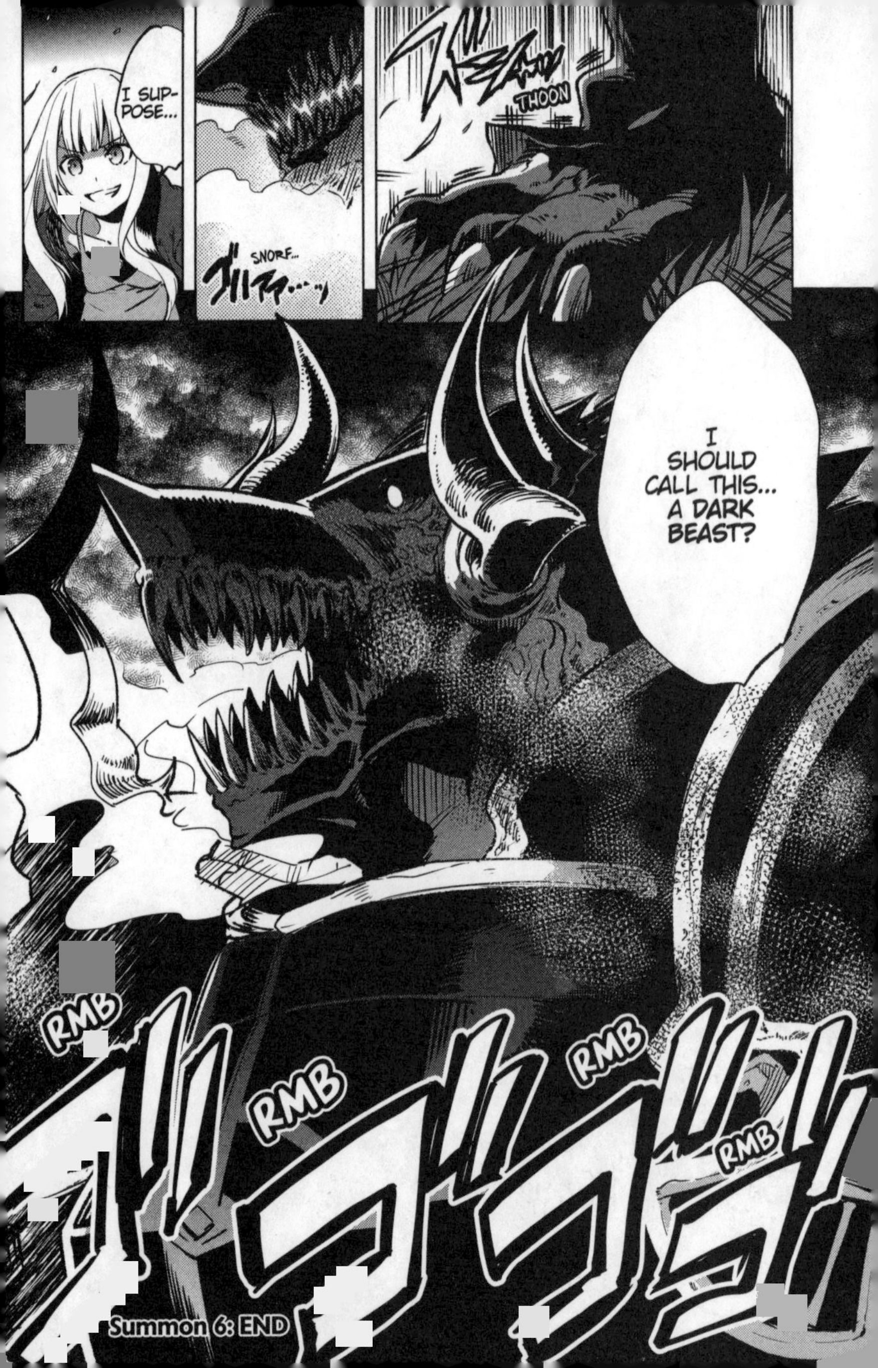
THOON
SNORF...
I SUP-POSE...
I SHOULD CALL THIS... A DARK BEAST?
RMB
RMB
RMB
RMB
Summon 6: END

She
Professed
Herself
Pupil of the
Wise Man

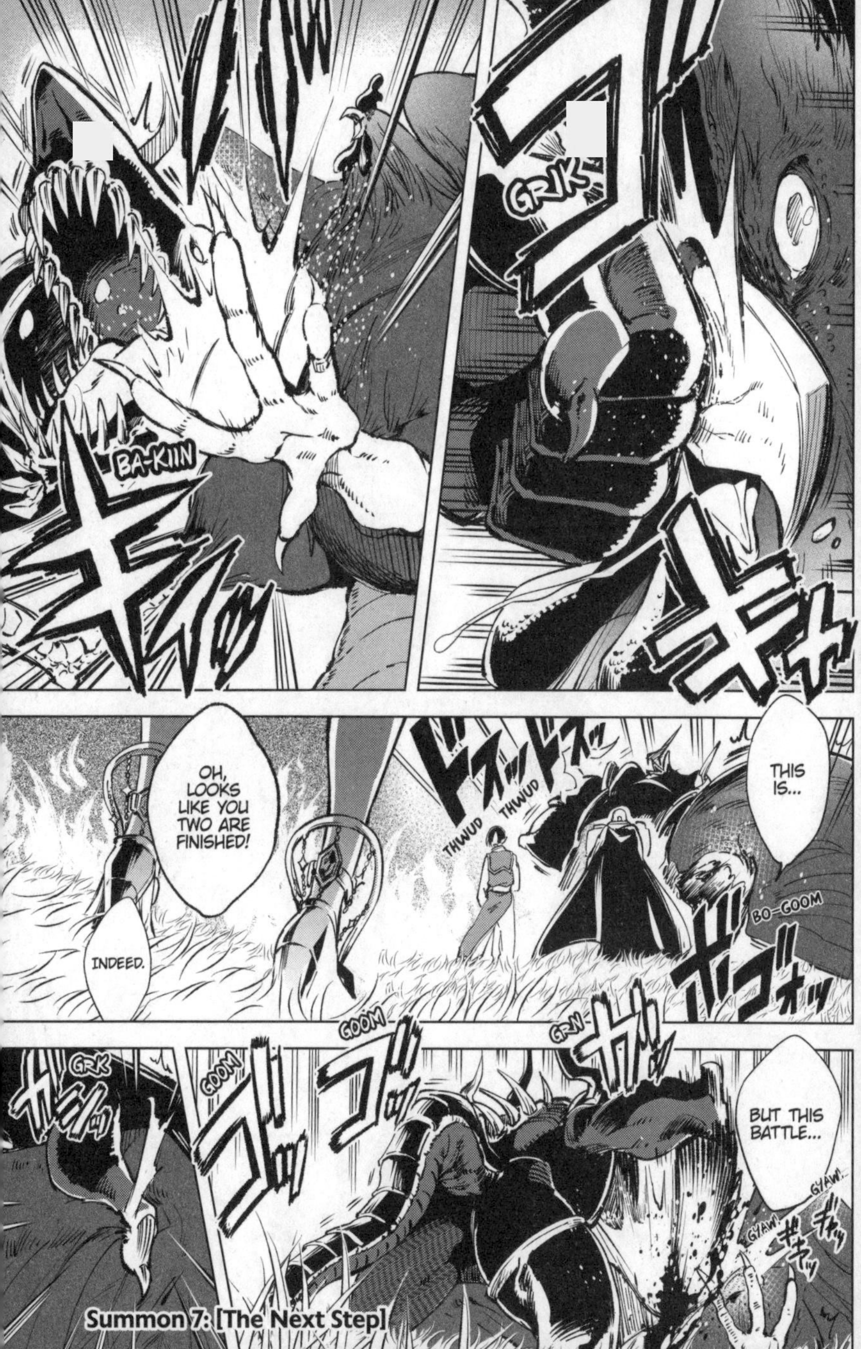
GRIK
BA-KIIN
THIS IS...
THWUD
THWUD
BO-GOOM
OH, LOOKS LIKE YOU TWO ARE FINISHED!
INDEED.
BUT THIS BATTLE...
GYAW!
GYAW!
GR-N
GOOM
GOOM
GRK

Summon 7: [The Next Step]

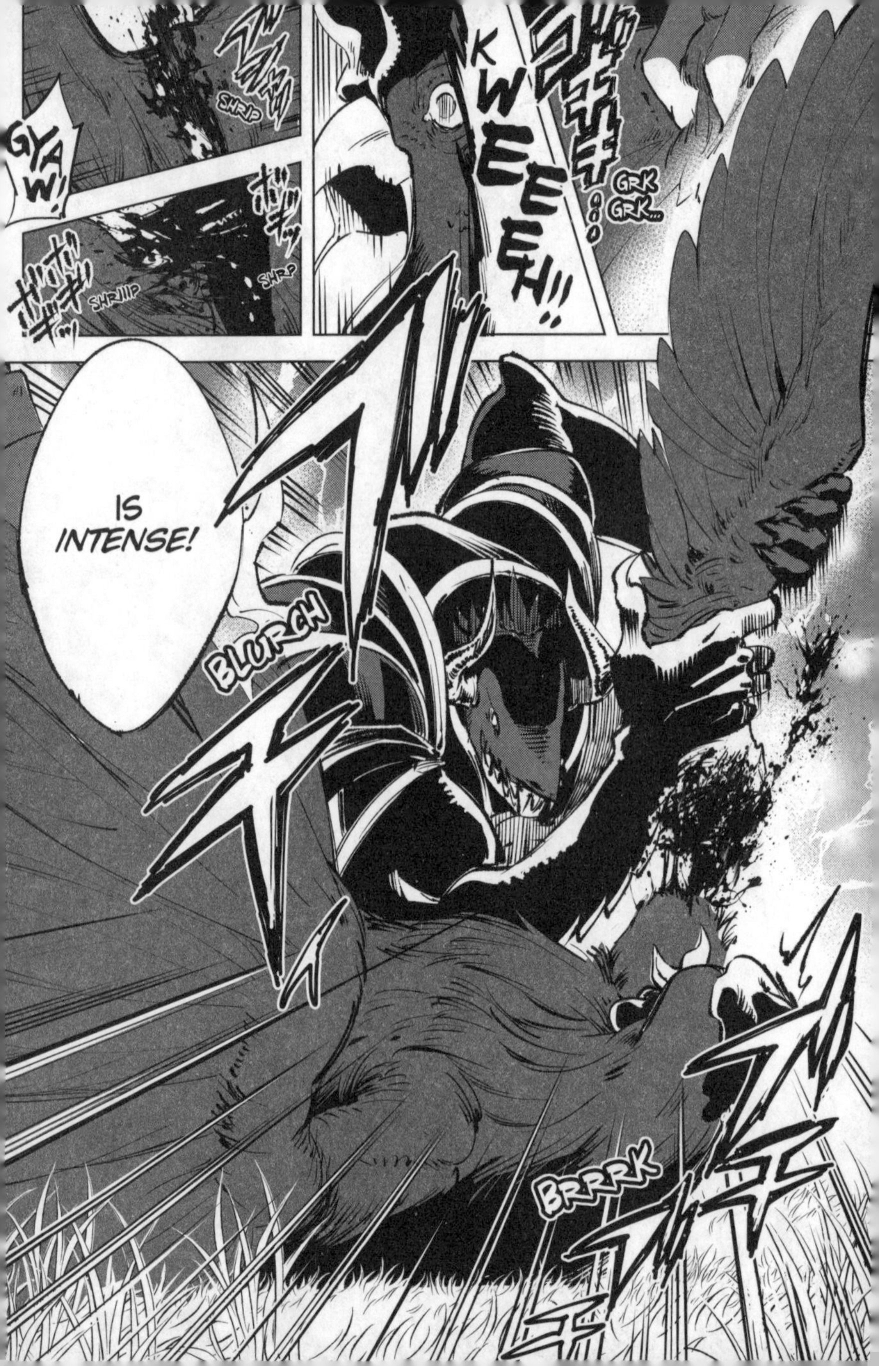
KWEEEEH!!
GRK GRK...
SHRIP
GYAW!
SHRP
SHRIIIP
IS INTENSE!
BLURCH
BRRRK

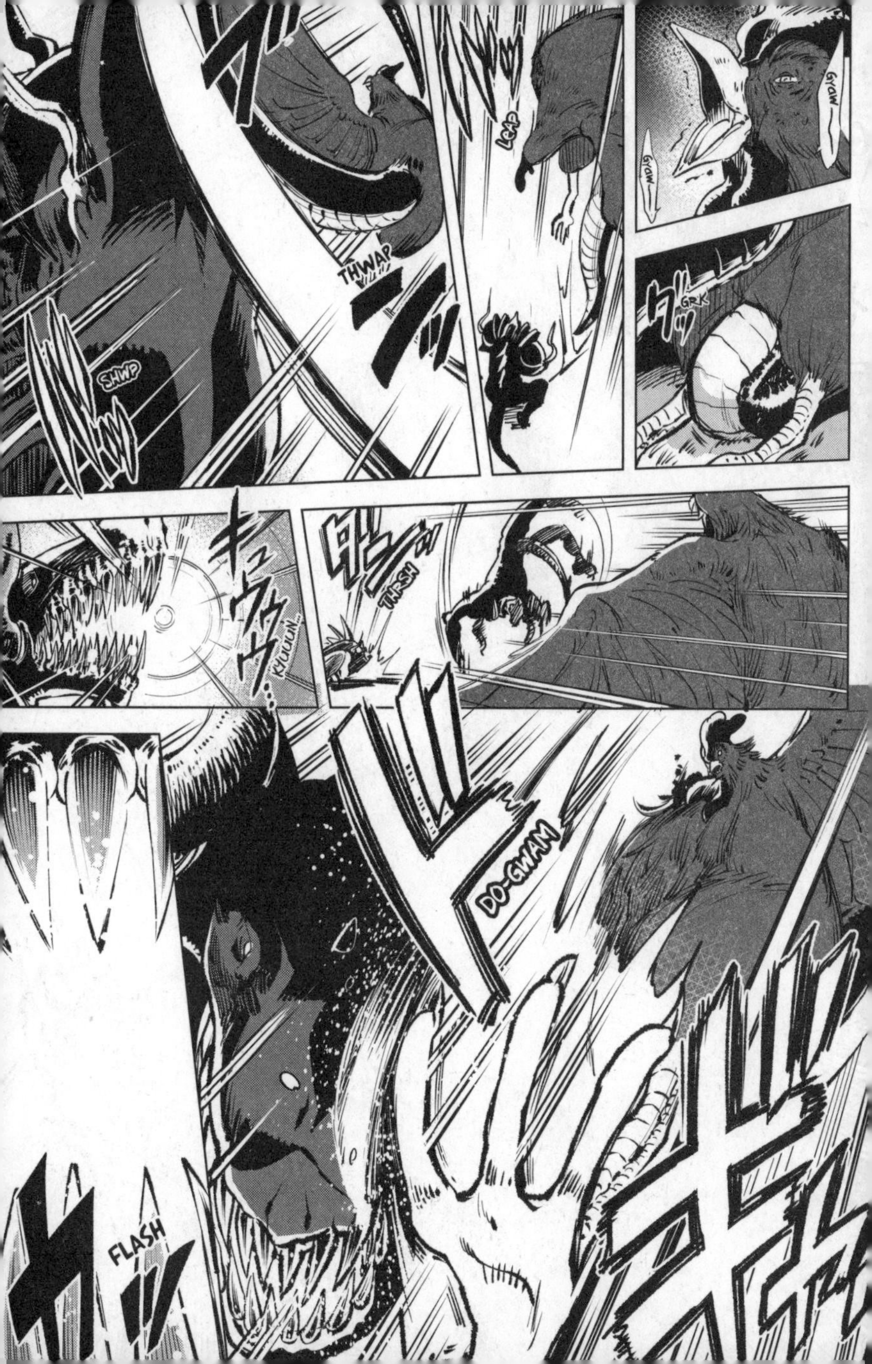
GYAW—
GYAW—
GRK
LEAP
THWAP
SHWP
THSH
KYUUUN...
DO-GWAM
FLASH

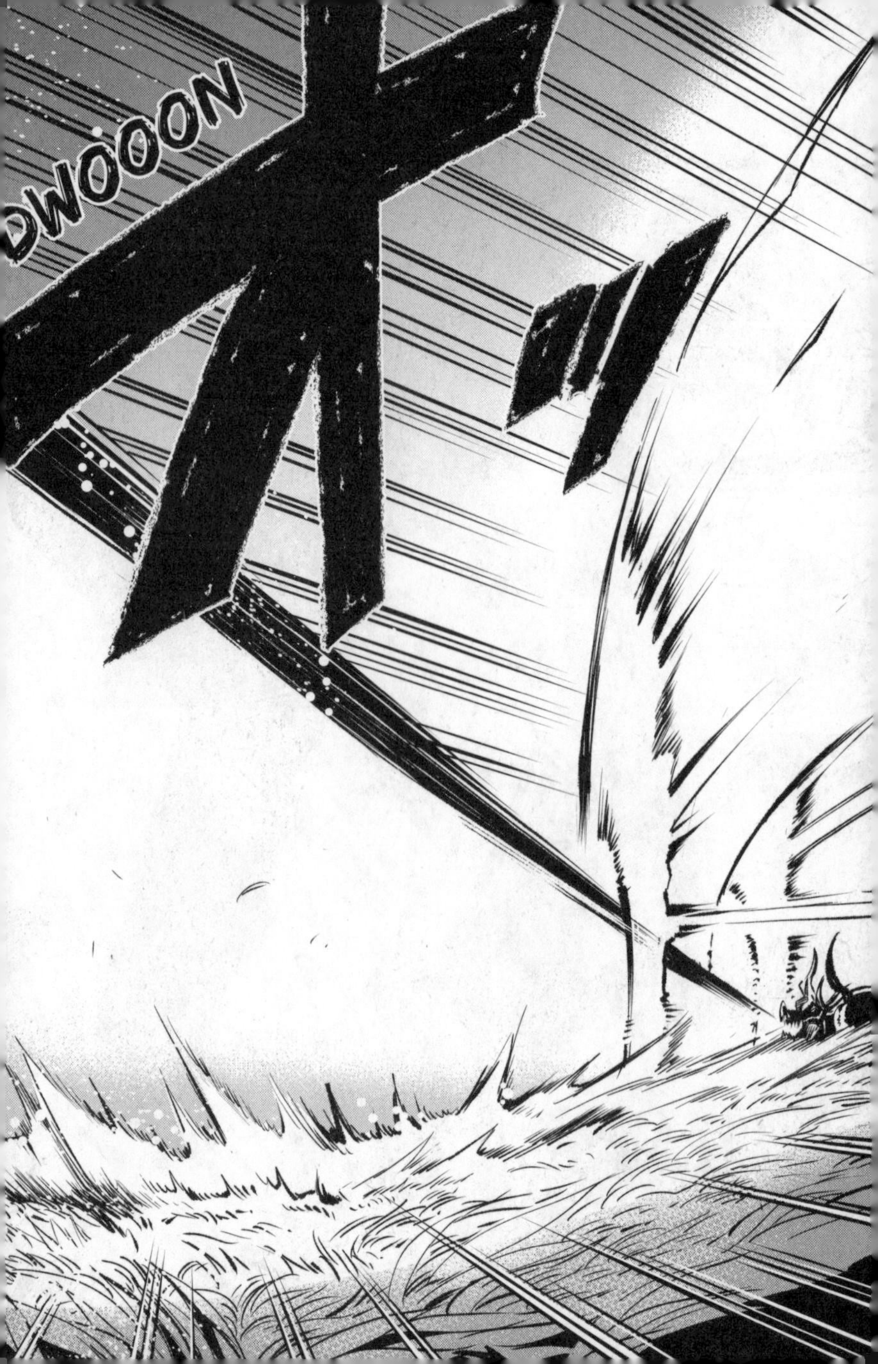
DWOOON

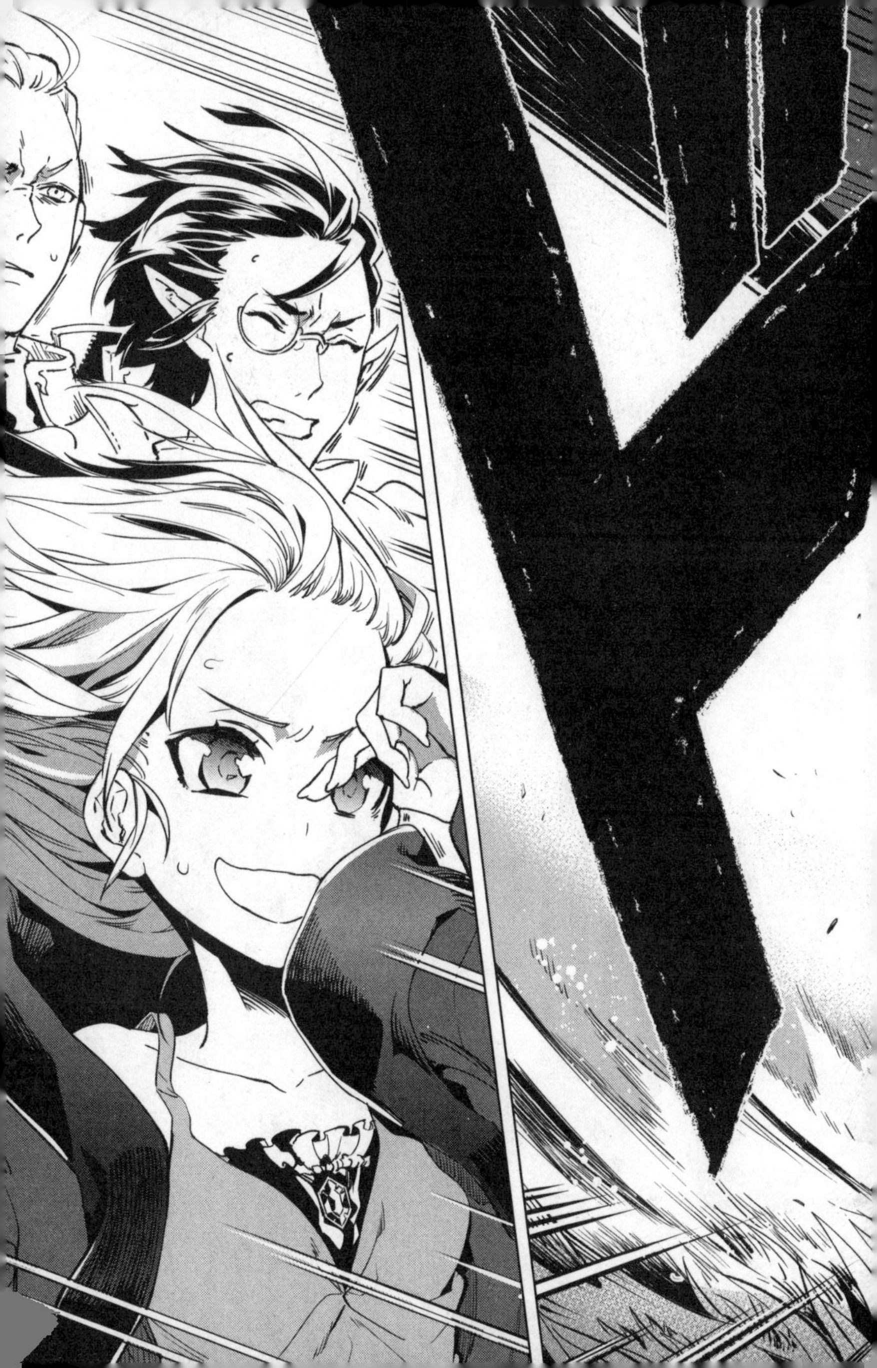

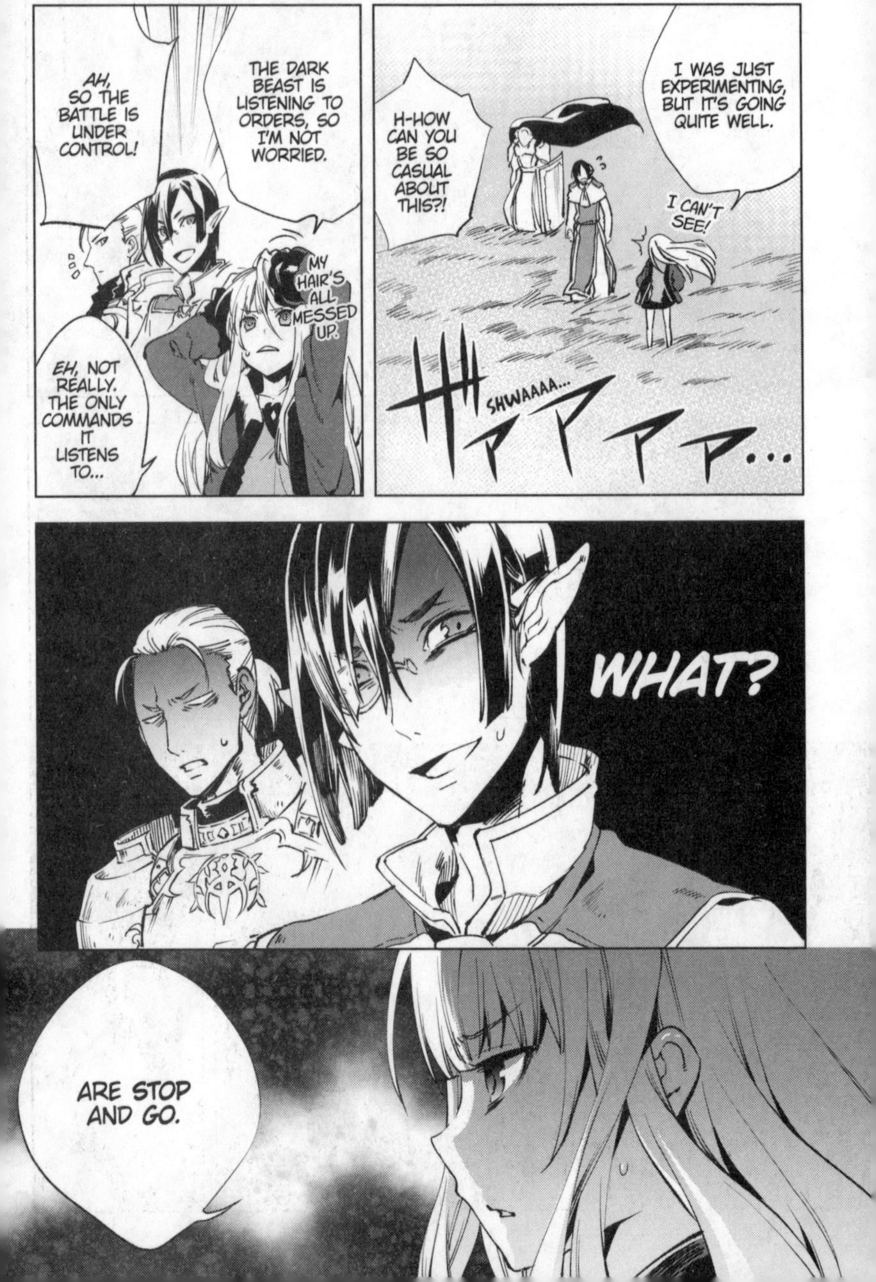
I WAS JUST EXPERIMENTING, BUT IT'S GOING QUITE WELL.
H-HOW CAN YOU BE SO CASUAL ABOUT THIS?!
I CAN'T SEE!
ザァァァ...
SHWAAAA...
THE DARK BEAST IS LISTENING TO ORDERS, SO I'M NOT WORRIED.
AH, SO THE BATTLE IS UNDER CONTROL!
MY HAIR'S ALL MESSED UP.
EH, NOT REALLY. THE ONLY COMMANDS IT LISTENS TO...
WHAT?
ARE STOP AND GO.

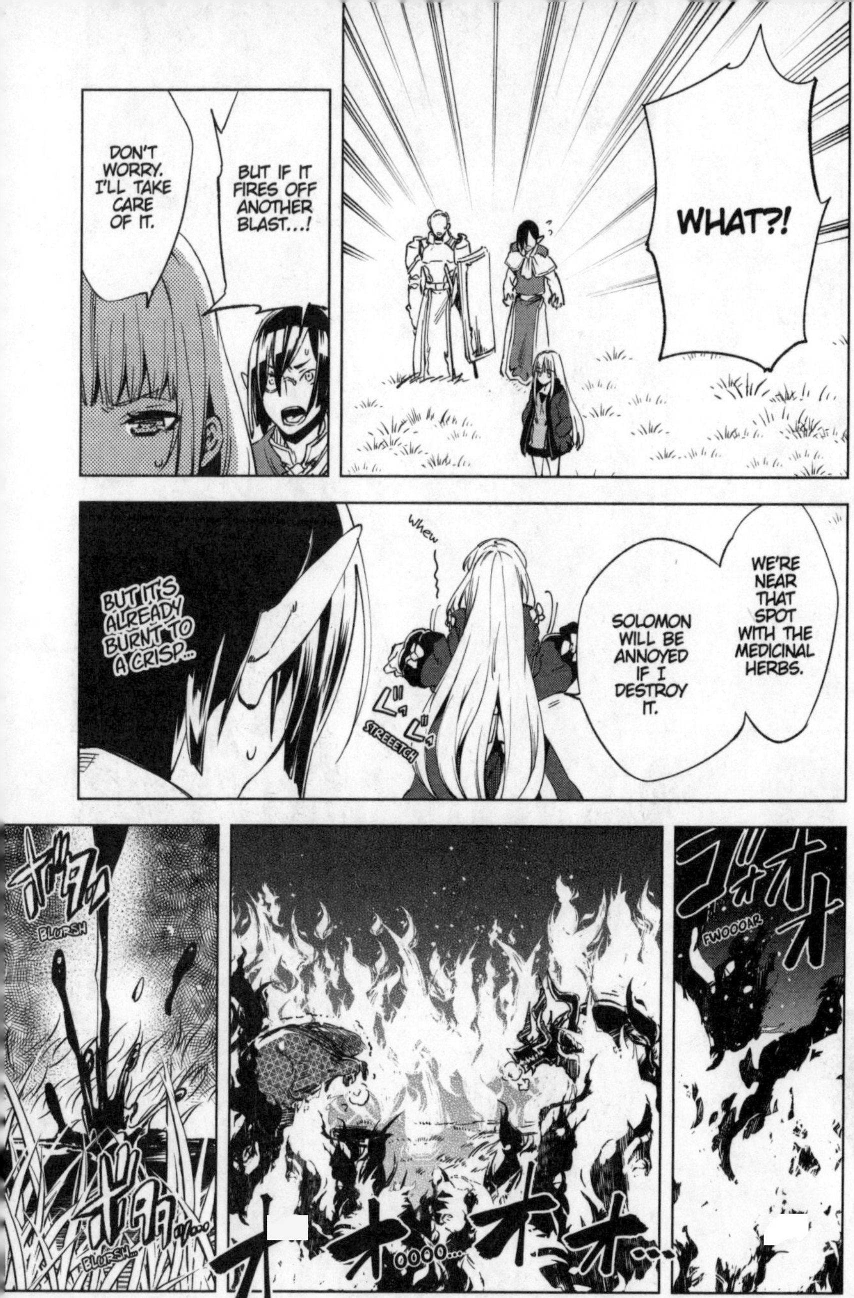
WHAT?!
BUT IF IT FIRES OFF ANOTHER BLAST...!
DON'T WORRY. I'LL TAKE CARE OF IT.
WE'RE NEAR THAT SPOT WITH THE MEDICINAL HERBS.
SOLOMON WILL BE ANNOYED IF I DESTROY IT.
Whew
STREEETCH
BUT IT'S ALREADY BURNT TO A CRISP...
FWOOOAR
oooo...
BLURSH
BLURSH...

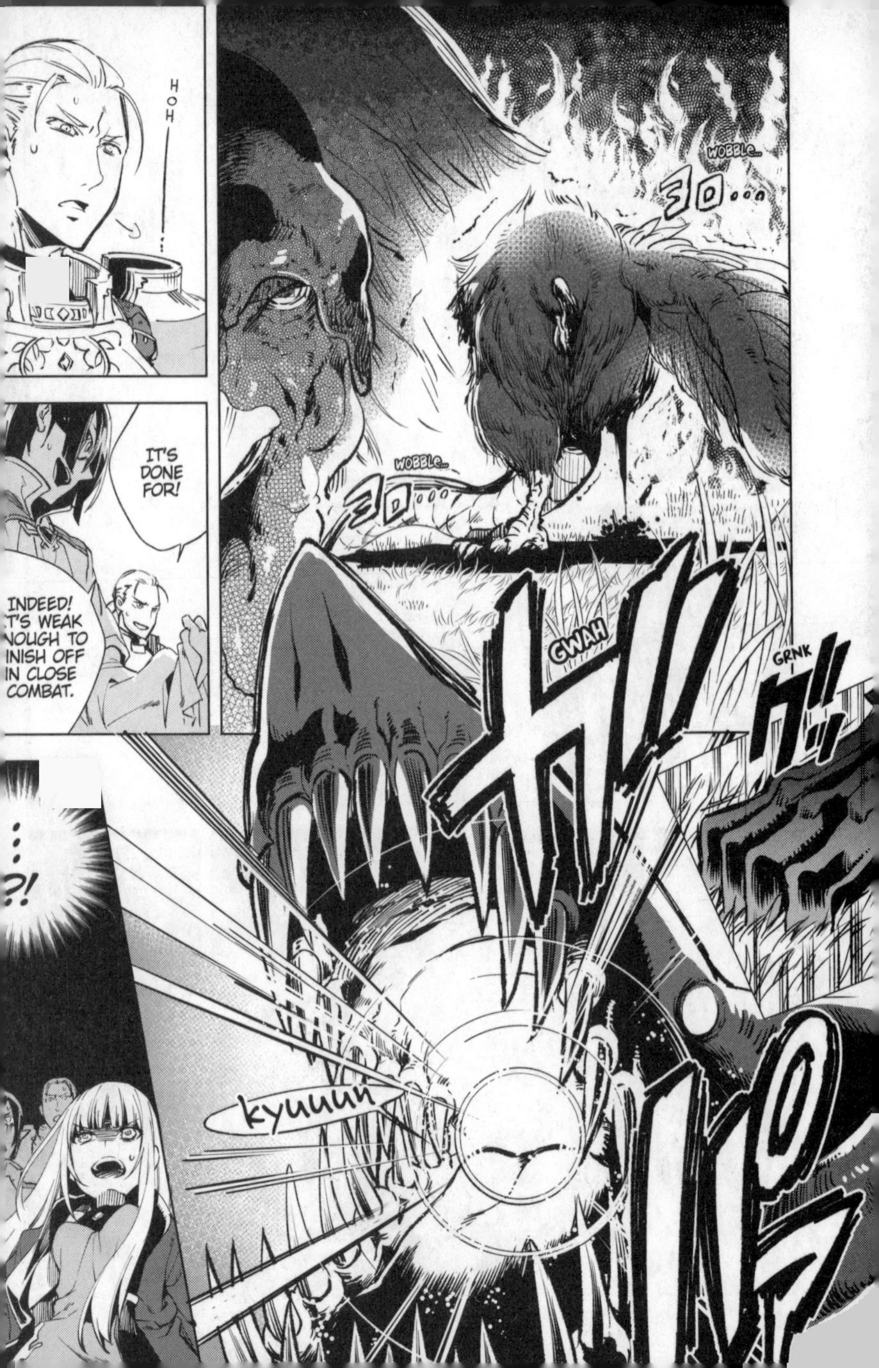
WOBBLE...
WOBBLE...
HOH---!
IT'S DONE FOR!
INDEED! T'S WEAK NOUGH TO INISH OFF IN CLOSE COMBAT.
GWAH
GRNK
kyuuun
...?!

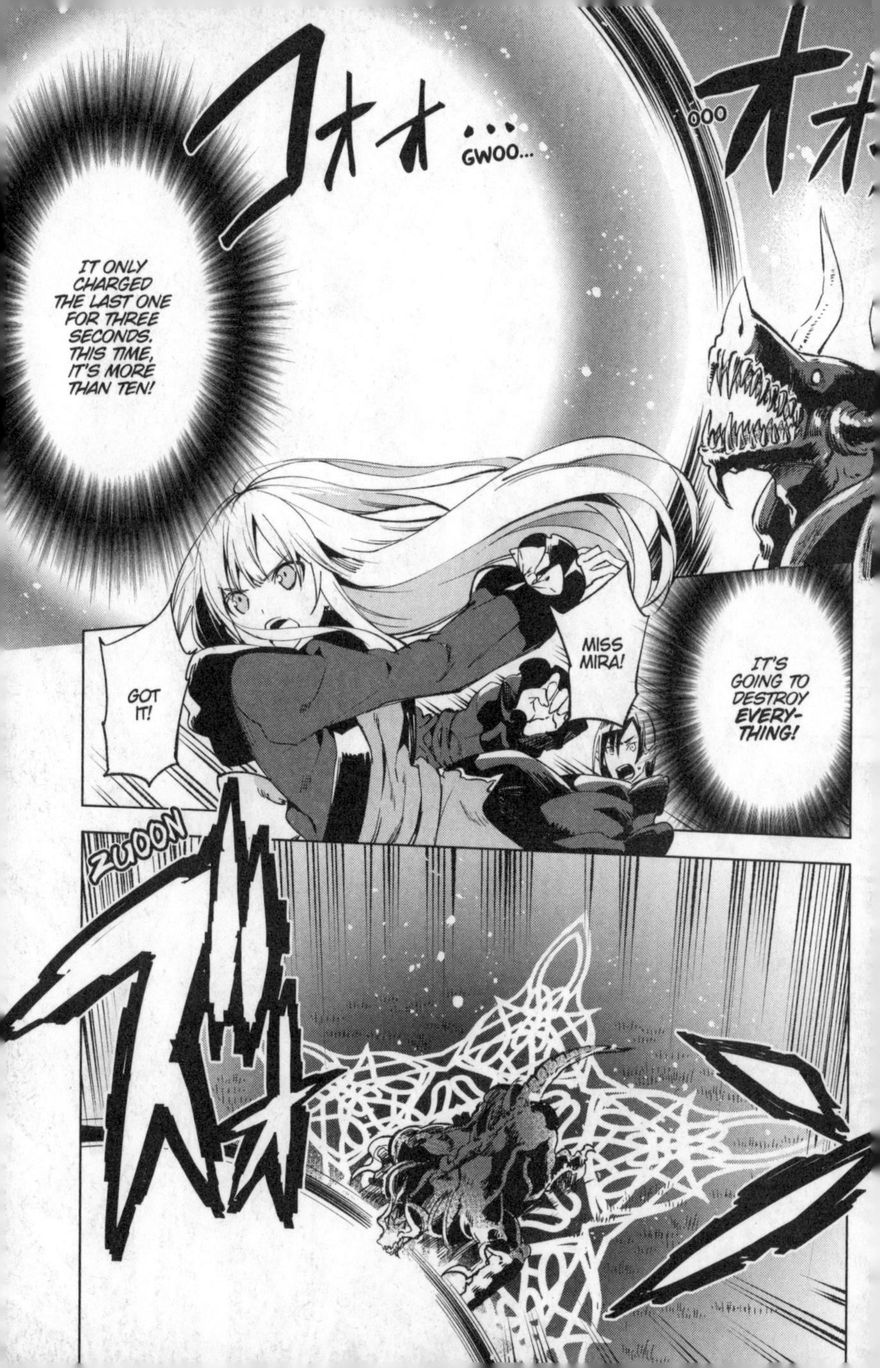
GWOO...
OOO
IT ONLY CHARGED THE LAST ONE FOR THREE SECONDS. THIS TIME, IT'S MORE THAN TEN!
IT'S GOING TO DESTROY EVERYTHING!
MISS MIRA!
GOT IT!
ZUOON

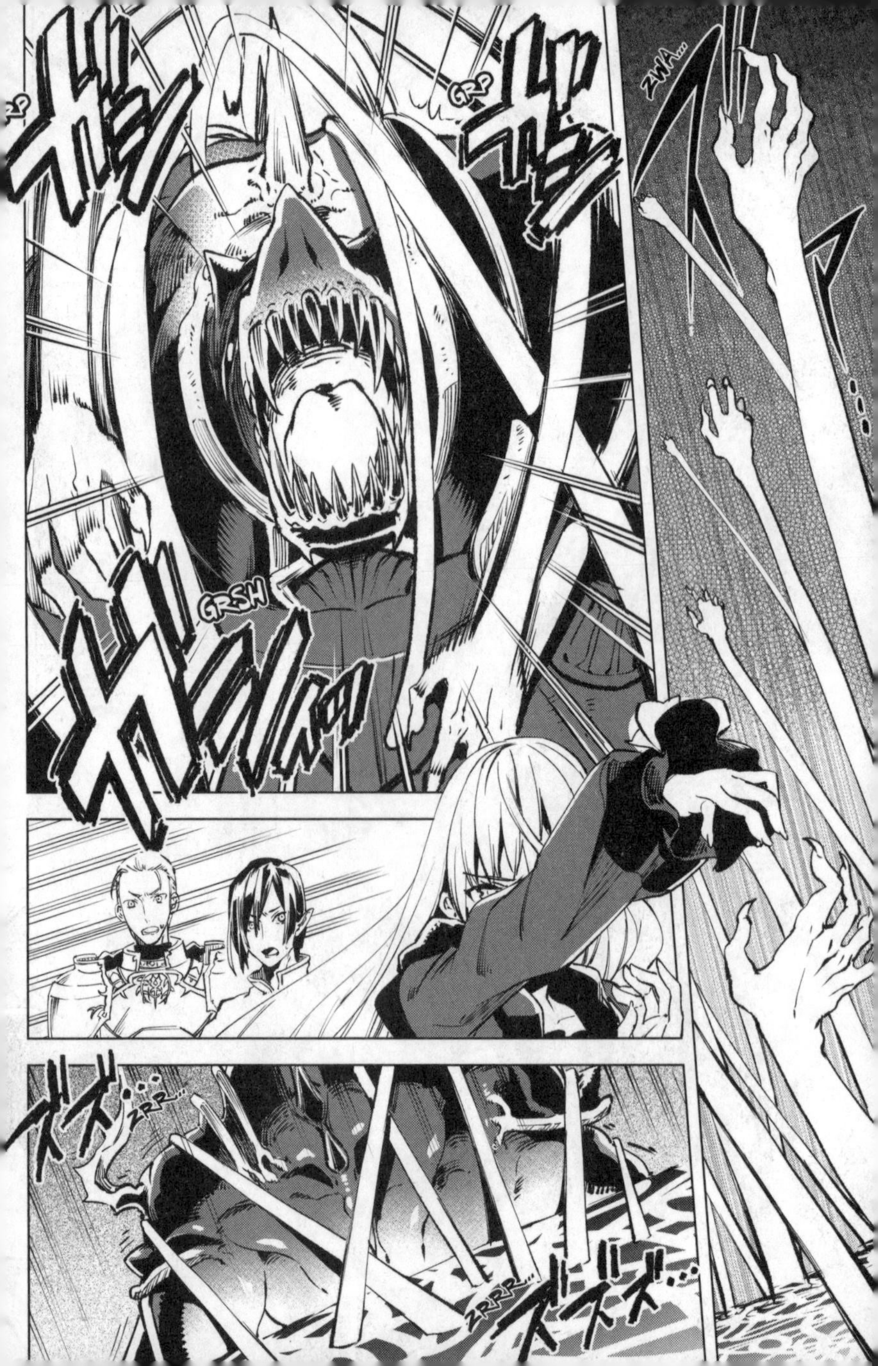
ZWA...
GRP
GRSH
ZRR...
ZRRR...

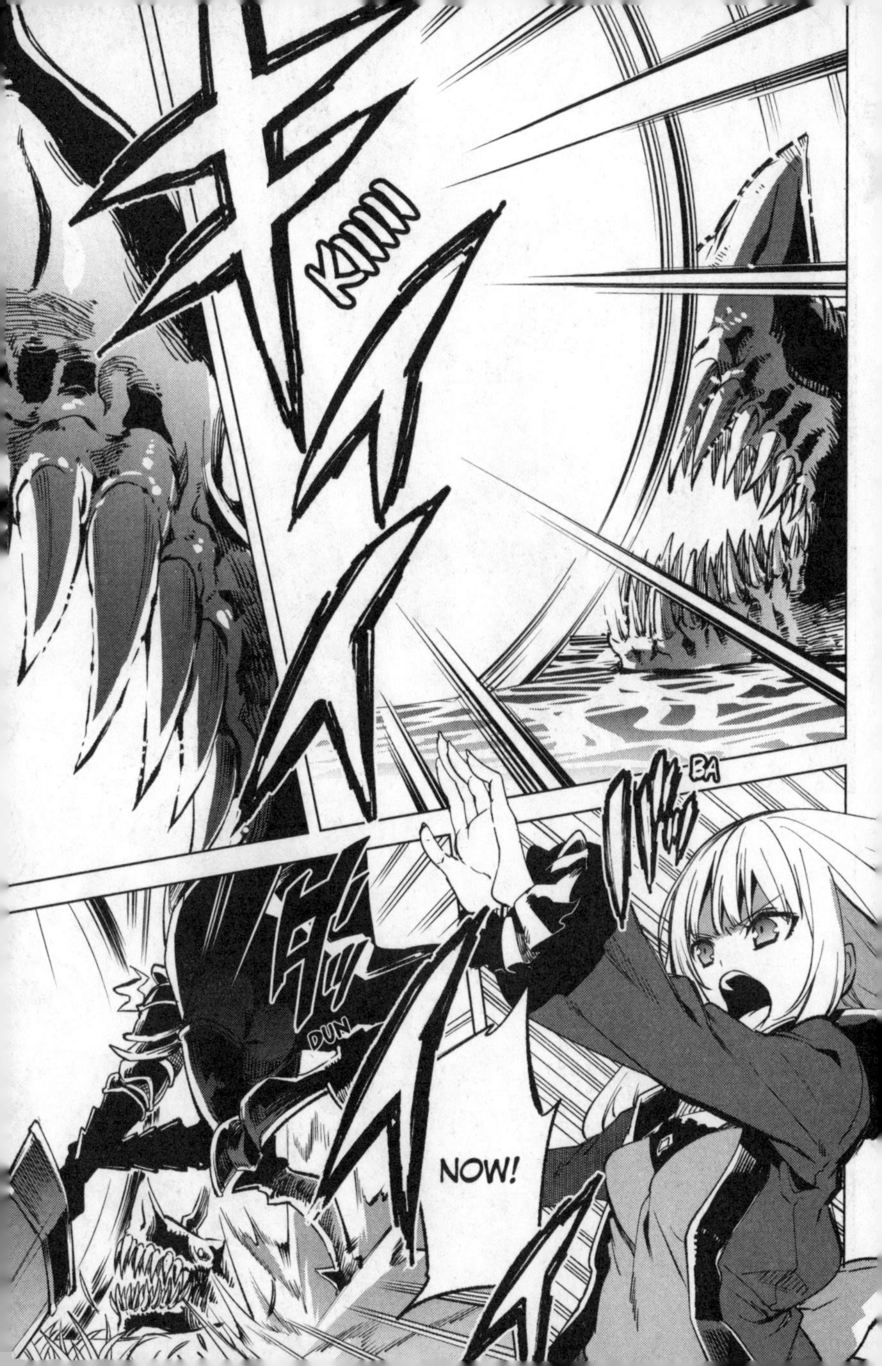
KDIIII
BA
DUN
NOW!

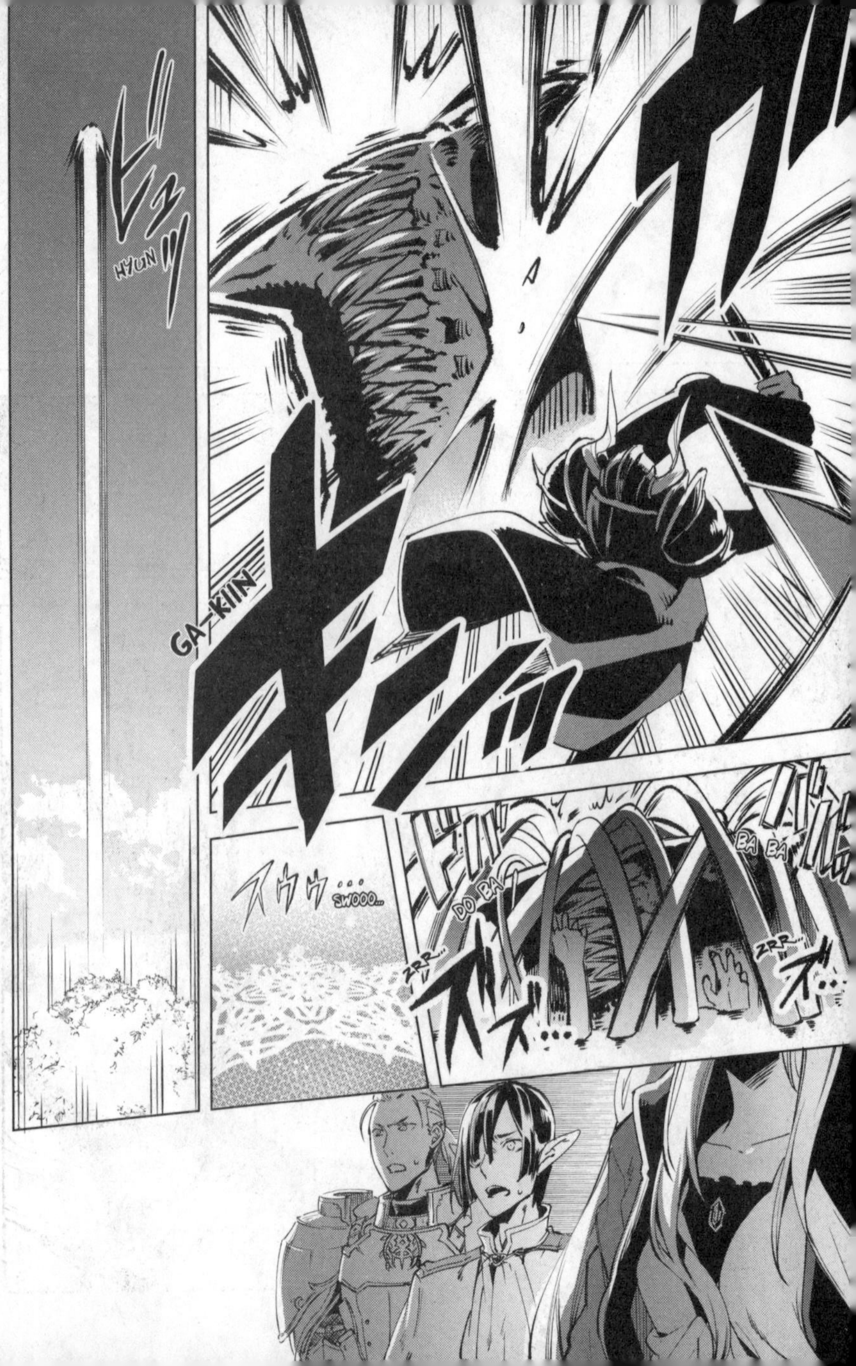
GA-KIIN
HYUN
BA BA
DO BA
ZRR...
ZRR...
スゥゥ…
SWOOO...

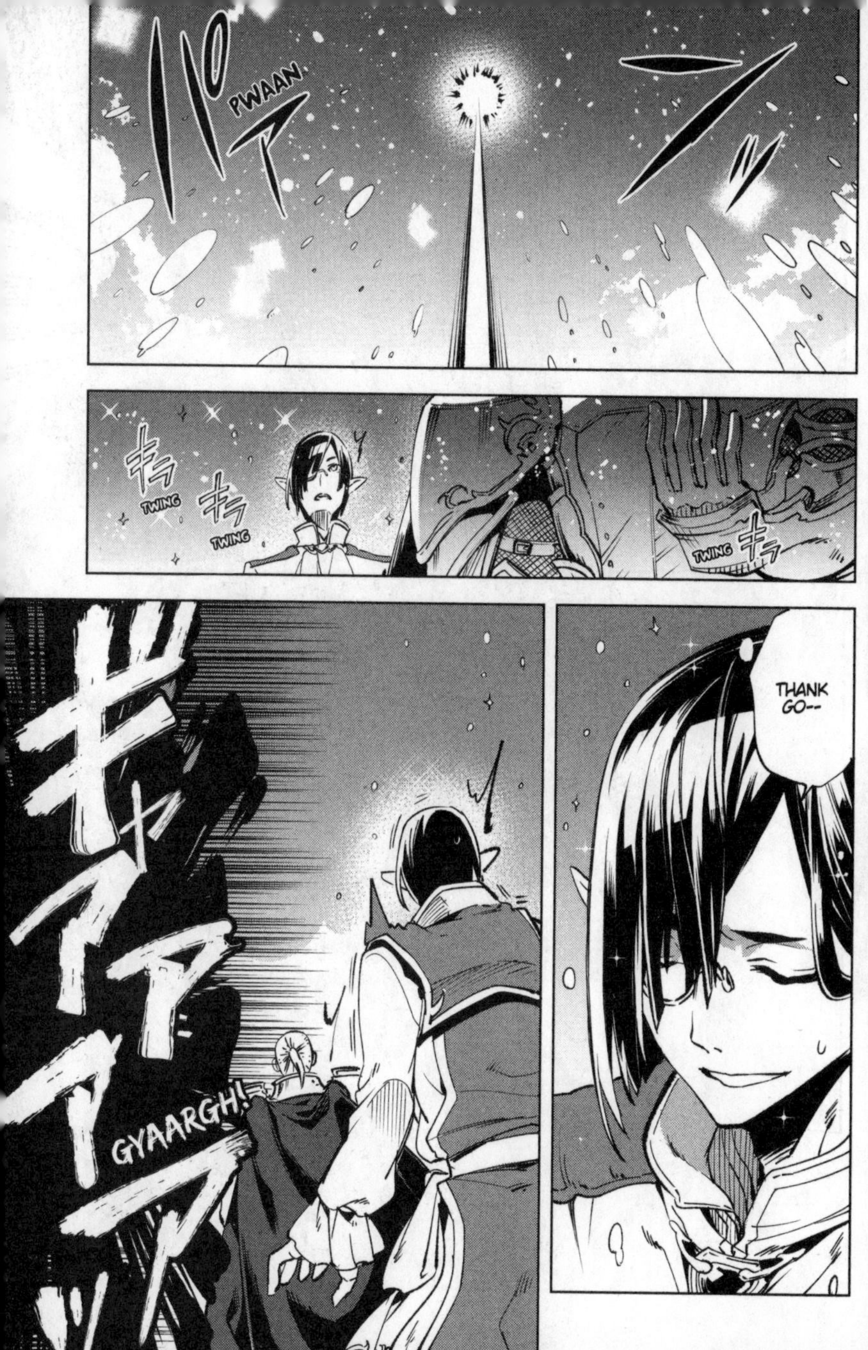
PWAAN
TWING
TWING
TWING
THANK GO--
GYAARGH!

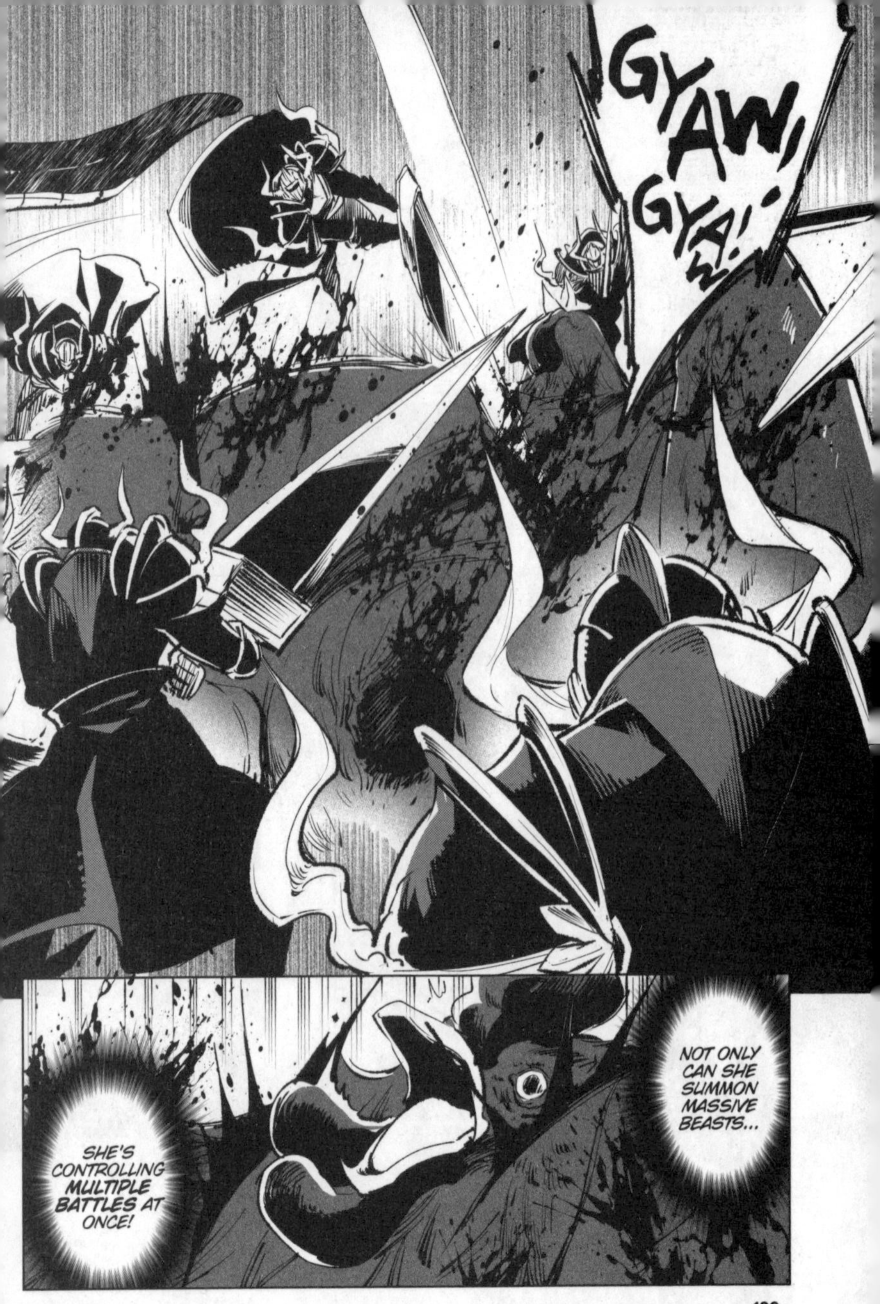
GYAW, GYA!
NOT ONLY CAN SHE SUMMON MASSIVE BEASTS...
SHE'S CONTROLLING MULTIPLE BATTLES AT ONCE!

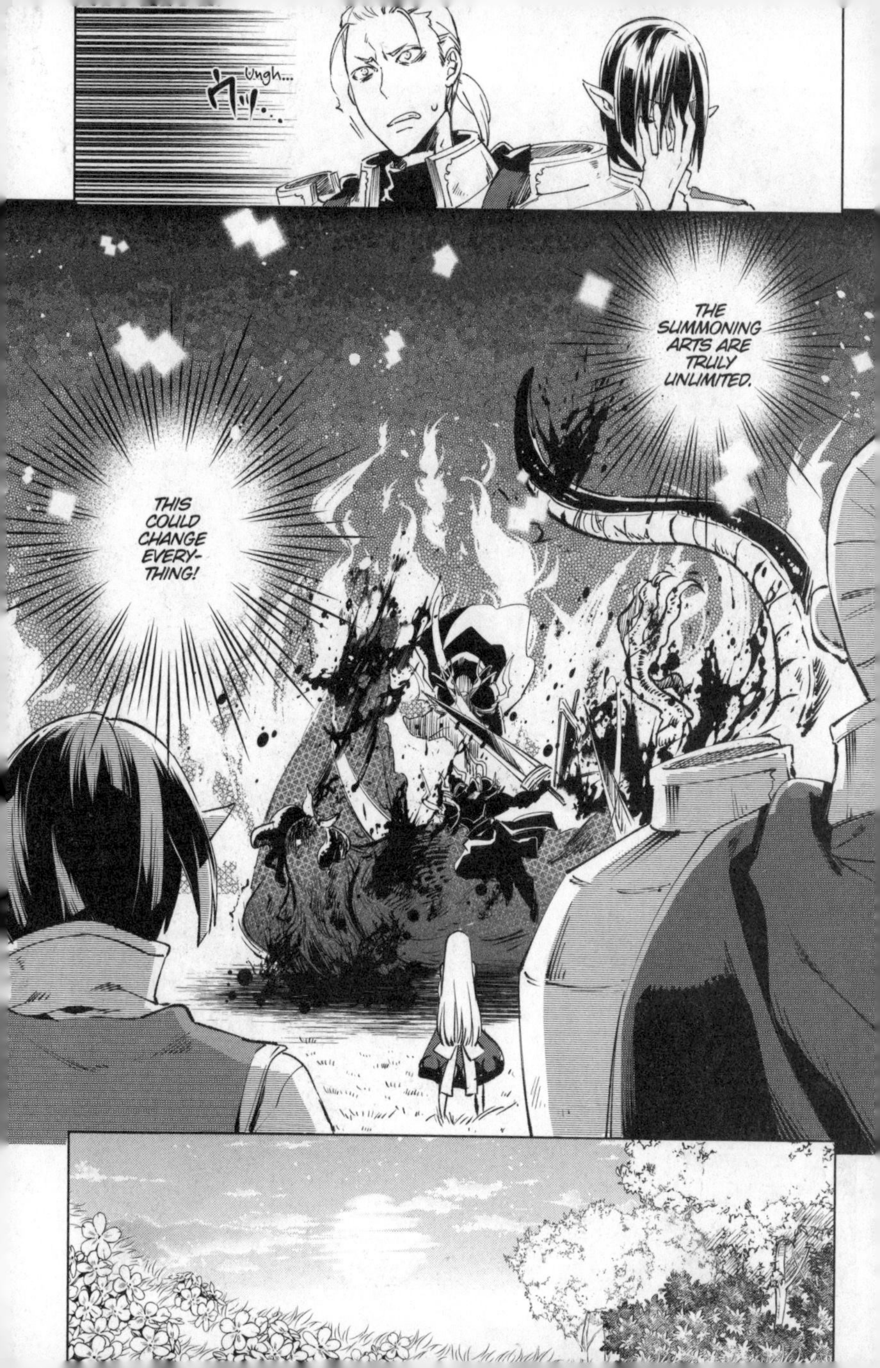
Ungh...
THE SUMMONING ARTS ARE TRULY UNLIMITED.
THIS COULD CHANGE EVERY-THING!

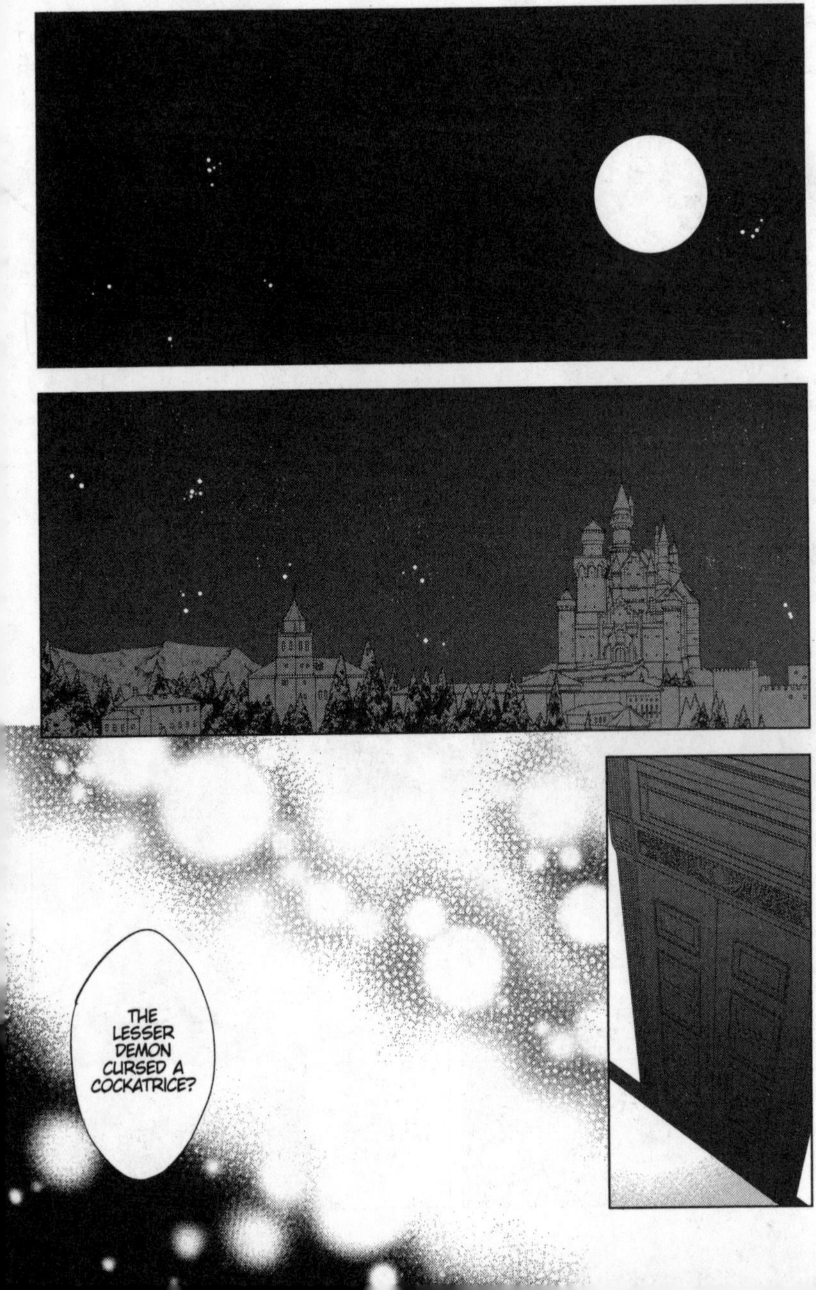
THE LESSER DEMON CURSED A COCKATRICE?

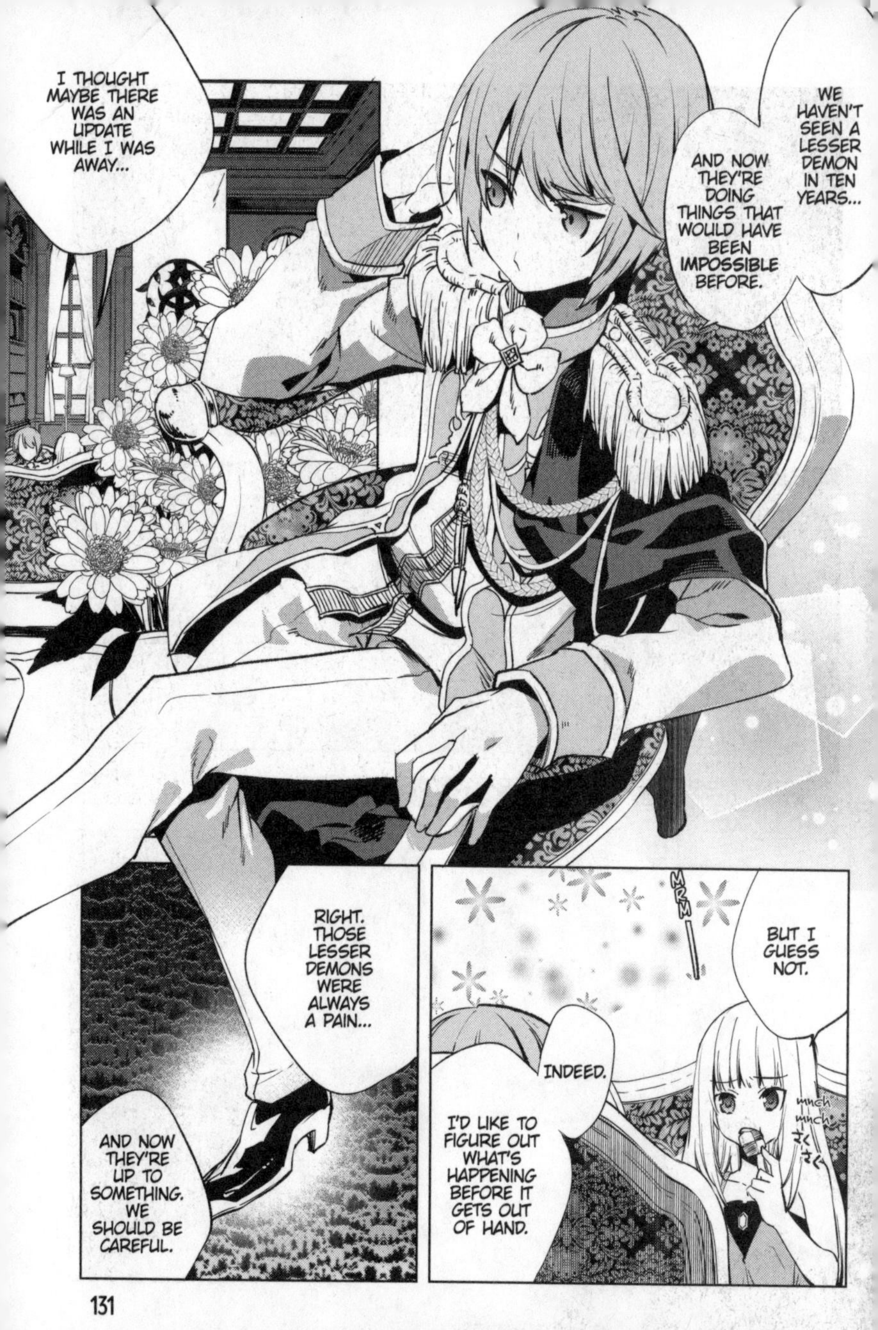
WE HAVEN'T SEEN A LESSER DEMON IN TEN YEARS...
AND NOW THEY'RE DOING THINGS THAT WOULD HAVE BEEN IMPOSSIBLE BEFORE.
I THOUGHT MAYBE THERE WAS AN UPDATE WHILE I WAS AWAY...
BUT I GUESS NOT.
MRM
INDEED.
I'D LIKE TO FIGURE OUT WHAT'S HAPPENING BEFORE IT GETS OUT OF HAND.
mnch mnch
さくさく
RIGHT. THOSE LESSER DEMONS WERE ALWAYS A PAIN...
AND NOW THEY'RE UP TO SOMETHING. WE SHOULD BE CAREFUL.

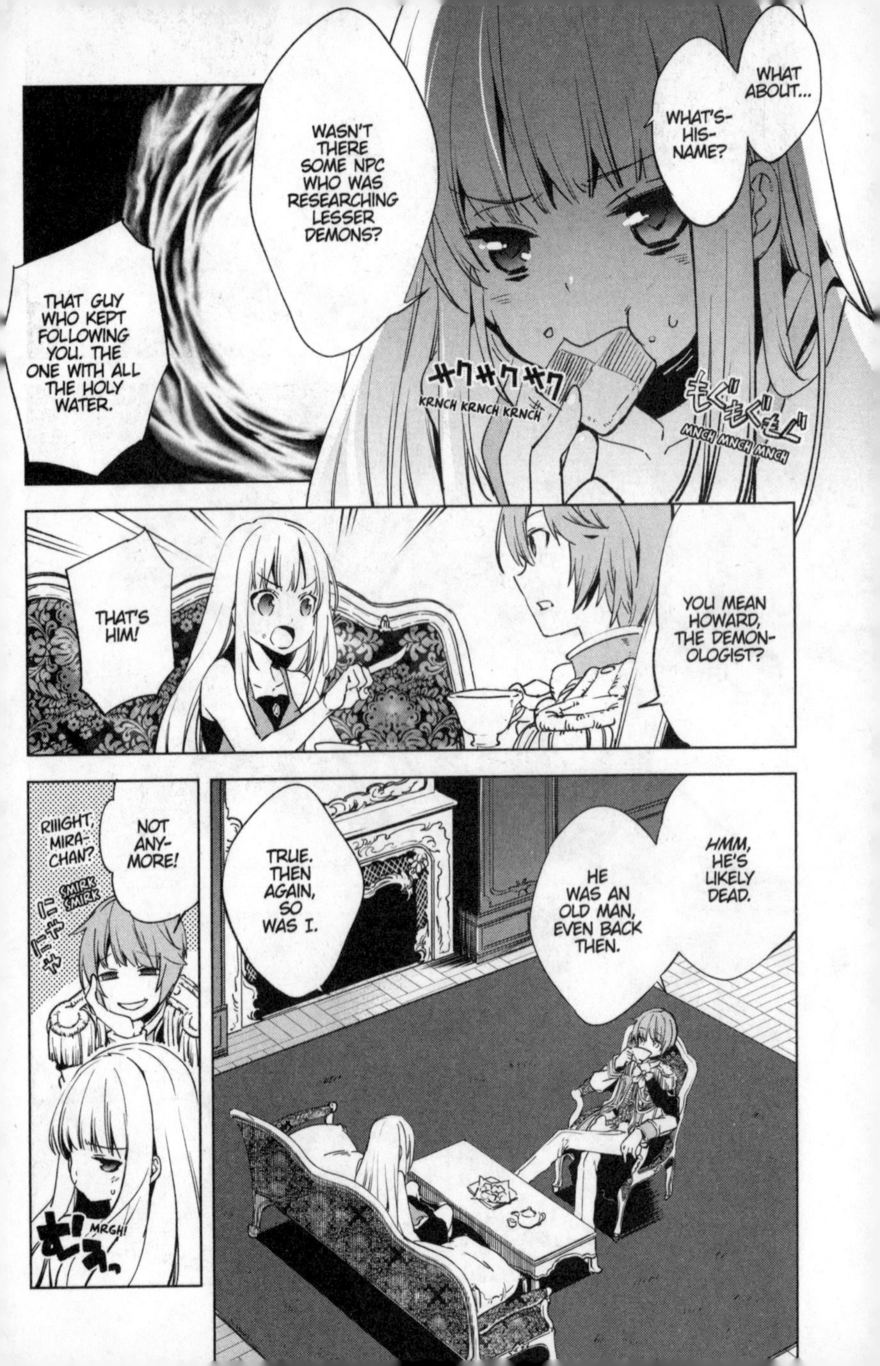
WHAT ABOUT...
WHAT'S-HIS-NAME?
WASN'T THERE SOME NPC WHO WAS RESEARCHING LESSER DEMONS?
もぐもぐもぐ
MNCH MNCH MNCH
サクサクサク
KRNCH KRNCH KRNCH
THAT GUY WHO KEPT FOLLOWING YOU. THE ONE WITH ALL THE HOLY WATER.
YOU MEAN HOWARD, THE DEMON-OLOGIST?
THAT'S HIM!
HMM, HE'S LIKELY DEAD.
HE WAS AN OLD MAN, EVEN BACK THEN.
TRUE. THEN AGAIN, SO WAS I.
NOT ANY-MORE!
RIIIGHT, MIRA-CHAN?
にやにや
SMIRK SMIRK
むぅっ
MRGH!

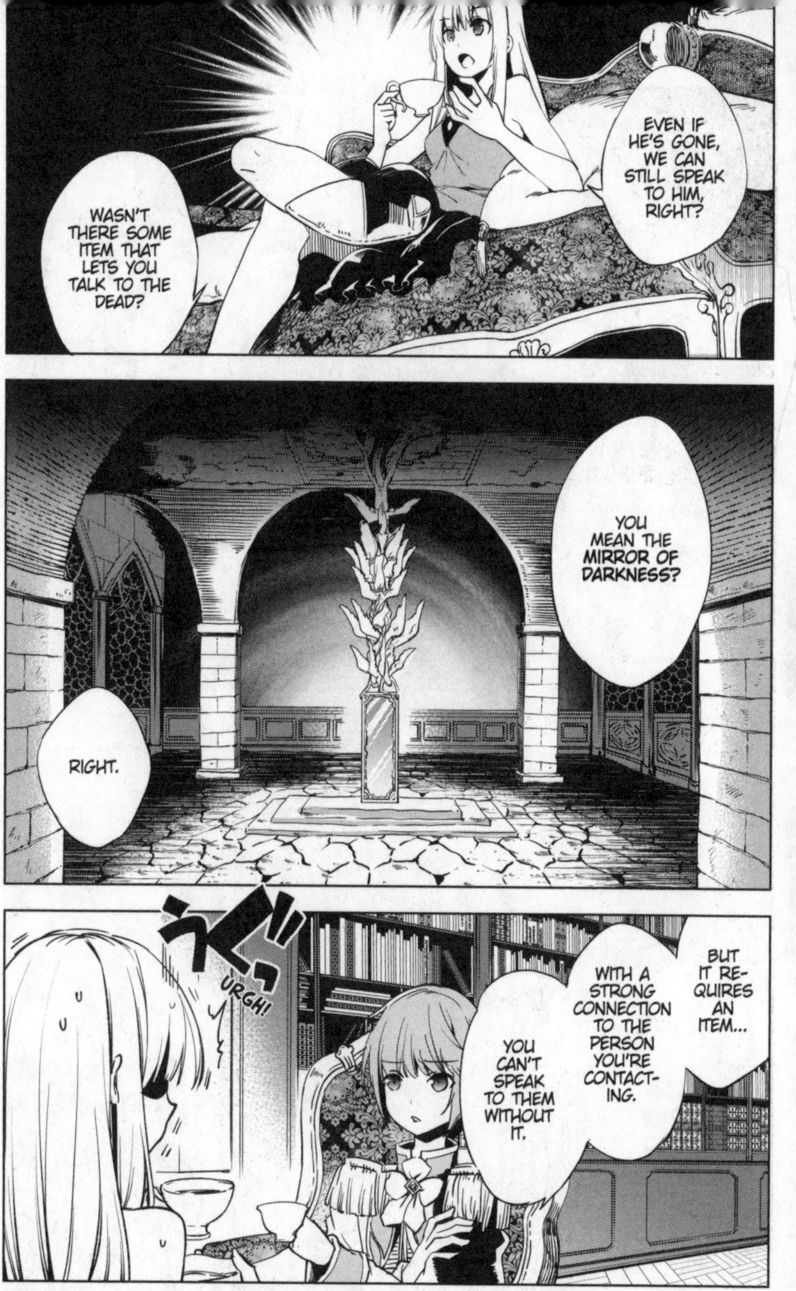
EVEN IF HE'S GONE, WE CAN STILL SPEAK TO HIM, RIGHT?
WASN'T THERE SOME ITEM THAT LETS YOU TALK TO THE DEAD?
YOU MEAN THE MIRROR OF DARKNESS?
RIGHT.
BUT IT RE-QUIRES AN ITEM...
WITH A STRONG CONNECTION TO THE PERSON YOU'RE CONTACT-ING.
YOU CAN'T SPEAK TO THEM WITHOUT IT.
URGH!

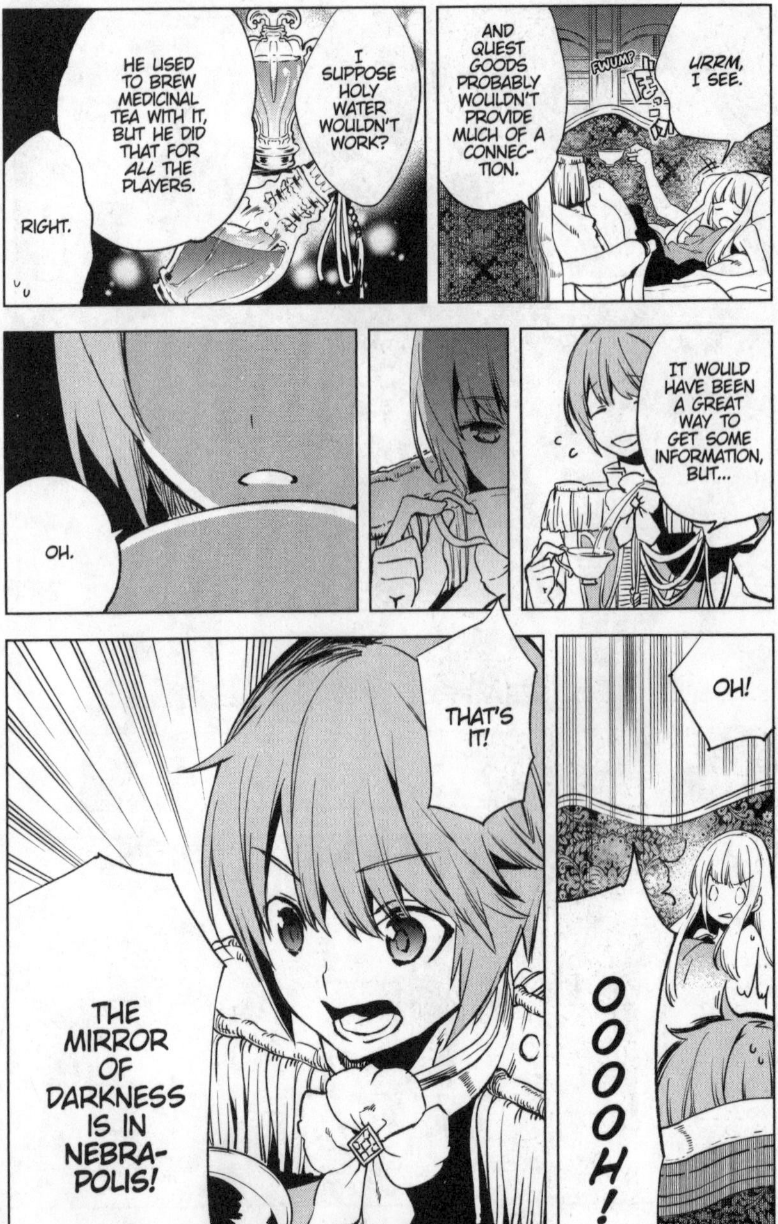
URRM, I SEE.
FWUMP
AND QUEST GOODS PROBABLY WOULDN'T PROVIDE MUCH OF A CONNEC-TION.
I SUPPOSE HOLY WATER WOULDN'T WORK?
HE USED TO BREW MEDICINAL TEA WITH IT, BUT HE DID THAT FOR *ALL* THE PLAYERS.
RIGHT.
IT WOULD HAVE BEEN A GREAT WAY TO GET SOME INFORMATION, BUT...
OH.
OH!
OOOOOH!
THAT'S IT!
THE MIRROR OF DARKNESS IS IN NEBRA-POLIS!

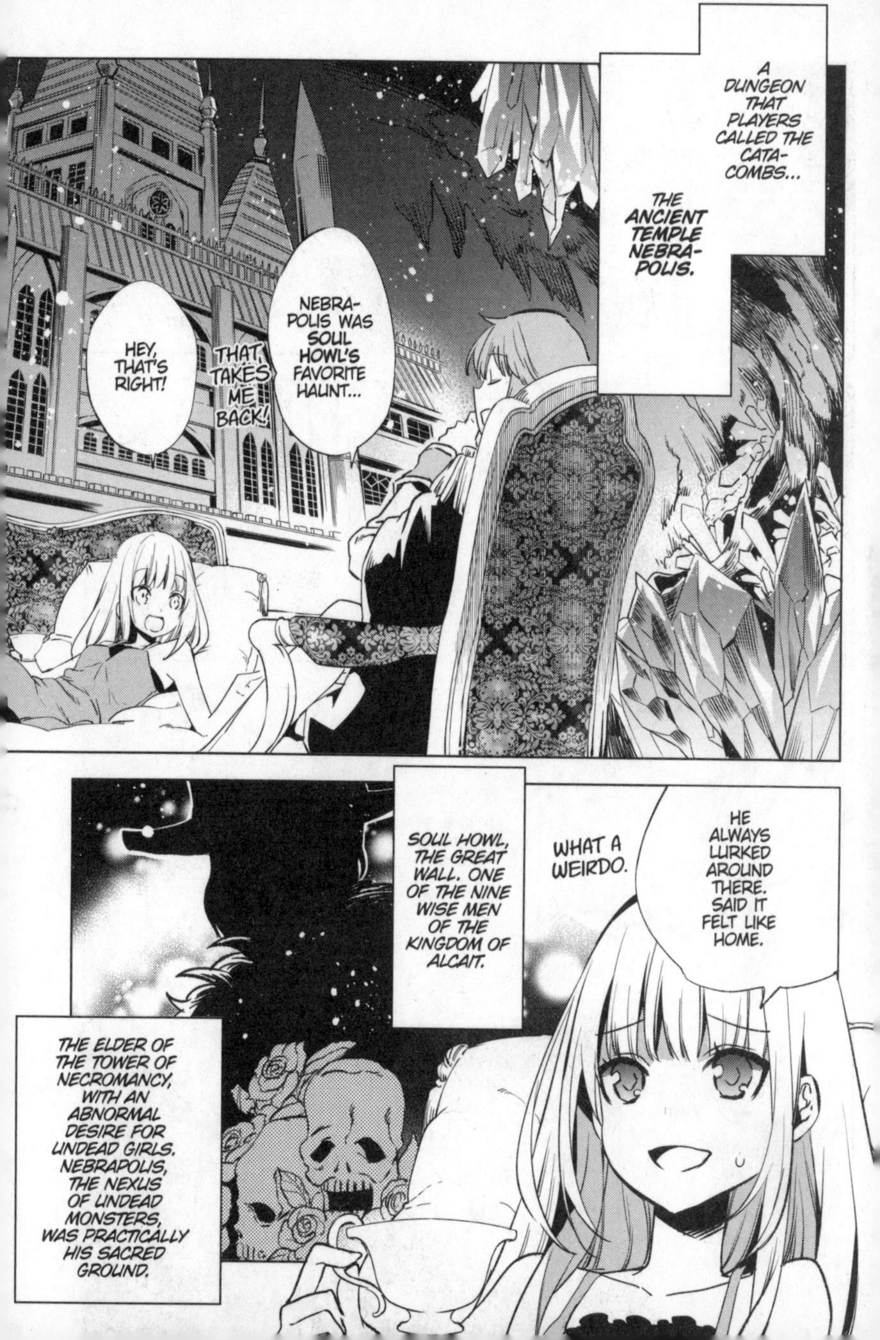
A DUNGEON THAT PLAYERS CALLED THE CATA-COMBS...
THE ANCIENT TEMPLE NEBRA-POLIS.
NEBRA-POLIS WAS SOUL HOWL'S FAVORITE HAUNT...
THAT TAKES ME BACK!
HEY, THAT'S RIGHT!
HE ALWAYS LURKED AROUND THERE. SAID IT FELT LIKE HOME.
WHAT A WEIRDO.
SOUL HOWL, THE GREAT WALL. ONE OF THE NINE WISE MEN OF THE KINGDOM OF ALCAIT.
THE ELDER OF THE TOWER OF NECROMANCY, WITH AN ABNORMAL DESIRE FOR UNDEAD GIRLS. NEBRAPOLIS, THE NEXUS OF UNDEAD MONSTERS, WAS PRACTICALLY HIS SACRED GROUND.

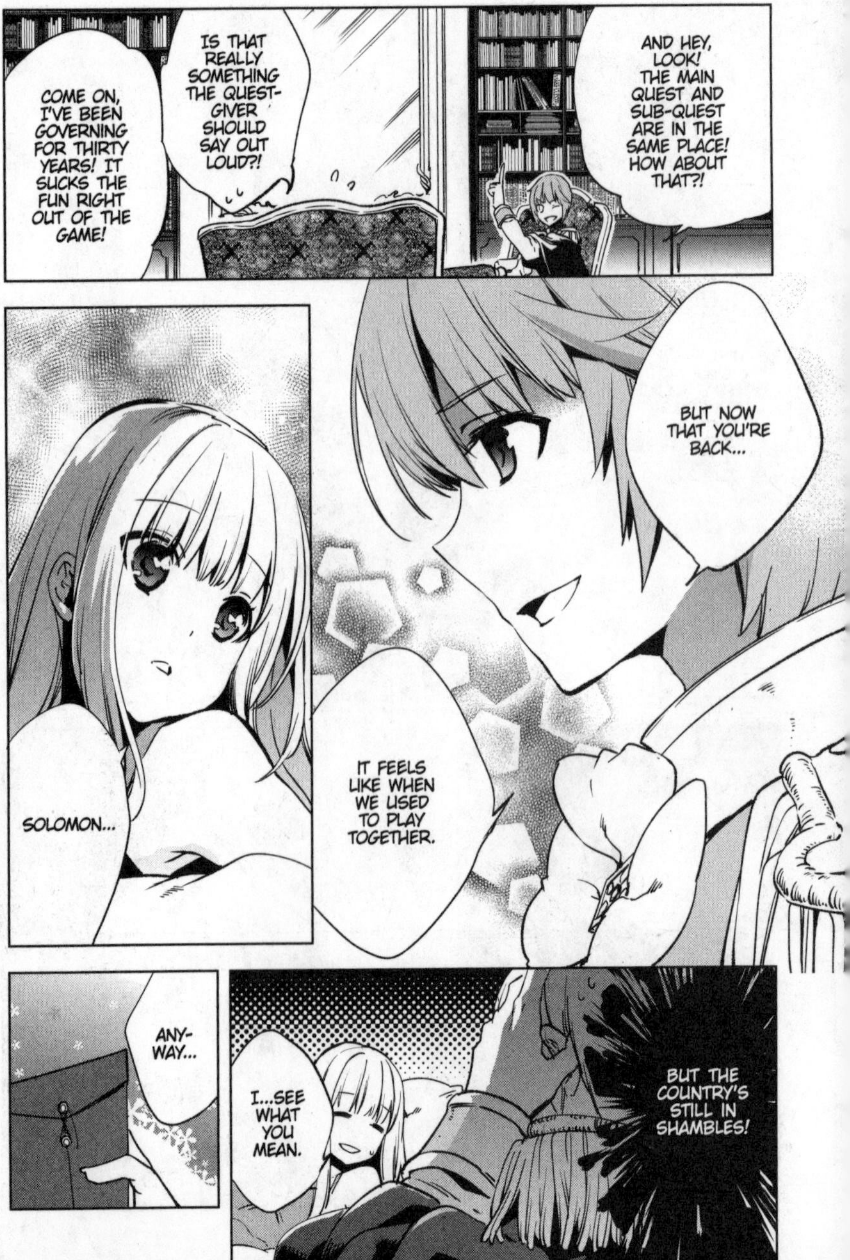
AND HEY, LOOK! THE MAIN QUEST AND SUB-QUEST ARE IN THE SAME PLACE! HOW ABOUT THAT?!
IS THAT REALLY SOMETHING THE QUEST-GIVER SHOULD SAY OUT LOUD?!
COME ON, I'VE BEEN GOVERNING FOR THIRTY YEARS! IT SUCKS THE FUN RIGHT OUT OF THE GAME!
BUT NOW THAT YOU'RE BACK...
IT FEELS LIKE WHEN WE USED TO PLAY TOGETHER.
SOLOMON...
BUT THE COUNTRY'S STILL IN SHAMBLES!
I...SEE WHAT YOU MEAN.
ANY-WAY...

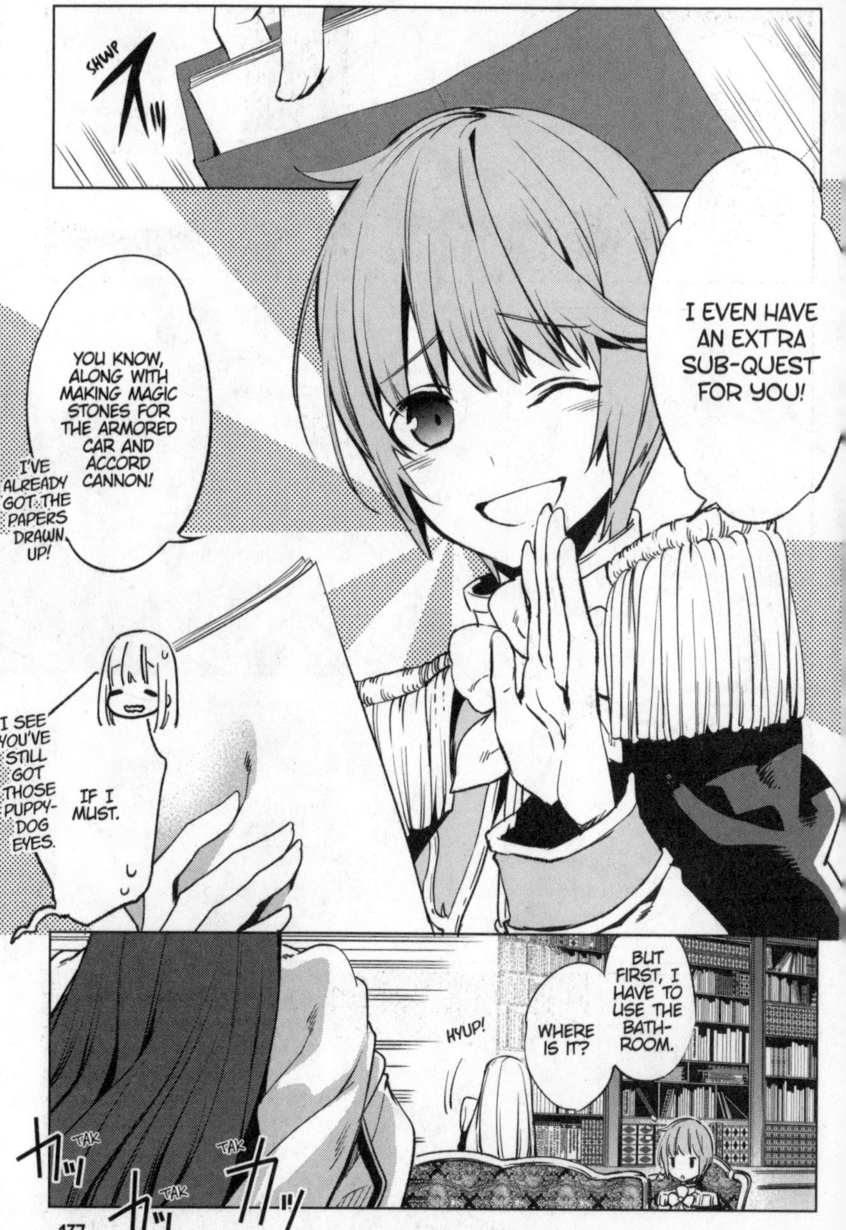
SHWP
I EVEN HAVE AN EXTRA SUB-QUEST FOR YOU!
YOU KNOW, ALONG WITH MAKING MAGIC STONES FOR THE ARMORED CAR AND ACCORD CANNON!
I'VE ALREADY GOT THE PAPERS DRAWN UP!
IF I MUST.
I SEE YOU'VE STILL GOT THOSE PUPPY-DOG EYES.
BUT FIRST, I HAVE TO USE THE BATH-ROOM.
WHERE IS IT?
HYUP!
TAK
TAK
TAK

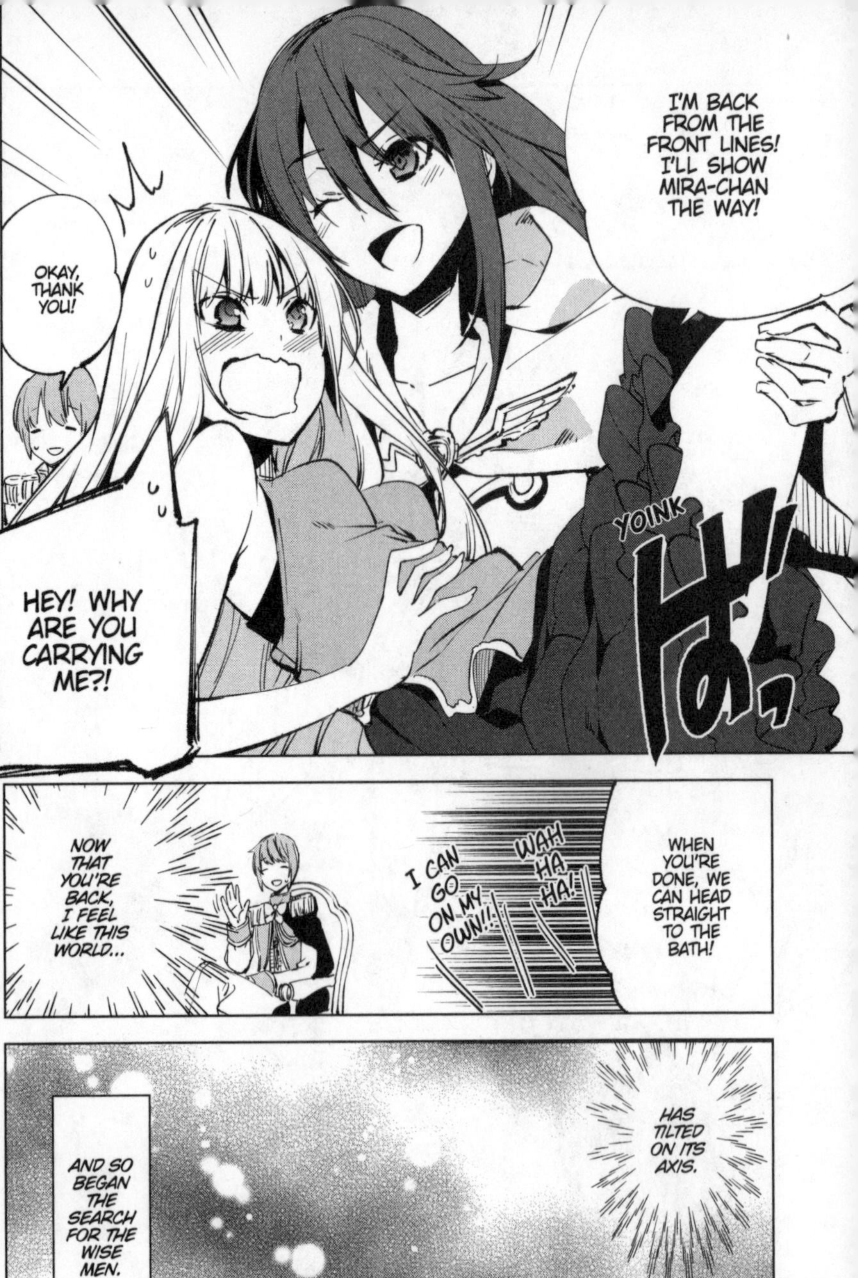
I'M BACK FROM THE FRONT LINES! I'LL SHOW MIRA-CHAN THE WAY!
YOINK
OKAY, THANK YOU!
HEY! WHY ARE YOU CARRYING ME?!
WHEN YOU'RE DONE, WE CAN HEAD STRAIGHT TO THE BATH!
WAH HA HA!
I CAN GO ON MY OWN!!
NOW THAT YOU'RE BACK, I FEEL LIKE THIS WORLD...
HAS TILTED ON ITS AXIS.
AND SO BEGAN THE SEARCH FOR THE WISE MEN.

Summon 7: END

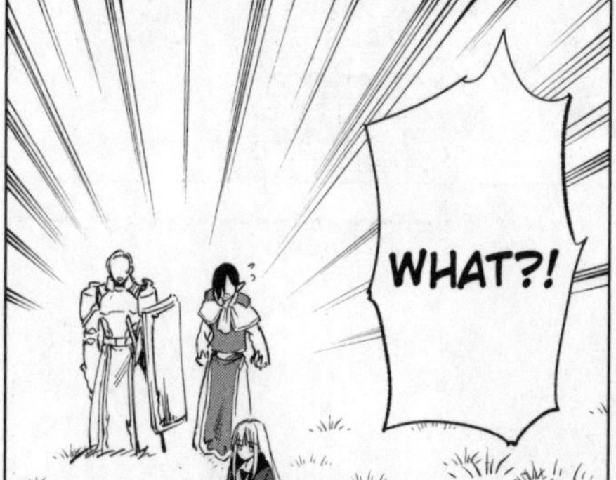
WHAT?!

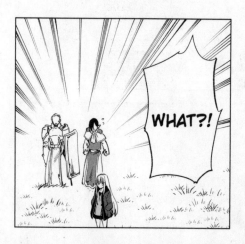

She
Professed
Herself
Pupil of the
Wise Man

She Professed Herself Pupil of the Wise Man

BONUS SHORT

A DAY IN THE LIFE OF KING SOLOMON

BY RYUSEN HIROTSUGU

Solomon sighed as he signed the last of the paperwork.

It was already mid-afternoon.

"Isn't it special training today?" he asked himself.

He rose to his feet and fetched the plate that had been prepared for him. It was only a sandwich, but the ingredients made it fit for a king.

The training would be physically demanding, so Solomon took a moment to finish his lunch and sip his tea. Then he headed for the training hall in the palace basement.

The room was large and sturdy, and everyone else was already there. Special training was a biweekly event, and it drew in all the kingdom's top soldiers. Joachim, Solomon's aide and personal mage, was already waiting for him. So was Reynard, knight commander of the King's Guard, and Garrett, vice commander of the Mobile Armored Division. A first-aid team was stationed in the corner, ready for duty. Solomon's blood ran a little hotter. This was going to be good.

"All right," he said, taking his place before the various commanders. "We're all here. Why don't we form up?"

He didn't need to say any more. Everyone knew what to do. They quickly assembled into their teams. The training hall was packed, but even so, they were ready in an instant.

The rules were simple: Each team would face off against one of the strongest warriors in Alcait.

The strongest, Solomon reminded himself.

After all, he had yet to find anyone in the kingdom who could best him.

No one here was about to waste the opportunity to learn directly from the king. The first team approached him. It was just a mock battle with blunted blades, but steel was steel, and a direct hit could still break bones—especially in the hands of Alcait's most accomplished warriors. Each weapon was custom-made for the commander who wielded it.

By contrast, Solomon looked much the same as he did in his office. The only difference was that he'd swapped his pen for a pair of practice swords. He was unarmored, and any direct hit would cause him grievous injury, but he stared at the men in front of him as though *he* was the one challenging *them*.

The starting signal sounded, and the first team attacked. Solomon might have been their king, but they did everything they could to strike him. Each and every one of them was a commander in the Alcait army, but they couldn't even touch him.

"Your second attack is a tad slow," said Solomon.

"Sir, thank you, sir!"

"You tip your attacks by raising your right shoulder."

"Sir, thank you, sir!"

"Your timing's not bad, but don't get pulled into your opponent's rhythm."

"Sir, thank you, sir!"

"Good, but keep track of your next move."

There was clearly an overwhelming disparity in ability.

Decades ago, when Solomon was with the Wise Men, he'd been their constant caretaker. They were always doing something reckless, and so he'd taken on the role of tank—drawing attacks from bosses and monsters, and even tackling top-level dungeons. He'd often found himself on the front lines. As a result, his skills were finely honed.

He had superb defensive abilities, and knew how to fight to survive, but it was more than that. Fighting alongside the Nine

Wise Men had awoken something inside of him. Not only did he have impeccable defenses, his attacking skills were unmatched. That was why, despite the fact that he was a paladin, Solomon had cast aside his shield and shifted to dual wielding. Still, the intuition he'd developed as a tank remained. His time with the Nine Wise Men had made him just as powerful as them. Even now, years later, those skills hadn't diminished.

When the first team had exhausted themselves, the second immediately jumped into the fray. Their tactics varied wildly, but Solomon knew how to handle them all the same. Under a barrage of his comments and observations, they fell just like the first.

The teams went down like dominoes, until only one remained: the pairing of Reynard and Joachim. Reynard put in an especially valiant effort, while Joachim supported him with a deluge of different spells. Together, they were magnificent. Even the highest-ranked monster would have fallen before them. But it still wasn't enough to beat Solomon. Like all the teams before them, they failed to land a single hit.

It had been ten years since they'd started training together like this. But although everyone was undoubtedly more advanced than they'd been at the beginning, they still couldn't reach Solomon's level. After all, he was improving, too.

"Fine move. You've gotten stronger, Reynard. You, too, Joachim."

And, with that, their four hours of training came to an end. Everyone, except Solomon, was battered and bruised. All the same, Reynard shot to his feet as soon as Solomon spoke his name.

"Thank you, Your Majesty."

He bowed at the waist, and it set off a chain reaction. Soon, everyone was bowing.

"Thank you, sir!"

"You're all showing great improvement," said Solomon. "Our country is stronger because of your efforts. Keep at it!"

Solomon turned and left the training hall, leaving cries of praise and dismay behind him. Many of the soldiers were already discussing how they would do better next time, and Reynard was grumbling to Joachim about how close they'd come. He, more than anyone, wanted to land a strike, even if it was only a scratch. Maybe then, Solomon would rethink this foolishness and at least wear some kind of armor.

"Perhaps if this was a little lighter, I could reach him," Reynard muttered, staring glumly at his sword.

"What is it that they say about poor workers blaming their tools?" Joachim asked.

Reynard groaned, a look of anguish spreading across his face. "Please, forget I said that."

"Oh, are you treating me to dinner, then?"

Reynard sighed. "Fine."

Having accepted Joachim's terms, Reynard got to his feet and swung his heavy practice sword about. He had to strike his king, if only to save him from injury. While that might seem contradictory, it made perfect sense to him.

Solomon strode through the palace, moving lightly and seemingly unfazed by fatigue. He was headed for the Technomancy Development Department, and his beloved Military Weapons Laboratory. The whole place had the look of a secret bunker. He exchanged greetings with the engineers and made his way to his target.

"Ah, I'm amazed every time I see it. Yes, excellent work."

As soon as Solomon saw the armored car at the center of the room, he broke into a grin. It had gone on its first test run a few days ago, and he'd come to check on the adjustments they were making as a result. As he stared at it, Garrett hurried across the lab toward him.

"Apologies for my tardiness, Your Majesty!" He'd come straight from the training room, and was still breathing heavily.

"Oh, there you are," said Solomon.

As vice commander of the Mobile Armored Division, Garrett had been one of the passengers in the test run, and would potentially become one of the car's regular operators.

"We've repaired all the parts marked as points of concern," reported the engineering director. "In theory, all problems should now be resolved."

He explained how the adjustments had been made, concluding that they couldn't make a final judgement without another test run. Solomon listened attentively.

"I see," said Garrett. "Well, Your Majesty, when should we schedule it?" He turned toward Solomon expectantly. Clearly, the test run had impressed him.

But Solomon offered him a troubled look. "I should like to hold it straight away, but there are…difficulties. Considering the number of Magic Stones required for the Accord Cannon, I don't know if we have enough," Solomon said, forcing a chuckle at the car's poor fuel economy.

"Oh, shoot. That's right."

The palace engineers were working night and day to produce enough Magic Stones, but the fact was, they couldn't keep up with demand. Refining them required a special technique created by Danblf, one of the Nine Wise Men. And despite all their work, he was the only one who really understood it.

Danblf had written a guide to refining, but his focus had always been on developing the technique further. The notes he'd left only took them to an intermediate level. At this rate, they would never make enough stones. They'd tried to compensate, of course—adding more engineers to their ranks—but most of those were still in training. It would take time before they were ready.

Despite these setbacks, Magic Stones were still an unparalleled energy source. If they could just make enough of them, they could power the Kingdom of Alcait almost indefinitely. But that goal was still a long way off.

For now, Solomon and Garrett could only stand beside the armored car, dreaming of future glory.

Before he left, Solomon took the time to inspect the other weapons in development. Afterward, he returned to his private rooms, determined to find a way to make the devices function.

Once in his chamber, he slipped on a simple outer robe, then opened an iron door in the corner of the room. The space behind had been heavily reinforced with mithril alloy. The metal glowed faintly green, the surfaces inscribed with special wards. Luminaria had worked painstakingly to carve a powerful anti-magic spell into the walls themselves.

"Perhaps just two hours today."

This was Solomon's private training room. A number of elemental swords sat in the corner. Solomon chose the ones he wanted and closed his eyes, imagining a powerful enemy he'd faced long ago.

It was time to get to work.

Two hours later, with one final swing, Solomon came to a stop. He relaxed out of his stance, staring down at his hands.

"I'm still not any better, am I? I can tell."

Just as he feared, he'd plateaued. No matter how much he trained, any further improvement had slipped away from him somehow.

"If only you were here," he sighed, opening his Friend List and staring at Danblf's grayed-out name.

His best friend, absent ever since this world had become real, was still missing.

Danblf had been one of the most powerful Summoners in the world. Even with all the freedom that Solomon enjoyed as ruler of Alcait, he couldn't think of a better training partner. With Danblf's refining techniques, they could even start mass-producing the Magic Stones that he needed for the armored car. Danblf would be a blessing, helping Solomon grow stronger, and furthering their advancement of Technomancy. But more than that…

"I miss you." Solomon just wanted to be reunited with his friend.

He had no idea that tomorrow was the day Mira would return to this world.

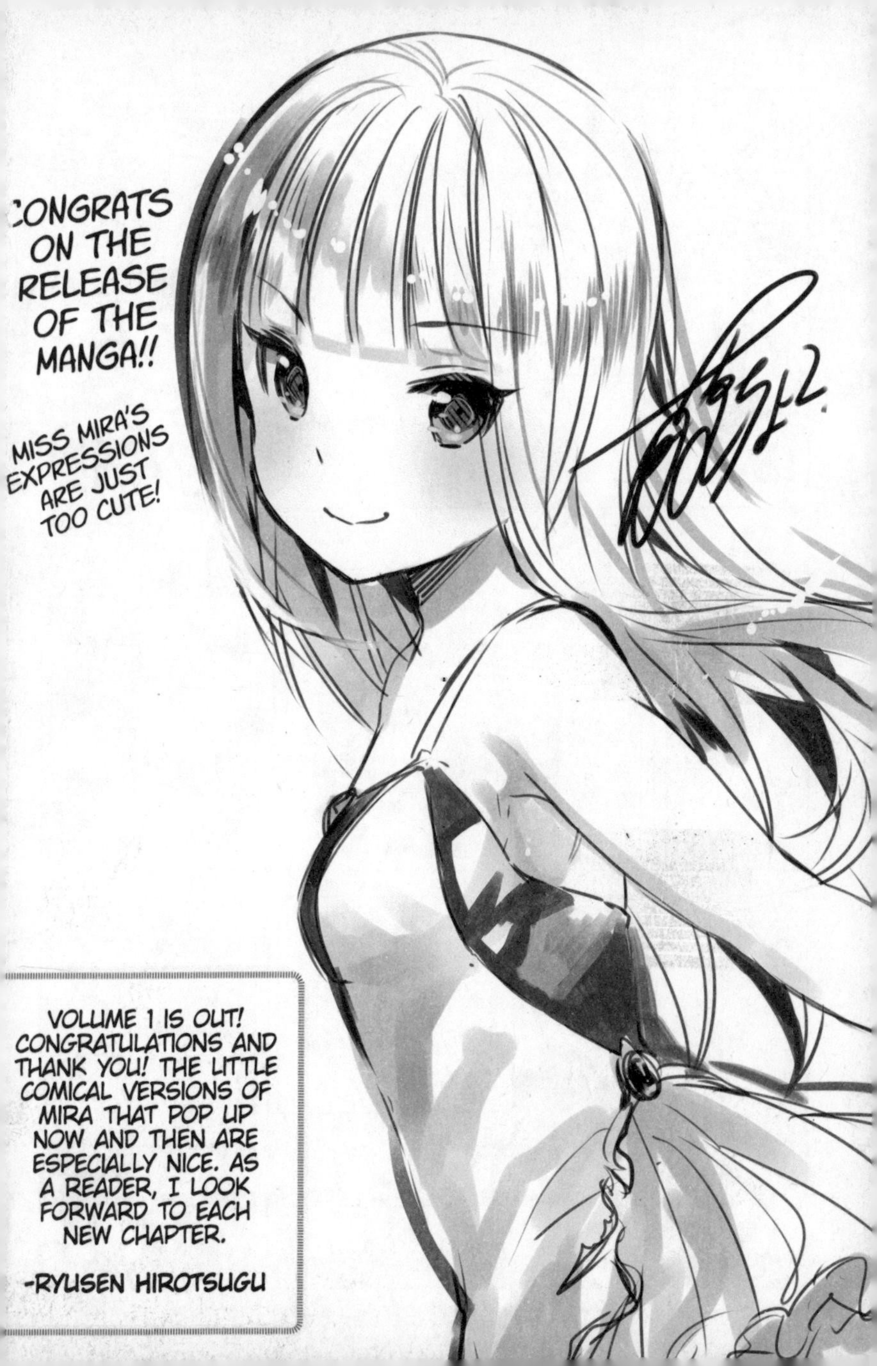
CONGRATS ON THE RELEASE OF THE MANGA!!
MISS MIRA'S EXPRESSIONS ARE JUST TOO CUTE!
VOLUME 1 IS OUT! CONGRATULATIONS AND THANK YOU! THE LITTLE COMICAL VERSIONS OF MIRA THAT POP UP NOW AND THEN ARE ESPECIALLY NICE. AS A READER, I LOOK FORWARD TO EACH NEW CHAPTER.
-RYUSEN HIROTSUGU

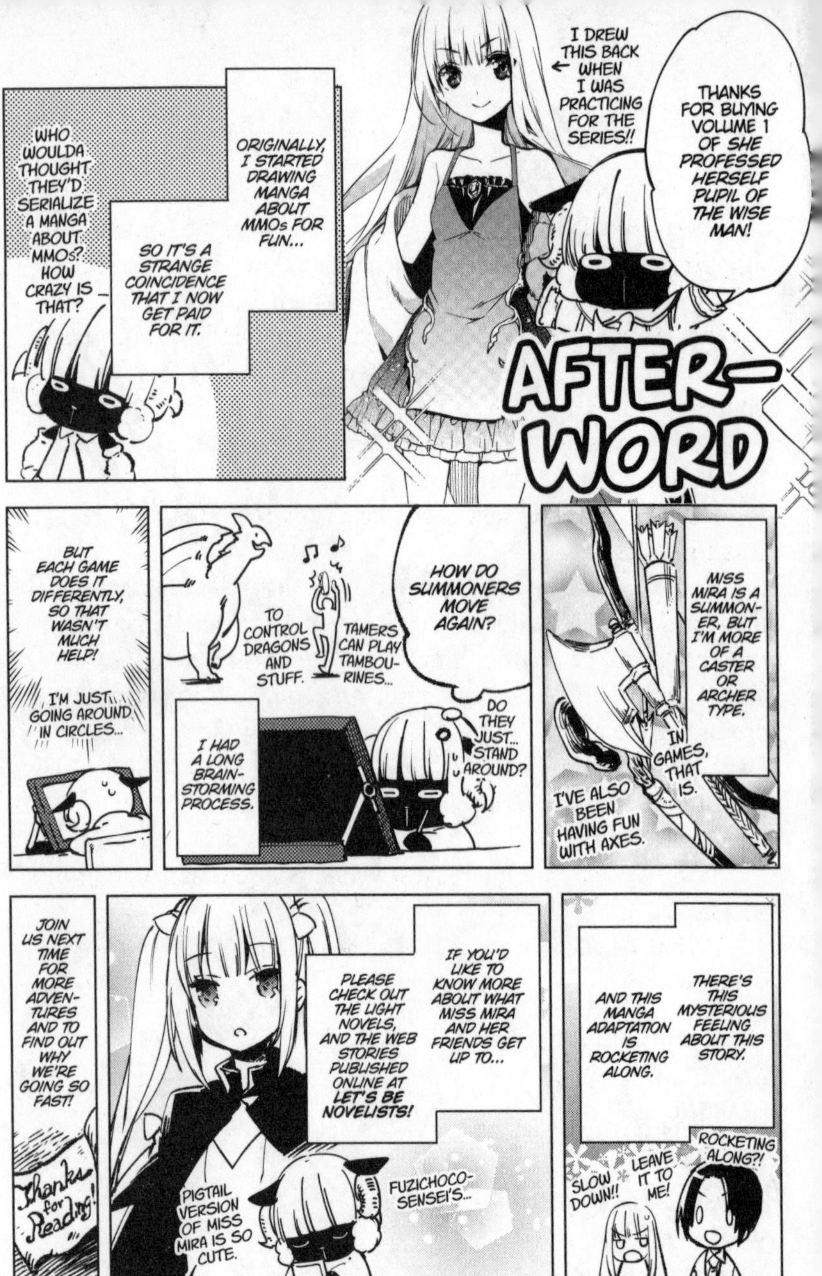
THANKS FOR BUYING VOLUME 1 OF SHE PROFESSED HERSELF PUPIL OF THE WISE MAN!
I DREW THIS BACK WHEN I WAS PRACTICING FOR THE SERIES!!
AFTER-WORD
ORIGINALLY, I STARTED DRAWING MANGA ABOUT MMOs FOR FUN...
SO IT'S A STRANGE COINCIDENCE THAT I NOW GET PAID FOR IT.
WHO WOULDA THOUGHT THEY'D SERIALIZE A MANGA ABOUT MMOs? HOW CRAZY IS THAT?
MISS MIRA IS A SUMMONER, BUT I'M MORE OF A CASTER OR ARCHER TYPE.
IN GAMES, THAT IS.
I'VE ALSO BEEN HAVING FUN WITH AXES.
HOW DO SUMMONERS MOVE AGAIN?
TAMERS CAN PLAY TAMBOURINES...
TO CONTROL DRAGONS AND STUFF.
DO THEY JUST... STAND AROUND?
I HAD A LONG BRAIN-STORMING PROCESS.
BUT EACH GAME DOES IT DIFFERENTLY, SO THAT WASN'T MUCH HELP!
I'M JUST GOING AROUND IN CIRCLES...
THERE'S THIS MYSTERIOUS FEELING ABOUT THIS STORY.
AND THIS MANGA ADAPTATION IS ROCKETING ALONG.
ROCKETING ALONG?!
LEAVE IT TO ME!
SLOW DOWN!!
IF YOU'D LIKE TO KNOW MORE ABOUT WHAT MISS MIRA AND HER FRIENDS GET UP TO...
PLEASE CHECK OUT THE LIGHT NOVELS, AND THE WEB STORIES PUBLISHED ONLINE AT LET'S BE NOVELISTS!
FUZICHOCO-SENSEI'S...
PIGTAIL VERSION OF MISS MIRA IS SO CUTE.
JOIN US NEXT TIME FOR MORE ADVENTURES AND TO FIND OUT WHY WE'RE GOING SO FAST!
Thanks for Reading!